Bedouin of Mount Sinai

Bedouin of
Mount Sinai

An Anthropological Study
of Their Political Economy

Emanuel Marx

berghahn
NEW YORK · OXFORD
www.berghahnbooks.com

Published in 2013 by

Berghahn Books

www.berghahnbooks.com

Library of Congress Cataloging-in-Publication Data

Marx, Emanuel.
  Bedouin of Mount Sinai : an anthropological study of their
political economy / Emanuel Marx.
     p. cm.
  Includes bibliographical references.
  ISBN 978-0-85745-931-2 (hardback : alk. paper) — ISBN 978-1-78238-
761-9 (paperback : alk. paper) — ISBN 978-0-85745-932-9 (ebook)
  1. Bedouins—Israel—Negev. 2. Bedouins—Egypt—Sinai. I. Title.
  DS113.75.M37 2013
  305.892′720531—dc23

2012032896

British Library Cataloguing in Publication Data

A catalogue record for this book is available from the British Library

Printed in the United States on acid-free paper

ISBN 978-0-85745-931-2 (hardback)
ISBN 978-1-78238-761-9 (paperback)
ISBN 978-0-85745-932-9 (ebook)

For
Egypt's Sociologist
Saad Eddin Ibrahim
An Advocate for Sinai

Contents

❖⟷◉〰❖

Illustrations

Maps

Tables

Acknowledgments

Over the years I accumulated many debts. Acknowledgments do not adequately express my gratitude to the many people who have helped me in every conceivable manner. My greatest obligation is to the many Bedouin men, women, and children who bore up with me and helped me understand their society. I cannot list all of them, but wish at least to pay reverence to the memory of three outstanding leaders: Mahmud Faraj, Hmed Salim, and Muhammad Mirdi Abu al-Hem.

Fieldwork in South Sinai was supported by the Ford Foundation, through the Israel Foundation Trustees. The Israeli South Sinai Administration greatly facilitated my work, and special acknowledgment must be made to one of its officers, Moshe Sela, for his wise counsel, steadfast support, and his many intriguing questions.

Friends and fellow anthropologists, including the illustrious band of Bedouin specialists, have been consistently helpful, and offered good advice and critical comments. I tested practically all my ideas on my wife Dalia, on Aref Abu-Rabi'a, Haim Hazan, Esther Hertzog, and Richard Werbner, and always benefited from their fair and constructive comments and sage advice. Dale Eickelman, Ugo Fabietti, Anatoly Khazanov, Smadar Lavie, Avi Perevolotsky, Philip Salzman, Frank Stewart, and Shelagh Weir read parts of the study and gave me detailed and often incisive feedback.

The following colleagues commented in detail on individual chapters: Joseph Berland, Clinton Bailey, the late Josef Ben-David, Frank Bovenkerk, Claudia Chang, Dawn Chatty, Erik Cohen, Gudrun Dahl, John Davis, Jerry Eades, the late Klaus Ferdinand, the late Raymond Firth, Ann Gardner, John Galaty, the late Ernest Gellner, the late Josef Ginat, Orna Goren, Don Handelman, Keith Hart, Shuli Hartman, Jörg Janzen, Iris Kalka, Bruce Kapferer, Joram Kufert, Stefan Leder, Tom Levy, Peter Little, Daan Meijers, Udo Mischek, Pnina Motzafi-Haller, the late Yehuda Nevo, Ida Nicolaisen, Yaacov Nir, Cédric Parizot, the late Aparna Rao, Nigel Rapport, Fred Scholz, Dina Siegel, the late Paul Stirling, Bernhard Streck, Pnina Werbner, and Damián Zaitch. Some of these esteemed friends and colleagues may not remember that they read my papers in the hoary past, and for some of them, alas, my thanks come too late.

I am deeply obliged to the following organizations, who have generously waived their copyright. The image on the book cover, El Greco's painting *View of Mount Sinai and the Monastery of St. Catherine,* is reproduced by kind permission of the Historical Museum of Crete © Society of Cretan Historical Studies. The painting shows imaginatively how monks, pilgrims, and local Bedouin have sanctified the region of Mount Moses (*Jabal Musa*) through the ages.

Chapter 1 has previously appeared, in another form, as "The Growth of a Conception: Nomads and Cities," in Haim Hazan and Esther Hertzog, eds. 2012. *Serendipity in Anthropological Research: The Nomadic Turn.* Farnham, UK: Ashgate, pp. 31–46. It appears here with kind permission of Ashgate Publishing and the editors.

Chapter 2 is a shortened and revised version of my article "The Political Economy of Middle Eastern and North African Pastoral Nomads," in Dawn Chatty, ed. 2006. *Nomadic Societies in the Middle East and North Africa: Entering the 21st Century.* Leiden: Brill, pp. 78–97. It appears here with kind permission of Koninklijke Brill NV and the editor.

Chapter 3 is a revised version of my article "Oases in South Sinai," in *Human Ecology,* vol. 27, no. 2, 1999, pp. 29–40. It is reprinted by kind permission of *Human Ecology.*

Chapter 5 is a slightly revised version of my article "Hashish Smuggling by Bedouin in South Sinai," in Dina Siegel and Hans Nelen, eds. 2008. *Organized Crime: Culture, Markets and Policies.* New York: Springer, pp. 29–40. It is reprinted by kind permission from Springer Science and Business Media BV and the editors.

I am grateful to Avigdor Orgad for preparing the maps. The three readers appointed by the publisher, Steven Dinero, Nancy Lindisfarne and Dina Siegel, suggested numerous important changes, for which I thank them. Finally, I am grateful to the staff at Berghahn Books for the efficient processing of the book, to Caitlin Mahon for wisely copy-editing the book, and to Marion Berghahn for years of steady encouragement.

Introduction

How I Came to Study the Bedouin of Mount Sinai

Soon after the Israeli forces occupied Sinai in 1967 the peninsula was inundated with many kinds of tourists and journalists. I avidly listened to their glowing accounts of the Bedouin of Sinai, yet for several years I hesitated to visit. I wavered between fear and hope that I would be tempted to study the Bedouin, and again experience the intellectual and emotional tumult of my earlier study of the Negev Bedouin. That first study had engaged my undivided attention for five exciting and memorable years. Between 1960 and 1963 I did eighteen months of fieldwork in the Negev, and then wrote a PhD thesis and a monograph (Marx 1967). The effort involved in living with and understanding the Bedouin had been considerable, and even at the time I knew that the experience was transforming my sociological thinking and would also deeply affect my life course.

On completing the study of the Negev Bedouin I decided to move in an entirely new direction, in order to add a second string to my professional fiddle. My vague desires rapidly took a clear shape when Max Gluckman from the University of Manchester invited me to join the Bernstein Israel Research Project, a comprehensive research project on the adaptation of Jewish immigrants to a new life. From 1964 to 1966 I lived in Maalot, a new town in Galilee. Most of the townspeople, as well as the immigrants who were still arriving in large numbers, were of Moroccan origin. A handful of officials catered to the basic needs of the new arrivals, such as housing, social welfare, health, and education. There was hardly any local employment, so the townspeople continued to depend on the assistance provided by the state. While there were many large households with growing needs, conditions in the town did not improve over time. The townspeople became so inured to subsisting for years on a combination of relief work, national insurance, and social welfare benefits that they considered the monthly welfare checks as equivalent to regular wages. The effects of this situation were, unsurprisingly, that the inhabitants came to depend on the officials and held the state responsible for their livelihood and welfare. They provided an extreme instance of the welfare state in action, showing how it controls and humiliates the people it presumes to help.

I found some of the social consequences of this situation quite surprising. Kinship ties, even those between members of the same household, were tenuous to the point where relatives were no longer prepared to help one another when in need. Parents often refused to support their grown-up children and siblings would not aid one another financially. Yet, if we may rely on the anthropological literature, Moroccan Jews were distinguished by strong family links. The town's schools were not very effective either. While some of the teachers were excellent, the pupils expected little from adult life and their scholarly achievements were quite low. It was strange to hear many townspeople complain bitterly about their utter dependence on bureaucrats and their poor life chances in the town. Yet they rarely moved away, even though many of them had kin and friends in more prosperous places. Finally, the relations between some of the officials and their clients were punctuated with minor violent incidents that, so I thought, generally ended inconclusively.

In short, the townspeople were for me an "exotic" society, quite distinct from the Negev Bedouin, whose actions had always made perfectly good sense to me. I could not fathom their behavior, and I found their often heated exchanges with officials especially perplexing. It was many months after leaving the field that I began to understand the complex structure of these violent encounters and, in the end, I concentrated my efforts on analyzing them

(Marx 2004c). Since then my interest in violent behavior, and its manifestations in bureaucratic practice, has never waned.

I mentioned above that when Israel occupied Sinai in 1967, I did not rush in to study the local Bedouin, as I feared to be drawn into a long-term commitment. As a preventive measure, I persuaded myself that these Bedouin were already familiar from the classic writings of Niebuhr (1799), Burckhardt (1992), Robinson (1867), Palmer (1871), Murray (1935), and Jarvis (1931), and that there was little I could add to the accounts of these acute observers. For good measure, I also refrained from joining any of the popular tours of Sinai. Instead, in 1968 I deliberately became involved in what was to become a long-term study of Palestine refugee camps under the Israeli occupation (Ben-Porath and Marx 1971). I followed the rapid integration of the camp dwellers into the larger economy, observed how the refugee camps evolved into regular urban quarters, how the refugees gradually transformed their simple shelters into decent dwellings and consolidated their ownership of the homes, while the flow of United Nations aid continued unabated. But I also learned that these developments did not affect the refugees' resolve to return to their ancestral homes, and became convinced that as long as the refugees and their descendants were not compensated for their sufferings, this moral issue would stay with us.

My self-imposed *cordon sanitaire* worked well, until the day in 1972 when Mr. Moshe Sela, an official of the Israeli Civil Administration in South Sinai, came to see me. He offered to arrange a short visit to the region, where he would show me the work of the administration with the Bedouin. Perhaps, as an experienced student of Bedouin, I could suggest improvements. He knew intuitively that there was nothing that I wanted more than to meet the Sinai Bedouin. No wonder I walked with open eyes into the baited snare. The short visit resulted in an extended period of fieldwork in South Sinai, during which Moshe Sela became a trusted friend, taskmaster, and interlocutor.

Between 1972 and 1982 I spent altogether twelve months in the field. It was a rather turbulent decade that comprised on the one hand rapid and uncontrolled Israeli colonization, and on the other a period of relative economic prosperity for the Bedouin, punctuated by several serious political and economic crises, including the 1973 war between Egypt and Israel. At an early stage I realized that the study should focus on the political economy of the Bedouin of Mount Sinai, particularly on labor migration, which I then considered to be the key to understanding the Bedouin. Only in the mid-1990s did I realize that the economy was more complex and variable than I had thought, and that drug smuggling, pastoralism, horticulture, and trade rivaled labor migration in importance. From then on all my thoughts concentrated on examining these aspects of the economy. The phases of this gradual transformation in my thinking are set out in chapter 1.

Military Occupation and Colonization

The eminent Egyptian geographer Jamal Hamdan has identified the strategic importance of Sinai for Egypt: "The northern strip of Sinai is the first and foremost entrance gate to Egypt, and most of Egypt's military history revolved around it" (1993: 6). This is an astonishing statement, considering the total dependence of Egypt on the sources of the Nile, as well as the general vulnerability of the Nile Valley to invasions from every direction. Even 2,400 years ago, the Egyptians knew that they were living in "an acquired country, the gift of the river" (Herodotus 1947: 82). They were always preoccupied with annual variations in the water supply, which made the difference between lean and fat years, periods of drought and plenty. While they depended on a steady water supply, they never feared that neighbors in the south would cut off the flow of their lifeblood. The threat that a developing Sudan would claim its full share of the waters of the Nile under the 1929 Nile Waters Agreement became real and significant only when oil production in the Sudan really took off in 1999 (United States Energy Information Administration 2007).

But invasions from the north were a recurrent feature of Egyptian history, and the invading armies always used the Sinai Desert as the passageway to the Nile Valley. The Mediterranean littoral was, and still is, the chief land route into Egypt (see map 1). It is a well-traveled route dotted with watering points (Cytryn-Silverman 2001: 4), and has never been an effective barrier against invaders. Therefore, Egyptians in every age viewed Sinai as their most

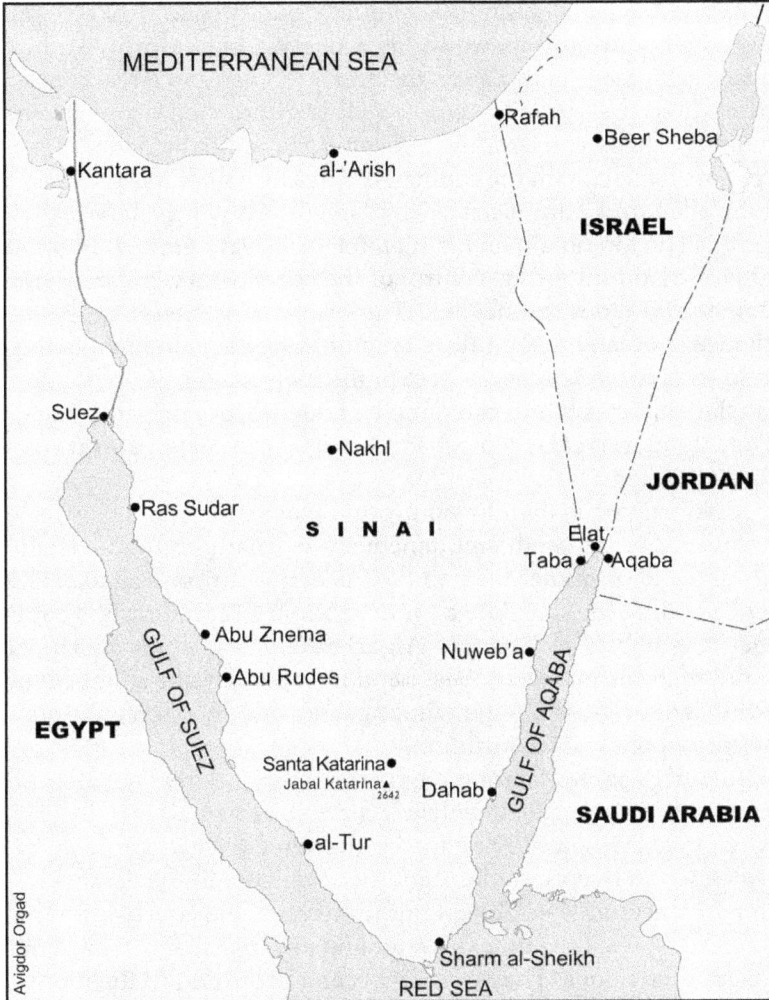

MAP 1. The Sinai Peninsula

problematic frontier (Mouton 2000: chap. 20); they constructed fortifications both along the coastline and in the eastern reaches of the Nile Delta in the hope of holding up the expected invaders. I doubt whether the Israeli authorities ever realized how sensitive the Egyptians were to the occupation of Sinai by a foreign power.

While the Israeli authorities initially had no policy of coloniz-
ing Sinai, and only viewed it as a negotiating chip in a future
peace settlement with Egypt, the scarcity of land in Israel created
irresistible pressures to colonize all territories occupied by the
military. The Israeli Land Administration nominally owns 93 percent of all the land in the country, but nearly half of it is in practice
controlled and administrated by Israel's army. Privately owned
land is hard to obtain and is therefore in great demand. In order
to wrest land out of the control of the bureaucracy, great staying
power and clout are needed. The ordinary citizen stands little
chance of obtaining the title to land of his own. Compared to this,
land in occupied areas, at least in the early stages of occupation,
is relatively cheap and can often be bought from private owners.
The situation creates almost irresistible social pressures to colonize occupied areas.

Colonization is therefore a process that starts from below, and
because it is initiated simultaneously by many individuals and
groups and at numerous points, it is almost uncontrollable, and
tends to drag the state into a running battle with colonists, a battle
that it is bound to lose (see Algazi's 2006 case study of Upper
Modi'in in the occupied West Bank for a similar situation). Some
politicians always join the winning side, and by degree the state
adopts a policy of colonization.

In Sinai's Santa Katarina region the rapid progress of colonization can be easily documented. It started in a small way in 1967,
when the Israeli occupying forces quartered a small garrison, between ten to twenty soldiers and two vehicles, in the Santa Katarina monastery. The soldiers put up tents in the courtyard of the
monastery, used the monks' water and electricity, and caused frequent altercations. They quickly became a burden to the monks,
who sought ways to get rid of them. Moshe Sela, an official of
the civil administration, the government agency responsible for
supplying services to the Bedouin population, tried in 1969 to establish himself in the Bedouin village of Milqa, near the approach
road to the monastery. He won the approval of the males of an
extended family of the Awlad Jindi section of the Jabaliya tribe
by offering to provide their compound with running water and
electricity if they permitted him to attach to it a small building
that was to serve as an office. When Moshe Sela began construc-

tion, the monks feared that they would lose control of the land in
the vicinity of the monastery, to which they claimed title, and the
tithes levied on the Bedouin orchards. Therefore, they instructed
the Bedouin, some of whom were permanent employees in the
monastery and did not wish to jeopardize their jobs, to put an
end to the building activities. The matriarch of the group showed
her disapproval by pouring rubbish onto the foundations of the
building, but could not really hold up the work while the males of
the family stood by. They assumed that the administration would
eventually move into permanent accommodation and that the new
building would then become their property. Instead, the building
became the nucleus of an ever-expanding administrative center,
and the Israelis stayed in it right up to the end of the occupation.

In 1970, Moshe Sela met the monks, led by Archimandrite
Dionysius, to settle the outstanding differences and come to an
agreement. Sela had informed two Israeli generals, Uri Baidatch,
head of the Nature Reserves Authority, and Abraham Yaffe, of the
army's southern command, of the negotiations. After he received
their blessing he, as well as the commander of the local garrison
and three of the monks, formally signed an agreement on 18 September 1970. This document, a copy of which is in my possession,
became the charter for more intensive Israeli colonization. It is
well worth an analysis.

The main motivation of the monks of Santa Katarina in signing
the agreement was to preserve their perpetual right in the lands
adjacent to the monastery. They had tenaciously held on to it for
centuries and under many consecutive regimes. They wished to
ensure that the Israeli occupation forces respected that right, so
that they could reclaim it from the regime that would supplant
the Israelis. That is why the monastery's right to the land is reit-
erated in this short document. Thus, the building that the Israeli
army was going to erect is "on land that is being hold [sic] by the
Monastery." If "in the future … the Army shall decide to leave
the building … the building shall be delivered by the Army to the
Monastery." The monks gave the Israelis "permission to search for
sources of water," and reserve any "excess of the water … for the
benefit of the Monastery. It is agreed that water shall not be delivered to the local beduins for irrigation of their plantations." This
last provision was intended to ensure that the Bedouin would not

acquire any residual rights to water through links with the Israeli authorities.

This document served as a charter for Israeli colonization. The officials worked on two mutually incompatible projects. On the one hand, they provided services for the Bedouin population, such as medical clinics, schools, and shopping centers. They dug new wells, installed an electric generator, and opened a car repair workshop. They also set up a dining room for their Bedouin employees. On the other hand, they built a "field school" (a hostel for Israeli hikers) and homes for the growing number of Israeli official service providers. By the early 1980s the number of permanent Israeli employees had grown to almost forty, while the Bedouin employees were hired and fired according to the needs of current construction projects. Their number was usually just below thirty. The Israeli employees were in a better position than the Bedouin to utilize such services as the car repair shop and the dining room, and eventually monopolized them. The settlement was rapidly becoming an Israeli colony that employed a peripatetic Bedouin workforce. By then the power relations in the Milqa area had changed to such an extent that the initial charter had become quite meaningless. While the local Israeli authorities continued to treat the monks with respect, they constructed buildings in the vicinity without consulting the monastery. The monastery lost control of the region and in practice now owned only the enclosed areas of the monastery and its branches. The monks could no longer collect tithes from Bedouin gardens. The gradual displacement of the Bedouin stopped only with the Israeli evacuation of Sinai.

About the Book

The book is the distillation of many years of work. The twenty-odd articles on the Bedouin of Mount Sinai that I published from 1977 onward became the groundwork for its eight chapters. The earlier articles, such as that on tribal pilgrimages (Marx 1977b), went through several revisions as my thinking on the Bedouin developed. For the purpose of including them in the book I made further changes, and they appear here as chapters 2, 4, and 7. Chapters 1, 3, 5, and 6 are of recent origin: they were published between 1999 and 2008. As I wrote them as segments of the planned book, they required only slight revisions. This introduction, as well as the conclusion, which reports on the dramatic changes I observed during my 2009 visit to Santa Katarina, are entirely new.

I chose the subtitle "An Anthropological Study of Their Political Economy" for two reasons. First, I wanted to indicate that this study is dominated by one theme: the reflection of global and regional politics and economics in the social forms and behavior of the Bedouin. I am particularly concerned with the question how the state's praxis of ruling, misruling, or neglecting the Bedouin is connected with their political economy, and especially with the various ways the Bedouin eke out a living. And second, I wished to stress that the study examines economic and political issues from an anthropological viewpoint. It deals with a particular collective, the people I lived with at a certain historical moment, and claims ethnological validity for just that moment. I do, however, attach some lasting value to the anthropological insights of the study.

I am not worried by the fact that a whole generation of neo-Marxist writers has associated the term "political economy" with political domination. While I have reservations about the tendency of these writers to attribute excessive power to the state—and hardly any to its suppressed and colonized subjects—I feel that their emphasis on power relations has generally been beneficial to a rather anemic anthropology. The concern with the power of the state is especially important in the case of the Sinai Bedouin. During Egyptian rule, as well as under Israeli military occupation, the governing state has regularly neglected their welfare, underserviced and overpoliced them, and in most respects ruled them from afar. The state's overwhelming power has nevertheless permeated every aspect of the Bedouin and their way of life. Should the state and its capitalist allies decide to intervene systematically in the affairs of the Bedouin, as they have done in the last two decades of the twentieth century, their brittle socioeconomic order is doomed to undergo a profound and perhaps irreversible transformation.

This orientation toward the political economy allowed me to see the Bedouin of Mount Sinai in a new light. For instance, I realized that they were not a bounded community on which numerous external forces impinged, and that the customary academic distinctions between society and environment, or text and context, were misleading. For these forces, whether they emanated from a distant or a nearby source, whether delivered by a soldier's peremptory orders or the persuasive message of a fizzy American drink (*kakule* in Bedouin speech) or a Seiko watch, profoundly affected the Bedouin's lives, and must therefore be treated as an integral part of their society. The constituents of this wide-open borderless social system that I had formerly relegated to the social background or context now dominate the ethnography and analysis. This approach may make some colleagues uncomfortable, for they will look in vain for the minutiae of daily life that constitute the core of traditional ethnographies.

This open system approach also permitted me to realize that the Bedouin were not just pastoralists, gardeners, migrant workers, and smugglers, but also engaged in a great variety of other occupations, and that their division of labor was akin to that of a city. They differed from city dwellers chiefly in their lack of formal schooling and occupational training, in the near absence of the services and infrastructures generally provided by the state, in low population density, and in wildly fluctuating economic and political conditions. These conditions forced the Bedouin to continually adapt to new exigencies and to switch from one livelihood to another.

The data also led me to engage with some popular theoretical themes, such as the nature of corporate groups and pilgrimage, and such fundamental socioeconomic problems as social security and labor migration. I realized that kinship and descent were less central to the Bedouin economy than links between trading associates, neighbors, and tribesmen, and so I kept their analysis to a bare minimum.

The book thus builds on the central theoretical understanding that the complex political economy of the Mount Sinai Bedouin is integrated in urban society and is part of the modern global world. This argument can be fully comprehended only by reading the book from cover to cover. I consider it important, however, that each chapter can also be read as a self-contained unit. Therefore, each chapter furnishes the geographical, ecological, and political information necessary for understanding the argument. I did eliminate redundant passages, but inevitably a certain amount of repetition remains. This arrangement has its advantages: it allows the book to be read in any preferred order, and not necessarily from beginning to end or from end to beginning. It also facilitates the use of individual chapters for teaching purposes.

The book seeks to be user-friendly and to respect the reading habits of a contemporary public. Therefore, I wished to present the information in chunks small enough to be contained in the average reader's relatively short span of attention. For the same reason I used the simplest and most direct language I could muster, and that required me to thoroughly think through the data and their interpretation and to clarify every concept to the point where I felt that the analysis had become clear and almost self-evident. Every author wishes his or her book to stay "modern," namely, that it should remain relevant even years after publication, and not be dated by the fashionable concepts it employs or by the up-to-date and therefore short-lived bibliographical references. This principle applies particularly to the Mount Sinai Bedouin, who have been around, and have been studied, for a long time. Where the existing travelers' reports and archival documents cover more than a millennium, there could be no question of resorting to an ephemeral "cutting-edge modernity" style of presentation. My study had to respond to the requirements of such a complex society: fieldwork extended over a decade, in which South Sinai underwent some rapid and far-reaching changes, and the analysis of the material lasted even longer.

While I insist that each chapter stand on its own and that the book can therefore be read in any desired order, I do make slight concessions to the traditional manner of presenting ethnographic material. Thus, I begin the book with reflections on how I came to study the Bedouin, and how my views on them changed in the course of study. I continue with a wide-ranging discussion of the essential characteristics of Bedouin societies. I move on to examine the ecology of Sinai, and then describe the main branches of the Bedouin economy one by one. The chapter on pilgrimages tries to pull together the separate strands of the analysis, while the conclusion brings the account up-to-date.

Here is a brief synopsis of the contents. This introduction explains, among other things, how I came to work with the Bedouin of Mount Sinai, and how the book gradually took shape. Chapter 1 tells the story of the slow and painful learning process that I had to undergo: it took me many years to realize that the Bedouin of Mount Sinai not only take part in an urban social order, but also that this urbanism is reflected in their complex specialized economy. Some of my earlier articles had not done justice to the varied and ever-changing occupations and trades of the Bedouin. Chapter 2 is devoted to a wide-ranging theoretical discussion of the political economy of Bedouin societies. It seeks to expose and correct various popular misconceptions about the Bedouin and other pastoral nomads. For instance, it shows that Bedouin are very efficient producers of meat and other animal products and make an important contribution to their nations' economies. Chapter 3 deals with the impact of the physical environment of Mount Sinai on the Bedouin population, as well as with the Bedouin's efforts to control their environment. It argues in particular that all oases are man-made, and that they are not necessarily established in the most fertile areas. Demands such as inaccessibility to outsiders or closeness to fellow tribesmen may be more important than the availability of water and pasture. For instance, when Bedouin construct orchards in the mountain vastnesses, they put more emphasis on inaccessibility than on the availability of soil or water. Chapter 4 shows how labor migration, which was during my fieldwork the most important source of income for the Bedouin, completely (if temporarily) transforms their social life. In particular, it turns Bedouin men into cosmopolitan proletarians. While all Bedouin are experienced in the ways of the world, only a few manage to accumulate an economic reserve. As migrant labor is rather insecure work in distant regions, the Bedouin invest great efforts in building up a system of social security at home. Chapter 5 shows how the Bedouin became involved in the great international hashish trade in the 1950s, why the drug trafficking stopped during the Israeli occupation, and how it resumed after the Sinai Peninsula was restored to Egyptian sovereignty. Chapter 6 looks at the mobile traders from al-'Arish, whose trucks rove over the countryside, supplying the Bedouin with most of the necessities of life, including wheat and corn, their basic foods. The Bedouin mistrust these strangers and complain that they exploit them systematically, although they could hardly survive without their services. Therefore, the traders should be viewed as indispensable members of Bedouin society. Chapter 7 examines the Bedouin's periodical personal pilgrimages to saints' tombs, as well as their regular annual tribal pilgrimages. It shows how the pilgrimages conjure up an orderly and just social world, how the tribesmen's annual gathering at the tomb of the tribal patron saint embodies the tribe, and how the pilgrimages momentarily bring together members of widely dispersed social networks. Finally, the conclusion deals with the radical changes that occurred in Santa Katarina region since the days of my fieldwork, based on a short stay in the region in 2009.

I am glad for having had the opportunity to exercise my mind on such an intriguing set of data and problems. I hope that the study offers a novel understanding of the complex and fascinating Bedouin of Mount Sinai, one that the Bedouin too may approve of. I look forward to reading the work of a budding new generation of mostly native ethnographers. These studies can be expected to make full use of the abundant historical and archival material and to bring forth intriguing new sociological insights.

Chapter One

The Growth of a Conception
Nomads and Cities

-<*==)(==*>-

My understanding of the Bedouin of Mount Sinai and, by infer-
ence, of pastoral nomads in general grew by painfully slow stages.
It has taken me the best part of thirty years to evolve a conception
of these Bedouin that encompasses the full range of data I observed and wrote down in field notes. Perhaps I should apologize
for being so slow-witted, but I naively believe that I am no different from other anthropologists involved in the extended process of conceptualization. As our conceptions determine which
aspects of reality we see and which we ignore, conceptualization
stands at the core of anthropological work. It requires us to engage in obstinate drilling in the hard rock of our mind, in order to
overcome our stereotypes and mental blocks, and to continuously
revise our interpretation of ever larger quantities of amorphous
data. Without this extended work and toil we would get stuck in
the fragmented commonplace knowledge created jointly by the
people we study and by us, their students. Only an incessant dia-
lectic between our selective observations and tentative interpreta-
tions can get us somewhat closer to understanding a reality that is
almost impervious to conceptualization.

The worst thing an anthropologist can do is to rely on her or his
stored-up research experience. He is then bound to go wrong. He

will easily recognize familiar landmarks, but fail to see the many intriguing new sights and insights concealed in his data. In order to make sense of his or her observations in a new field, the anthropologist must make a radical fresh start. First, she must develop an initial conception of the social aggregate studied, being well aware that it is simplified, even stereotyped, but will inevitably change and grow as work progresses; second, she must focus on a sociological question that touches the lives of the people she lives with; and third, she must devise a methodology that precisely fits the problem and the people studied. Only such a three-pronged approach gives the anthropologist a chance to achieve his or her ultimate aim: to get the ethnography right, in the sense that a large amount of data become meaningful "facts," hang together and explain one another, thus enabling him or her to understand at least a limited aspect of an elusive reality. As we all know, this is easier said than done.

In my earlier work on Bedouin cultivators and pastoralists in the Negev (Marx 1967) I argued that, in as far as they specialize in pastoralism, Bedouin are full participants in a complex city-based market economy. While cereal farming provides them with some economic autarky, their labor-intensive pastoral activities produce expensive commodities, such as meat, milk, wool, and hides. They consume only small quantities of these products, as they can sell them for a good price in cities. With the proceeds they buy their staple foods, such as cereals, oil, and sugar, and the numerous goods they require in daily life. On the face of it, the nomads can transact their business during one or two annual trips to the city. They may even dispense with personal visits and, instead, trade with itinerant merchants. Yet they depend on the city for sheer existence, and can remain pastoralists only as long as the city dwellers are wealthy enough to buy their products.

When Bedouin become labor migrants in cities and in industrial enterprises they become even more involved in urban society. Ironically, while they are only sojourners in the city and work in the lowliest occupations, they are more exposed to the city's economic and political vicissitudes than most other city dwellers, for in a recession, they are the first to lose their jobs. Then, they may return home to their flocks and fields and sell the produce on the market, thus reentering the city economy by another door.

Thus, when I began fieldwork in South Sinai I already knew that Bedouin depend on cities. It took me some time to realize that these particular Bedouin do not only rely on the city; they also fully participate in urban civilization. This insight helped me in formulating a first conceptualization of their society. It took me much longer to work out a more advanced second conceptualization. That happened when I finally grasped the significance of a reality I had seen for many years: that these Bedouin had developed an urban civilization in their midst. Only then did I realize that this urbanism was evident in every aspect of their lives, as in their complex division of labor, their total dependence on foods and other commodities produced in cities and villages, their heavy reliance on income from migrant labor and drug smuggling, and their submission to the indirect rule of the state.

The dependence of the Mount Sinai Bedouin on the city was even greater than that of the Negev Bedouin. They never achieved any economic autarky, and could not survive in their mountain reaches without a steady supply of imported grain and other basic commodities. Even their small flocks and orchards could sustain them for only a few weeks. They were "pastoral nomads" only in a very limited sense, and had developed a quite complex multifaceted monetary economy, whose further growth was not so much limited by scarce capital as by a lack of schooling and technological training. In order to drive home my point I argued, provocatively, that they were a specialized segment of urban civilization (Marx 1992: 256).

These understandings led me to concentrate more and more on the complex economy of the Sinai Bedouin. I soon discovered numerous groups that engaged in a wide range of social activities. While most of these groups were corporate, the descent groups that are so prominent in ethnographic studies of pastoral societies were in this case neither corporate nor very active. This induced me to look more closely at the workings of the corporate groups, which often included clusters of kinsmen, and to pay less attention to descent groups and kinship networks. I was aware that I was parting ways with colleagues who considered kinship and descent to be basic elements of "social structure," as I had in *Bedouin of the Negev* (Marx 1967).

The First Conception

Between 1972 and 1982 I spent altogether about twelve months in South Sinai, mostly among the Jabaliya Bedouin in the Mount Sinai region. It did not take me long to realize that they were quite different from the Negev Bedouin, whom I had studied earlier. In the Negev my theoretical starting point had been that the Israeli military administration had a critical impact on Bedouin society. Its officers believed in the notion, so common among administrators of pastoralist groups, that the Bedouin produced animals and grains mainly for their own subsistence and contributed little to the national economy. Therefore, they did not hesitate to remove most of the Bedouin from their land and to confine them to a native reservation. They did not wish the Bedouin to enter the labor market, which was to be reserved for the masses of destitute Jewish immigrants. They issued only a small number of short-term labor permits to the Bedouin, and allowed them to enter the market town of Beersheva just once a week. Thus, they reduced people who had previously participated in a complex economy to pastoralists and dry land farmers.

In Sinai such a conception did not work, for neither the Egyptian authorities nor the Israeli occupying forces that replaced them put much effort into administrating the Bedouin population. While the Jabaliya did raise flocks and tended orchards, in contrast to the Negev Bedouin they did not derive an income from them. Theirs was a token pastoralism that, they were at pains to tell me, only caused them losses, and a horticulture that only produced fruit and vegetables for home consumption. They treated the fruit especially as "sweets," and not as a staple food. They earned their cash income mostly as labor migrants, as they had done, so the elders insisted, for many generations. This claim is fully corroborated by ancient documents stored in the Santa Katarina monastery and by travelers' accounts (Marx 1987). They maintained the flocks and orchards as resources to fall back on in bad times, a kind of economic reserve or insurance policy. Experience had taught them that in the recurrent economic and political crises that befell the region, the labor migrants were always the first to lose their jobs. Whenever there was a wave of unemployment, they would return home and reactivate their flocks and orchards, thus rejoining the market economy by an alternate route. During my fieldwork there were two occasions when the reserve economy came alive; one was the October 1973 war between Egypt and Israel, and the other, ironically, was US Secretary of State Henry Kissinger's shuttle diplomacy between Cairo and Jerusalem in 1976, which was to lead to a peace treaty between the two states and, incidentally, to end the Israeli occupation of Sinai. On both occasions the labor migrants returned home and worked hard to increase their flocks and raise the yields of their orchards and vegetable patches.

Most Bedouin considered labor migration to be a fundamentally unattractive type of work, as it forced men to spend long periods away from family and home and also because it generally offered insecure and low-paid employment. While almost every Bedouin man spent many years of his working life as a migrant laborer, he never intended to remain one for long. He eagerly looked forward to the time when his sons would be old enough to take over and he could stop working. Then he would return home to South Sinai, to tend his gardens and raise a small flock, and be subsidized by the income of his sons. In practice, these long-term projects hardly ever worked out as planned. When work opportunities were abundant the older men too would again go out to work as labor migrants, and when work was scarce the flocks and orchards could not rapidly enough be converted into profitable enterprises.

For a long time I thought that labor migration was the key to understanding this society. It certainly was, and had been for generations, the Bedouin's major source of cash income. As labor migration typically offers only insecure employment, the Bedouin invested great efforts and resources in building up a system of mutual assurance at home. This was an economy in reserve, in the widest sense of the word. It consisted of the gardens and flocks that were maintained in a state of readiness for rapid development. Furthermore, it included carefully fostered ties with kin and friends, who would provide aid in time of need. Lastly, it included the maintenance of tribal membership through which the Bedouin acquired important territorial privileges, in particular the right to construct gardens and homes in their tribal territory, as well as free passage through, and access to pastures in, South Sinai, the region of the Tawara tribal confederation.

While the men were away at work, the women and children operated the reserve economy. The women kept the gardens and flocks just ticking over, so that when the men returned home they would put greater efforts in them and turn them into profitable ventures. Women also took care of relationships with kin and friends, the people who would support them in time of need. The men too would periodically take time off from work, in order to visit their kin and friends and bring them small gifts. During the date harvest in autumn many men would return home to accompany their families on the annual tribal pilgrimage to the tombs of the tribe's ancestor and other saints. That was the only time when the members of the tribe, who had all year been scattered among many distant workplaces, were reunited. Together they reembodied the tribe and reaffirmed its territorial rights, while each individual consolidated his or her relations with the saints, the intercessors with a provident God.

The Second Conception

This was the conception I used in my first articles on the Bedouin of Mount Sinai (Marx 1977b, 1980, 1984, and 1987, on which chapter 3 is based), and it seemed to explain most of the data. But soon I was writing several papers that did not fit the conception. The change was precipitated by a comparative study of pastoralists in the Arab Middle East that I had begun at the time (Marx 1992, 1996, and 2006a, on which chapter 2 is based). A major finding of that study was that pastoralists are so deeply involved in the market economy that they should be seen as a specialized sector of a complex city-based economy. In the city they market their produce, such as meat, hides, and wool, and they buy all the necessities of life, including most of the grains that are their staple food. They depend so heavily on cities that any economic or political turbulence there may change their entire way of life, to the extent that they may temporarily or permanently cease to be pastoralists. This new viewpoint allowed me to account for the two dramatic political events that occurred during my fieldwork:

the 1973 war between Egypt and Israel and the negotiations between the two countries conducted in 1976 by Henry Kissinger,
then the US Secretary of State. Both events had caused political
upheavals that sent home the Bedouin labor migrants. Such trau-
matic events, I realized, had occurred quite regularly in the course
of the peninsula's history, for Sinai has for millennia served as a
land bridge between Africa and Asia, and was the scene of many
battles between invaders from the north and Egyptian defenders,
neither of whom cared much for the native population (Eckenstein 1921; Mouton 2000: 27–36).

The desire to understand how Bedouin coped with these re-
curring crises made me examine the available historical material.
The Santa Katarina monastery in the Sinai Mountains preserves
a unique collection of ancient documents, many of which concern the Bedouin. The documents cover, very unevenly, the last
one thousand years. Most of the documents have been copied
on microfilm (see Stewart 1991: 98), but only some of the Arabic and Turkish documents have been deciphered and translated
(Humbsch 1976; Schwarz 1970). An interesting history of Sinai
(Shuqair 1916) used these and other documents to good purpose,
but left room for further study. There also exists a long series of
reports by travelers and pilgrims to South Sinai, going back to
the fourth and fifth century (Hobbs 1995: chap. 8; Deluz 2001).
The earliest surviving accounts are those of Egeria (or Etheria), a
Frenchwoman who visited Mount Sinai in 385 CE (Éthérie 1957;
see Eckenstein 1921: 114), and the hermit Nilus, who lived in Sinai
around 410 CE (Henninger 1955). Some of the learned and dis-
cerning travelers of the eighteenth and nineteenth century, such
as Niebuhr ([1774–78] 1968), Burckhardt ([1822] 1992), Robinson
(1867), C. W. Wilson and H. S. Palmer (1869–71), and E. H. Palmer
(1871), have left valuable accounts of the region and its people. I
could not afford to neglect such rich material, which could add a
historical dimension to the study.

The new conception led me to review my earlier work. I realized that the economy of the Bedouin of Mount Sinai was more
diversified than I had thought, and that they were profoundly
involved in world events. My writings had not portrayed all the
complexity and adaptability of their society.

The reexamination of the ethnographic material resulted in several articles. The first article dealt with oases (Marx 1999, on which

chapter 4 is based). It showed that there were various kinds of oases, all of them man-made. As some oases had been established as hideouts for bands of smugglers, the paper touched marginally on the importance of the smuggling of narcotic drugs to the Bedouin economy before the Israeli occupation. Smuggling had driven economic development in South Sinai, and smugglers had even created several new oases in the mountains. While smuggling was at low ebb during my fieldwork, it remained an important though submerged aspect of Bedouin society that demanded a fuller treatment (Marx 2008, the source of chapter 5).

Another set of articles (Marx 2004b and 2005a, the sources of chapter 6) dealt with the critical contribution of roving traders to the economy of the South Sinai Bedouin. The traders supply the Bedouin with grain and almost all the other necessities of life. While grain is the Bedouin's staple food, it is not grown in the region, and had it not been for these traders, the Bedouin would not have survived in arid Sinai. Under Egyptian rule, this trade had been in the hands of South Sinai Bedouin cameleers, later to become truck drivers, who worked closely with Egyptian shopkeepers in Suez. Only during the Israeli occupation was the trade taken over by the urban merchants of al-'Arish in North Sinai, and after Sinai returned to Egyptian sovereignty in 1982, Bedouin truckers became involved in it once more.

All these articles prepared me for this book, which is an attempt toward an explicit theoretical statement about the Bedouin of Mount Sinai (for an earlier version, see Marx 2005b). Once I understood the complex occupational specialization of the Bedouin, I realized that the secure base of Bedouin society, such as the tribe and kinship links, the flocks and orchards, and the tribal pilgrimage, could no longer be treated as an economic standby, or as a response to the exigencies of labor migration. They were just another way of life, one of many possible ones. Philip Salzman had tried to convert me to this viewpoint (Salzman 1980: 7–10), but at the time I did not heed his good advice.

It took me a long time to realize that the Bedouin not only participated in the great society and its market economy, but also were an integral part of it. This was especially evident in their diversified occupational structure. While practically every household raised flocks and tended orchards, and most men were either labor migrants or involved in smuggling, quite a few men and women also engaged in a specialized trade. They were well diggers, builders, cameleers, truck drivers, mechanics, and vegetable farmers, including several men who produced the local variety of tobacco and thus infringed upon a state monopoly. They were pollinators of date palms, fishermen, boat builders, storekeepers (stores were called *kantin*, as in British army camps), and owners of coffeehouses. Some men worked for the government, as tribal chiefs, teachers, and police informers. Others were tribal judges, healers, jewelers, tailors, basket makers, and tourist guides. There were also up to thirty permanent employees of the Santa Katarina monastery, whom the monks called *subyan al-deir*, lads of the monastery. They included an electrician, driver, carpenter, and cook, and a number of menial workers. Nearly all the above-mentioned Bedouin specialists were men, but there were also women specialists, among them healers, fortune-tellers, and midwives. The services of all these men and women were remunerated in cash.

Specialization was even reflected in such matters as the services of local healers and in the powers attributed to various saints. Each healer treated a specific set of complaints; one was an expert on diabetes *(sukkar)*, another specialized in circumcisions and extractions of the uvula *(zor)*, operations to which every boy and girl was subjected, and another again cured mental illnesses. Saints too were thought to specialize in dealing with certain problems. Bedouin often approached one saint when their children fell ill, another was visited by barren women, a third saint could bring back a lost camel, and yet another could assure the welfare of the flocks.

This does not imply that the economies of the city and of the Bedouin were almost identical. The low population density, the relative poverty and illiteracy of most of the inhabitants, the peculiar combination of labor migration, pastoralism, and horticulture, all these produced a special brand of complex economy. It required the inhabitants to cover great distances to perform the simplest economic transaction; it induced them to use locally available materials, and to exercise great ingenuity in operating modern technologies. Thus, a visit to a healer, often combined with a personal pilgrimage to a saint's tomb, might take several days of travel by foot or by car. The basket maker al-Rifi of Wadi Firan used only locally produced materials, the fronds and fibers of palm trees. Even where industrially produced cords were available, he preferred to twist his own ropes. His products were quite different from those marketed in the cities and villages of Egypt: he made containers for dates, baskets for coffee-making utensils or for clothing (to be hung from the rafters of the house or the roof of the tent), chicken coops, and a kind of incubator for newly hatched chicks. While Egyptian villagers too used the material from local palm trees for the manufacture of numerous household goods, the only item made in both regions was cords made of the fibers (Henein 1988: 179–94). Similarly, local car owners who had no access to spare parts carried out ingenious improvised repairs with odd pieces of wood and ends of barbed wire left behind by the armies passing through Sinai. In addition, in order to benefit from the full range of urban services, the Bedouin would in the course of the year still make numerous excursions to Suez and Cairo or, respectively, Eilat and Tel Aviv.

There were other persons whose presence made Bedouin society possible. The roving merchants from al-'Arish were obviously part of the society. So were the tourists, who bought trinkets from Bedouin children or stayed in holiday camps run by Bedouin, the government officials who provided essential services, the soldiers and security officers who interfered in the Bedouin's' way of life and, incidentally, drove up the price of narcotics, and the Greek monks who had inspired the Bedouin's horticulture during centuries of coexistence and who, after having in the past claimed to own all the land in the vicinity of the Santa Katarina monastery, now supported the Bedouin's claims to the ownership of orchards and building sites.

Therefore, it is essential to treat Bedouin society as a complex and economically differentiated social agglomerate, whose members participate in various ways in an urban civilization. A study of the Bedouin must take into account the impact of rapid and often dramatic changes in the wider political arena on the Bedouin economy. It must show how various economic pursuits produce numerous sectors and lifestyles within this Bedouin society, existing side by side and yet linked up with one another, each sector adapting in its particular manner to changing political and economic circumstances. The study is therefore quite unlike the standard anthropological monograph. It works with an open system that examines how numerous social forces not just impinge on people but become part of their lives. The ethnography thus becomes exceedingly complex, wide-ranging, and seemingly disjointed, and therefore lacks the dramatic unity of persons, time, and plot that makes a good read. The personal and tribal pilgrimages (Marx 1977b, 2006b, on which chapter 7 is based), however, reflect and fuse many of these disparate strands of society.

The Bedouin of Mount Sinai illustrate one solution to the profound connection between nomads and cities: their society is an attenuated version of the city's complex economic specialization. The Syrian Rwala Bedouin (Lancaster 1997: 166–67) exemplify a very different type of dependence on cities: their major specializations in sheep raising, commerce, and trucking require them to constantly move between the cities and markets of four countries (Saudi Arabia, Iraq, Jordan, and Syria). But they too have for generations had numerous specialized artisans and traders living in their midst. Therefore, I argue, in chapter 2, that all social aggregates in which pastoral nomadism is an important part of the economy share the city's diversified economy.

The basic understanding that urban civilization pervades every aspect of Bedouin society made me question some of my own theoretical positions. I shall briefly discuss just two issues. First, I look at the diverse corporate groups found among the Bedouin, because my findings may harbinger a theoretical reorientation. Second, I discuss the great geographic mobility of the Bedouin because, paradoxically, it helps us understand why Bedouin can, for the time being, remain in the Mount Sinai region. The prevailing myth of demographic stability of the Bedouin population may make us oblivious to the threatened extinction of the Bedouin as pastoralists and horticulturalists.

From Corporate Descent Groups to an Abundance of Corporate Groups

My ideas about corporate groups changed twice. I first found that corporate descent groups played an important role in Negev Bedouin society. On examination I realized that, in spite of appearances, these groups were not founded on kinship. While many members were related as kinsmen, they acted as partners in an egalitarian corporate group that dealt with clearly defined issues. In contrast, relationships among kin were generally dyadic, and one could call on a kinsman for any imaginable kind of assistance. Then, in Sinai I found that Bedouin descent groups were neither important nor corporate; instead, in the manner of city dwellers, people associated in numerous and varied corporate groups. I began to wonder whether earlier anthropologists had not given too much weight to descent groups and failed to appreciate the significance of the many other corporate activities.

During fieldwork in the Negev, Bedouin friends often tried hard to convince me that the corporate descent group *(khams)* was concerned only with the defense of its members, and was clearly separate from the domestic group. When they insisted that the members of the descent group were "close" *(qarib)* to one another, I assumed they were talking about kinship, because the Hebrew term for closeness *(qirva)* derives from the same root and denotes, among other things, kinship. When I asked them whether maternal and affinal relatives were "close," my Bedouin informants said that they were definitely not; on the contrary, they were distant *(ba'id)*. It took me some time to realize that closeness *(qaraba)* referred to agnation, the putative descent link that conferred membership in the corporate descent groups. It also covered the relationships between two allied and intermarrying descent groups (Marx 1967: 174–76). I also discovered that while the Bedouin recognized numerous categories of kin, they thought about each kinsman or kinswoman as a potential partner in a useful dyadic, or at the utmost triadic, relationship. Thus, a mother's brother was someone who could be fully relied upon, more than even a father or brother, to help his sister's son in any contingency. Brothers were expected to assist one another; in practice, a man or a woman could make practically any demand on each of their siblings, according to his or her capabilities and resources. The Bedouin felt that their connections with these individuals were the outcome of sharing, or having recently shared, the same domestic environment. They never thought of kinship as a way of ordering relationships, or as the organizing principle of groups. They did not even think that kinsmen participated in an ego-centered network of close-knit or loose-knit relationships. It did not occur to me at the time that kinship was a Western concept that anthropologists were applying, by hook and by crook, to all societies. While David M. Schneider's *American Kinship* (1968) showed conclusively that the anthropologists' conception of kinship was embarrassingly similar to the American man-in-the-street's ideas about kinship, we have not yet fully embraced the lesson that kinship is a Western ethnocentric construct. Many anthropologists still consider kinship to be a special field of study (see, e.g., Peletz 1995).

After reading Eickelman's (1989: 156–61) discussion of "closeness" in Morocco (there too, as elsewhere in the Arab world, it is called *qaraba*), I came to the conclusion that the term *qaraba* is better translated as corporateness, while being aware that other scholars translate *qaraba* both as kinship and agnation (see Abu-Lughod 1986: 51). Eickelman shows that in the urban neighborhood he studied, the term closeness may refer to "participation in factional alliances, ties of patronage and clientship, and common bonds developed through neighborliness" (1989: 156). Members of these corporate groups recognize common interests and have the capacity to act jointly in their implementation. Their association is often expressed as a blood tie, especially when it deals with defending the members' bodily safety. The group is then activated whenever a member's blood has been spilled. The principle applies even when only a drop of blood was drawn, and in the absence of a wound they can be relied upon to discover a scratch and define it as a wound. Such associations may then be further elaborated as joint descent groups, so as to fit them into the image of a segmentary society made up of a series of ever more encompassing descent groups.

The Sinai Bedouin forced me to discover the many varieties of corporate groups that were operating all around me, for their descent groups were noncorporate, and functioned mainly as imaginary links between households and the territorial tribe. Bedouin said that the tribe was corporately responsible for blood revenge, but could not cite any examples from the recent past. On the contrary, they often argued that "for the last fifty years there has not been a single instance of murder in South Sinai," so that it was hard to see the tribe engage in violent action. Yet I could "see" the tribes when members gathered at the various annual pilgrimages. Only when I managed to break away from the notion that corporateness was linked to descent could I see the many ongoing corporate activities.

As a necessary step toward understanding the meaning of corporateness, I examined the prolific literature on corporate descent groups. In the Arab world the corporate descent groups go under various names, such as *hamula, khams, qom, batn, fakhdh,* and *bayt,* and in daily conversation people nonchalantly employ further terms that ordinarily denote other types of groups, like *'a'ila* (family), *ahl* (often used for the extended family), and *qabila* (tribe) (see Aswad 1971: 49–50). The multiplicity of terms is due partly to variance of regional linguistic usage and partly to people's sociological understanding. They think of descent groups as evolving self-transforming entities: families may branch out into descent groups, and descent groups may be promoted into tribes. Therefore, the use of "incorrect" terms is not as imprecise as it may appear.

Most anthropologists would go along with the following working definition: a corporate descent group is an egalitarian group of adult men who claim descent from one (male or female) ancestor; its task is to assist any member or members who have been physically attacked or whose property rights (mostly in land, but also in human beings and herds) have been infringed upon by members of another descent group (for various definitions and more references see Fried [1957: 23], Befu and Plotnicov [1962: 64], Buchler and Selby [1968: 70], and Hayden and Cannon [1982: 133–35]).

Now that we possess a definition, we must examine and deconstruct it. The six chief characteristics of the group are, according to the definition, that it is composed of men only, its members are recruited by descent, it is egalitarian, it functions in defense of persons and property, it is activated by acts of aggression and, being a "corporation," it may exist in perpetuity. Let me examine the attributes one by one.

1. The group is made up of men only. The members often claim that only agnates, the men descended of one named ancestor, are admitted. Many anthropologists would therefore consider them to be kin. By using this term, which includes

both men and women, they beg the question of why membership is open to men only. It is curious how kinship is used to define an organization that a priori excludes most of the persons we call kin, namely, all kinswomen and all maternal and affinal male relatives. Therefore, I argued in a study of the Negev Bedouin that agnation is quite distinct from kinship: agnates are members of groups recruited by descent (Marx 1967: 183). Many of them may, of course, also be kinsmen, and as such are expected to help each other in every conceivable way. But as members of the group, they are only required to act when a member is assaulted or his land is invaded.

The men are mobilized whenever trained fighters are needed. The women are excluded mainly because they do not possess, or rather are not allowed to acquire, martial skills. But when the men are absent or when reinforcements are needed, women may take their place even in fighting. Thus, Beck (1991: 95) reports that the women of the Qermezi, a Qashqa'i descent group, rushed to defend their farmland against peasant invaders until the men caught up with them: "At the height of the conflict, 13 Qermezi men and 30 women faced 150 peasants and their supporters. Both sides, including women, sustained injuries." A "males only" rule applies mainly to martial groups. Corporate groups that engage in other activities may include both men and women. For instance, among some Bedouin pastoralists all the members of a household, whether young or old, male or female, jointly care for the flock. In this context they may act corporately (Abu-Rabi'a 1994: 69–72).

2. Members are formally recruited by descent from a distant ancestor. One might therefore assume that they were all kinsmen. In reality, no member can furnish the full details of his own connection to the ancestor. There is always a structural gap in his genealogical knowledge, separating the apical ancestor from his descendants who have remained in living memory (Peters 1990: 99). Even when the genealogy shows that the ancestor is only five generations removed from the members living today, they will admit that they have no memory of his or her direct descendants and that

in all probability the ancestor is much further removed, certainly "many more than five generations" (Marx 1967: 188). Because of this genealogical amnesia none of the members can prove a precise kinship connection to the ancestor, so that all the members are equidistant from him or her. Thus, the ancestor is no longer a kinsman, but rather a figurehead who symbolizes the boundedness of the group, and the unity and formal equality of its members. Many members have kinship links with each other, but their obligations as kin may clash with the group's purposes and may impede its functioning.

Furthermore, membership is not necessarily determined by descent. True, a man becomes a member by birth. But this does not mean that he will always take up the membership or remain a member all his life. As an adult he can choose not to join the group. All he has to do is move to another location, or join another group. He can indicate to fellow members at any time that he wishes to leave the group by simply not fulfilling his contractual obligations. The group can also decide to expel a troublesome member, for instance, one who has had too many violent encounters (Marx 1967: 199–200, 239–41; Ginat 1987: 90–112; see also Moore 1978: 122–24). The group may also extend membership to strangers or merge with another descent group. We must therefore conclude that, in practice, membership of the group is almost voluntary, and that even persons born into the group choose if and when to join it and when to leave. What unites the group is the joint purpose of its members; their actual descent is of little importance.

3. The group is corporate, in the sense that all members share the same rights and obligations (Fortes 1970: 306). It cannot be otherwise, for if members are expected to risk their lives for their fellows, they must be sure that this is done on a reciprocal basis and that the group will stand by them when their turn comes. Many groups take active steps to ensure the commitment of members, especially of the younger men who do most of the fighting. That is why Negev Bedouin parents are expected to give each son soon after marriage his due share in the family's farmland and flocks. The out-

come is usually that they not only hand over part of their productive resources, but also tend to lose the son's labor. As this clearly goes against the parents' interests, they delay the transaction as long as possible. But it serves the requirements of the corporate descent group to turn young men into property owners, and thus make them equals of their property-owning fathers. This will induce them to risk life and limb to protect their own as well as the group's interests. Therefore, the other members of the group encourage reluctant fathers to hand over the productive resources, "as custom demands." While life inheritance appears to enhance the corporateness of the group, it also exposes the internal differentiation between the elders who make the policy decisions and the younger men who bear the brunt of the fighting (Marx 1987: 172). In practice, there are other differences that make for inequality among members, as Fried (1957: 23–24) and Salzman (2004: 43ff.) have pointed out, such as ranking and ethnic stratification. There are also individual differences between wealthy and poor members, between clever men who persuade their fellows to support them even in doubtful cases and simple men who are bound by the formal rules (Marx 1967: 182–83), between men who can count on the individual and corporate support of family members, friends, neighbors, and other corporations and others who stand almost alone (Peters 1990: 134). Egalitarianism thus struggles against heavy odds, but its form is maintained. Weber (1947: 133) has pointed out another factor leading to inequality: there can be no corporation without a leader or leaders. To this should be added that a group cannot operate without internal articulation; it must be subdivided into sections and cliques of unequal power.

4. Formally, the group serves only one purpose: to protect its major values, the lives, land, and property of its members. In practice, it behaves very much like other interest groups: while it has been set up for a specific purpose, its interests can shift and change in due course. Michael G. Smith (1974: 96) disagrees with this position. He believes that the corporateness of a group is expressed in every aspect of its operation, the implication being that a group cannot easily adapt

to change. A noncorporate group (he uses choruses as an example) or any other group that is essentially nonpolitical, he believes, is not and cannot become a corporate group. I cannot accept this argument, for even groups that perform aesthetic or recreational activities always engage in politics and are in some respects corporate. Furthermore, they may at any suitable moment transform themselves into purely political groups. Choruses, African Zionist churches, or celebrations of the Prophet's memorial day in Manchester have not only been known to turn overnight into cells of militants (P. Werbner 2002: 157 ff.), but they may even have been set up in the first place as front organizations (Mafeje 1975). It should not come as a surprise to learn that the corporate descent groups of the Negev Bedouin continued to function after the members lost all their land and flocks and moved into new towns. There the descent groups engaged in political resistance and their members were represented in local political arenas (Jakubowska 1992). A group that has been set up to perform a particular task may then quite easily and rapidly assume other duties and yet remain corporate.

5. The group responds to external acts of aggression, and thus acts only intermittently. In between actions it exists mostly in the minds of its members. Of course, they do receive daily reminders of their obligations as members, for instance, whenever they gather at the group's meeting place and drink coffee together, or when interlocutors require them to state a "family" name. The members are activated by a cue: when they hear that the blood of a member has been shed, they put aside whatever they are doing at the moment and rush to the site of the fighting. The member is called a protector of blood *(dammawi)*. The common blood is the ideology underlying the group's organization: the members believe that they share the same blood and defend the blood of fellow members, for are they not descendants of one ancestor? As there must be bloodshed before the group can be mobilized, blood is drawn in every fight, even if it later on turns out to be an almost imperceptible scratch. The fact that outsiders have encroached on their members' lands, herds, or other property may underlie the group's going into action, but

members do not consider this as sufficient ground for mobilization. They first need to see blood. An astute leader can, therefore, easily provoke or even simulate a bloody clash and draw members into ill-considered disputes, including ones that are outside the group's interests.

6. The group continues into perpetuity, even when its membership changes or is altogether replaced by another generation. Many students of the corporation have stressed this trait, from Henry Maine, who speaks of "the leading attribute of Corporations—Perpetuity" ([1861] 1917: 110), to the more skeptic Michael G. Smith, who speaks a century later about "presumed perpetuity" (1974: 96). The continued existence of the group is said to be assured by its presumed joint ownership of land and other resources. The property is handed down to the next generation, thus allowing the group to continue in existence independently of the more or less brief lives of its members (Fried 1957: 18).

This belief in continuity, however, is not borne out by the ethnographic data. These show, on the contrary, that both groups and property are in constant flux. A group that has grown too large tends to split up (Peters 1990: 106); one that is too small may disband; groups are racked by internal squabbles and may split; members who feel that the group deserted them may secede and establish new groups (Marx 1967: chap. 7). In the wake of such splits, the eponyms of the corporate descent groups may also change. Besides, there are corporate groups that do not hold property in common. Among the Negev Bedouin, for instance, farmland is owned individually, and pastures are owned by tribal federations. But that has never prevented corporate descent groups from protecting either private or communal property. Even where there are customary methods for redistributing joint property, such as the common land (musha') of the traditional Palestinian village, corporate descent groups effectively protect their members' interests. Perpetuity is, then, no more than a legal fiction that disguises the temporary and dynamic nature of any human collaboration. Most corporate groups are short-lived affairs, and enduring ones are the exception.

The gist of the argument so far has been that corporate descent groups are flexible interest groups, which may be perpetual, but are more often short-lived. In the course of time they may undergo a variety of transformations, and may even change structure from one situation to the next. Membership is almost voluntary, and is certainly not confined to the direct descendants of an ancestor. There is considerable movement of individuals in and out of groups. Groups develop internal status differences; they have leaders, are divided into sections, and cliques and members compete among themselves for resources. In all these respects they resemble other types of groups that have been studied by anthropologists, such as factions, camps, voluntary associations, business partnerships, and even domestic groups. Conversely, I argue that all these noncorporate groups may on occasion become corporate and engage in all the activities that corporate descent groups specialize in. I would even go further and argue that corporate groups perpetually change their structure and practices in the course of interacting with other groups. The image of an amoeba that constantly changes shape, splits, and fuses with other amoebas may fit them well. It may thus be quite misleading to classify a group as a corporate descent group, faction, etc., without inserting an immediate temporal and situational qualifier.

To sum up, nearly all the joint economic activities of the Bedouin, such as organized migrant labor, drug smuggling, and transportation, are carried out by a variety of corporate groups, much as in cities. The corporate descent groups so beloved in the anthropological literature are there, but play an insignificant part in the lives of the Bedouin.

Why Some Bedouin Remain in South Sinai and Why Others Leave

I would like to take the argument that Bedouin partake in urban civilization one step further, and claim that the Bedouin can live in South Sinai only because they are urbanites. If they were not, they would simply disappear from the face of Sinai. Consider that the ten thousand Bedouin living in South Sinai find very little pasture for their flocks, and invest much money and labor in herding and in buying supplementary feed for their animals. Their orchards, wrought at great expense out of the rocky ground, do not produce enough fruit and vegetables to satisfy their own needs. Most of their income derives from the city, and almost all their consumption goods are imported from the city. If this argument is correct, then why do the Bedouin bother to stay in an environment as arid and inhospitable as South Sinai? Would one not expect them to move to the city instead?

There is a twofold answer to these questions. First, at least half the members of each generation of Bedouin do actually leave Sinai, or rather, they do not return to Sinai from their labor migration period. They settle their households permanently in the cities of the Nile Valley or in other regions of Egypt, but even there live among their own tribesmen and retain links to the homeland. They retain the option of a return to the fold of the tribe.

Second, those Bedouin who remain in South Sinai participate in the market economy in many ways, besides horticulture and herding. There are several categories of Bedouin for whom the region holds attraction.

First, South Sinai is good for those Bedouin who use the region as a haven of retirement. When their sons are old enough to take over from them as labor migrants, which may be from the age of fifteen onward, these men may be thirty-five or forty years old. They look forward to many years of life at home, in the intimate circle of family, relatives, and friends, and expect to enjoy the social security net provided by these links. They partly rely on the fruit and vegetables grown in their own orchards, drink of their own wells, and look forward to the occasional meat dish, preferably from an animal slaughtered by neighbors. For the rest, they are subsidized by the work of their labor migrant sons and through them remain connected to the market economy. By maintaining the orchards and small flocks in good condition, the elders prepare the ground for the time when their sons in their turn choose to retire. As there is one Bedouin whose flock of sixty sheep and goats allows him to eke out a living, and several vegetable farmers in Tarfat Qadren, west of Santa Katarina, who make a living from the sale of vegetables and fruit to local customers, they possess "living proof" that this economy is workable.

Second, it is good for men engaged in the smuggling trade, which offers large incomes and honor to the entrepreneurs, and small but often quite regular wages for their employees. The drug trade contributed an estimated 30 percent to the national economy of South Sinai in the 1950s and 1960s. It has played a major role in the development of oases and orchards in South Sinai. It has convinced the Bedouin tribes that they must live in peace with one another, as a precondition for conducting smuggling operations across tribal boundaries and for keeping the state authorities at bay. This situation has shaped the Bedouin's self-image of being peaceful people among whom, they say, "there has not been a case of murder for fifty years." Smuggling has also led the leaders of gangs to establish close links with representatives of the army, police, and other agencies of the state. Through these links the smugglers have been able to not only keep the smuggling routes open, but also to avert dangers such as the alienation of tracts of land, and to protect themselves against the arbitrary acts of local officials. While smuggling was very limited during the Israeli occupation of Sinai (1967–82), the smuggling organizations were not disbanded. The smugglers lay low, waiting for a change in the political situation.

Third, South Sinai is good for most women. Strange as it may sound, women have an interest in continuing the system of labor migration. While most of the men work outside the region, the women stay at home and lead relatively protected, and yet independent, lives. They have many responsibilities: they raise the children, run the household, maintain the gardens, and, with the help of their daughters, take the flock out to pasture. They foster the links with kin, collect and store much important information, and spend the money remitted by their husbands. Thus, they accumulate considerable power, which is shown in their self-assured interaction with both members of their own circle and outsiders, such as tourists. Should their men return home for good, they would lose much of their power and freedom of action. As life in the mountains is good for the wives of labor migrants, they do all they can to make the husbands extend their work periods. Returning husbands not only mean living at a reduced income; they also deprive the wives of their power and independence. No wonder most women are dissatisfied with the husband who returns home (see Lavie 1990: 122). Women are also quite reluctant to give up their relative independence when the husband desires them to resettle near his place of work.

Fourth, it suits the numerous men and women who produce goods or perform paid services for others. We saw above that there is a great variety of such specialists.

It appears that a large number of Bedouin wish to remain in, or return to, South Sinai. Yet their number is likely to dwindle over time, as military and commercial installations encroach on their land and, even more critically, on their water supply. The amount of water available to the Bedouin is strictly limited. When the army sets up installations in Sinai, it taps the local water supply with little consideration for the needs of a disenfranchised civilian population like the Bedouin, but also trucks in water from large distances. Hotels on the seashore will also use some local water, but supplement it with desalination plants. The Bedouin have access only to the water left in the ground by these stronger contenders and have no supplementary sources. Therefore, wherever a successful hotel is set up and the number of tourists grows (Hobbs 2001: 212), the Bedouin's water supply is reduced. This happened in the Santa Katarina area, in Nuweb'a, Dahab, and elsewhere. The amount of water available to the Bedouin for irrigation and even for drinking declined in all these areas. When the Bedouin themselves seek to increase cultivation the results are similar. When the owners of gardens in the Firan oasis installed mechanical pumps and increased the cultivated areas in the 1950s, the water level fell rapidly and all the wells had to be repeatedly deepened. When Bedouin developed the Tarfat Qadren oasis near Santa Katarina in the 1960s, the water supply in the downstream Firan oasis declined even faster. Eventually the gardeners dispensed with the pumps and returned to the less wasteful manual watering devices.

Neither the hotels nor the agencies of the state employ many Bedouin; they prefer to bring in their own workforce. The Bedouin are not literate enough and their traditional skills are not required by these city dwellers (Aziz 2000). Both the Bedouin's chances of employment and of improving their indigenous economy thus decrease as South Sinai is "developed." The outlook for the Bedouin is bleak. If the young labor migrants do not return to South Sinai, the chain of generations built on the fragile indigenous economy of flocks and orchards will break. The vivid orchards, which have for almost two millennia been an outstanding feature of the high mountains, and are today a major tourist attraction, will dry up. Then the Bedouin will gradually abandon the mountain ranges of South Sinai. More and more of them will join the many Qararsha, Huwetat and 'Aleqat Bedouin who have already settled in the cities and villages of mainland Egypt. Others will gravitate toward the tourist centers along the east coast of Sinai. As there will no longer be work for all the specialists who were part of the Bedouin economy, they too will gravitate to the mainland or to the tourist centers in Sinai. Even the smugglers will move away, as there will no longer be a law-abiding population to provide them with cover and services. The Bedouin as individuals will survive and adapt to the changed conditions, as they have always done (Lange 2003), but a unique and complex social formation will be no more; it will be reabsorbed by the city from which it emerged.

This chapter has dealt with the development of my thinking on Bedouin. I shall end it on a personal note. Underlying my work on Bedouin is a profound interest in their continuous adaptation to changing conditions and their quest for basic security. I feel that this is not simply the result of the fact that my fieldwork extended over a decade and thus encompassed a series of economic and political crises. It may also be due to my being a refugee from Nazi Germany, as Richard Werbner so perceptively pointed out (R. P. Werbner 2004: 340). Like so many refugees, I sought in vain to sink roots in new surroundings. The endless and hopeless search for a secure home became a lifelong preoccupation. It pervades all my work, but is particularly salient in the study of the Mount Sinai Bedouin.

Chapter Two

The Political Economy of Bedouin Societies

-<×⟹ ⟸×>-

In this chapter I formulate some generalizations about the political economy of pastoral nomads in the Middle East and North Africa, based on my work with Bedouin in the Negev and the Sinai Peninsula, as well as on my reading of the rich anthropological literature on pastoral nomads. As a starting point I take the notion elaborated upon in chapter 1: that pastoral nomads are a specialized sector of urban civilization. This idea has far-reaching implications, namely, that pastoralism alone is not feasible in a subsistence economy; that people take up pastoralism when there is a market for their animals; that they depend on the settled population for nearly all the necessities of life, including basic foods; that they are susceptible to control by the state; that in order to reduce their dependence on the market and on the state they usually engage in a variety of economic activities; that conditions may force them to give up, either temporarily or permanently, their pastoral activities; and that nomadic peoples therefore become pastoral nomads only in a limited sense and at particular times. I do not argue that the concept of pastoral nomadism has outlived its usefulness. On the contrary, I claim that it can be infused with new life once the study of the rapidly changing economic and political environments in which the "pastoralists" operate is given greater analytical weight than hitherto.

Pastoral Nomads Participate in Urban Economies

To begin with, a new type of classification is required. It should, first, distinguish between those groups whose economy is largely based on animal breeding and those for whom animal breeding is only one of several productive activities. Pastoralism may go hand in hand with a wide range of economic activities and, of course, these combinations may fluctuate or change dramatically over time. When a group largely depends on herds—whatever the species—it merely becomes a specialized sector in a complex and differentiated economic system. It depends on city markets and agents of the state, and is exposed to the vicissitudes of the political and economic environment, to war and famine, economic recession, and technical change. This dependence derives from the fact that pastoralists produce meat and other animal products mainly for affluent city dwellers, and only incidentally for their own consumption. In order to reduce the risks involved in a pastoralist specialization, most groups tend to combine herding with other economic pursuits, such as dry farming, trading, craft work, migrant labor, and smuggling. I do, however, concede that some pastoralists may subsist on meat, milk, and blood. Thus, colonial and postcolonial regimes in East Africa and elsewhere have from time to time prevented the access of cattle pastoralists to markets and left them no choice but to subsist on animal produce (Dahl and Hjort 1976: 23; Spencer 1988: 8–9; McCabe 1994), or markets have closed due to political upheavals, as in Mongolia today (Bruun 2006: 58–62).

Second, the new classification should consider the ways in which pastoralists adjust to changing market conditions. They do so both by calibrating their market involvement and by shifting around investments. During an economic slump or social turmoil, when city dwellers may not be able to afford meat, pastoralists may drastically reduce pastoral production or stop it entirely, only to resume it when conditions improve. We must therefore take a long-term view that can comprehend these changes in systems of production. We must realize that such "economic" adaptations bring in their wake extreme changes in every sphere of social life. For instance, a shift in emphasis from pastoralism toward labor migration in the 1970s caused the Bedouin of Mount Sinai to cease moving around with their flocks and to settle in nucleated villages, to give up their tents and to build solid stone houses. The wives of labor migrants took over not only the management of the household, and of the flocks and orchards, but also maintained the networks of social relations with neighbors and relatives. They carried out all these tasks with great self-assurance and aplomb. Yet as soon as the husbands returned home for good, they took charge of the household. The women rapidly lost much of their power and submitted to their husbands' authority.

Defining Pastoral Nomads

A look at the definitions of pastoral nomadism found in widely used scholarly publications may serve as a useful starting point for a revision. A standard textbook definition might run like this: pastoral nomads are tribal peoples who engage in animal husbandry in marginal environments; their movements are governed by the constant quest for pasture and water (Barfield 1993: 4; Coon 1960: 872; Gottwald 1979: 437; Johnson 1969: 4; Montagne 1947: 11; Spooner 1973: 4). The definition is ecologically biased and also tends to treat the tribe as an inclusive and undifferentiated social entity. While admitting that the ethnographies of all the authors cited go well beyond this definition, I nevertheless claim that the definition affects their analyses. It may lead them to make tacit, and sometimes even explicit, assumptions about the nature of pastoral nomadism, such as:

1. Pastoralists usually live in arid regions unsuitable for agricultural exploitation. Take Coon, for instance: "Pastoral nomadism is a sophisticated system of exploiting land incapable of cultivation" (Coon 1960: 872; see also Montagne 1947: 30; Patai 1971: 42; Scholz 1995: 27).
2. Pastoralists mainly breed animals and have no other important source of livelihood (Musil 1928). Montagne (1947: 12) makes it very plain that "[t]he whole pastoral economy relies on the raising of camels." Other ethnographers, however, recognized that most pastoralists rely on numerous sources of livelihood. Thus, Barfield states that "the historical and ethnographic record is full of nomads who also farm, trade,

serve as soldiers, smuggle or drive trucks" (Barfield 1993: 4). But they often subscribed to the pastoralists' own viewpoint that these activities were mere "adjuncts to pastoralism which remained the key element of their social and cultural identity" (Barfield 1993: 4), and treated the nonpastoral activities as haphazard, occasional, and of little significance to the national economy.

3. Pastoralists' nomadic movements are mainly determined by the natural environment, by climate, soil, and water, and not so much by political and economic factors. Thus, Bencherifa and Johnson claim that "seasonal herd relocations were based on detailed awareness by pastoralists of the different temporal and spatial availability of fodder and water" (1990: 396; see also Caskel 1954: 36; Lewis 1987: 3; Scholz 1995: 27).

4. Pastoralists are autonomous tribal peoples who depend neither on settled farmers nor on state authorities. They are often depicted as enemies of law and order, waiting for moments of weakness to invade and destroy agricultural communities (Johnson 1969: 3; Shmueli 1984: 18; Spooner 1973: 6). When projected back into history, this becomes the battle between *The Desert and the Sown* (Bell 1907; Reifenberg 1955), a presumed relentless fight between the destructive forces of the desert nomads and a civilized and productive sedentary population (Lewis 1987: 12).

5. If not today, then at least in the recent past pastoralists engaged in an almost autarchic subsistence economy, based mainly on animal products such as milk, meat, and wool; and they were more interested in building up their herds than in the sale of animals, so that their participation in the market economy was limited and developed only lately. Thus, Scholz argues that the "main purpose [of pastoralists] is to assure subsistence ... [and not] the increase of herds for marketing or gain" (1995: 26–27). This viewpoint is quite common in studies of East African pastoralists (but see Kerven [1992] for a rebuttal). Some Africanists recognize that today's pastoralists produce for markets, but believe that "the process of commercializing livestock and livestock products ... took place in most pastoral societies in the world during the

second half of the twentieth century" (Dietz et al. 2001: 194). Others refer, in the spirit of Herscovits's "cattle complex" (1926), to "the symbolic value placed on cattle ownership as an end in itself" (Barfield 1993: 24–25). Even Middle Eastern ethnographers, who are well aware that animals are raised for sale in markets, may occasionally argue that the nomad "is interested in maintaining not his cash profits but the number of head of his cattle" (Cunnison 1966: 38; see also Asad 1979: 420), or that, at least in days past, his production was oriented "towards the requirements of subsistence" (Khazanov 1984: 16; see also Janzen 1980: 59; Salzman 2004: 1).

6. Pastoralists always remain pastoral nomads. This profoundly unhistorical point of view assumes that their traditional way of life continued, and will continue, unchanged through the ages. The most extreme adherents to this position are, ironically, scholars who concede that economic change may seriously affect the tribe and even cause its demise (Scholz 1995: 28). When Barth claims that among the Basseri of Iran unsuccessful individuals may have to settle down as farmers, while wealthy herdsmen may become landowners (Barth 1961: 111), he implies that the core of the tribe remains immutably pastoral.

Each of these points has been refuted by students of Middle Eastern pastoralists. My task now is to construct a model of pastoral nomadism that is more in line with realities on the ground. It covers the following points:

1. To the extent that pastoralists produce meat, wool, and other animal products for urban and rural markets, they depend on the city and the state;

2. Their movements are determined as much by political and economic considerations as by climatic and ecological factors;

3. They cannot function as autarchic societies or subsistence economies except in certain colonial conditions;

4. All but the most highly specialized pastoral nomads engage in a variety of occupations, the relative importance of which varies due to continual economic change;

5. During economic recessions and political turmoil, pastoralism may be eclipsed by other economic activities, such as agriculture or trade;

6. When conditions permit, some members of the population—not necessarily former nomads—will again specialize in pastoralism; and

7. The term "tribe" refers to two distinct types of organization that are very often found side by side: it is both an administrative division of the state and an organization that controls a home territory.

The Political Economy

Now I must put the parts of the argument together. A good starting point is to look at the market value of pastoral products. It has often been reported that pastoral nomads consider themselves superior to settled agriculturalists (Musil 1928: 45; Bates 1973: 22; Hobbs 1989: 30). This attitude may be based on good economic grounds, for the market generally pays higher prices for animals and animal products than for farm produce, and makes pastoralism a relatively profitable business. A rough and ready computation by Schwartz (1986: 229) indicates that "while the body of a goat feeds a household for a maximum of three days, the equivalent counter-value of 45 kg of corn meal lasts as ration for half a month." In other words, the market price of meat is about five times greater than that of grain. Furthermore, Dietz et al. (2001: 198–201) have shown that, contrary to popular belief, the caloric value of meat is lower than that of an equivalent measure of grain: there are 2,300 calories in a kilogram of beef, as compared to 3,500 calories in a kilogram of maize or sorghum. In nutritive terms meat is then a luxury, whose price is partly determined by people's taste for proteins, and partly by the high input of labor and feed in animal rearing. Only affluent city people can regularly afford such expensive food.

Meat cannot be produced cheaply, due to the intrinsic difficulties of caring for large numbers of living creatures. In the hot season animals are watered frequently and require supplementary feed until well into the rainy season. The lambing and shearing seasons demand especially heavy concentrations of labor. In a study of sheep herding households in the Negev, Abu-Rabi'a (1994) shows that only an extended family with children old enough to work, and often reinforced by a hired shepherd, can raise the labor required for a flock of up to two hundred sheep (similar conditions are reported for East Africa [Sperling and Galaty 1990: 83]). Libyan Bedouin solve similar manpower problems through the joint efforts of residents of camps (Peters 1990: 213). The problem is exacerbated by the selection practices of the nomads. Herdsmen cull animals so as to maximize the number of lactating females and their offspring, to keep a minimum of young males, and to eliminate the older and experienced animals (Kavoori 1999: 115ff.). Therefore, herds lack lead animals and are vulnerable to predators (Khazanov 1984: 28), and must be herded and protected both day and night.

In contrast, rain-fed cereal farming needs only a fraction of this labor. Crop farmers may put spurts of heavy work into a short plowing and sowing season, and another equally brief harvesting and threshing season, but they may enjoy some leisure in between. An ordinary farming household can cope with all the work and does not need to recruit workers from outside. As Meillassoux (1981) has shown, peasants congregate in villages for joint consumption and defense, but not in order to share labor.

As meat is relatively expensive, and usually easily marketed, pastoralists consume very little of it. They prefer to sell it in urban markets in exchange for grains and other necessities. Most ethnographers of the Middle East would go along with this almost trite statement; but some East African colleagues still claim that at least some "herders ... are able to subsist exclusively on their animals" (Sperling and Galaty 1990: 73). Thus, the Maasai and Turkana are often said to subsist on animal products (McCabe 1994: 207–8; Spencer 1988: 9; Galvin 1985). The patterns of long-term food consumption are probably more complex. For instance, McCabe notes that a Turkana pastoralist with whom he worked for several years "sold goats and sheep frequently to buy maize and slaughtered many for food" (2004: 156). Even when colonial and postcolonial authorities prevented pastoralists from selling animals in the main markets, they seemed to consume more cereals than meat, for even these groups sold animals to traders and villagers and thus obtained the cash to buy cereals and other goods. Among the Rendile, East African pastoralists whose food consumption has been studied for five years by Schwartz (1986)—we do not possess an equivalent study for Middle Eastern or North African pastoralists—there was considerable fluctuation in the relative amounts of meat, milk, and maize consumed. In order to compare the consumption patterns of the three types of food, I multiplied the quantities consumed each year (as per Schwartz 1986, table 10) by the caloric values of each food, as given by Dietz et al. (2001). The data permitted me to calculate the proportion of calories in the Rendile diet derived from grain in each year (see table 1).

TABLE 1. Caloric values of milk, meat, and maize consumed by Rendile households in the years 1978 to 1982

Year	Milk	Meat	Maize	Total calories	Calories provided by maize (percent)
1978	101,500	331,200	1,008,000	1,440,700	70
1979	179,200	269,100	896,000	1,344,300	67
1980	56,000	414,000	448,000	918,000	49
1981	102,200	117,300	766,500	986,000	78
1982	219,100	303,600	2,044,000	2,566,700	80

Sources: Schwartz (1986: 316) and Dietz et al. (2001: 197–201).

The table shows that there was considerable variation in the total amount of calories these pastoralists consumed each year, and that the amount of meat and milk in the diet fluctuated. Schwartz does not report on the number of animals consumed by the households, but although a long drought had brought down the price of animals, the figure appears to be quite small. The salient point to emerge from the table is that maize was regularly the most important food, accounting for 50 to 80 percent of the annual caloric intake. A study of pastoralist households in Somalia supports these findings: meat and milk represent less than 30 percent of their caloric intake (Ahmed 1990: 137). The same trend has been observed in the Negev, where Abu-Rabi'a (1994: 122) found that nomadic Bedouin families slaughter 7 percent of their lambs for home consumption, whereas settled households slaughter 21 percent. The Bedouin eat meat either on festive occasions (which may include unwelcome visits of senior government agents), or when there is no market for animals, as in famines, animal epidemics, or economic slumps.

Evidently, pastoralists raise animals chiefly for sale in the marketplace. The anthropologists who took the trouble to look into animal sales found them to be "the primary source of income" (Asad 1970: 248; see also Black-Michaud 1986: 54–56; Fabietti 1984: 150). We know that large numbers of animals were sold in regional markets. The merchants of Aleppo alone handled in the beginning of the twentieth century 400,000 or 500,000 sheep per year (Lewis 1987: 28). An estimated 550,000 sheep and goats were slaughtered in Palestine in 1937 (Brown 1938: 175), and over 60,000 camels from the Sudan, equal in weight to half a million sheep, are sold annually in the camel market of Imbaba, Cairo (Stephens 1992: 82). The most recent figures on production and sale of animals are assembled in table 2.

TABLE 2. Production and sale of camels, sheep, and goats in the Middle East and North Africa in 2003

	Camels	Sheep	Goats
Live animals	4,688,000	184,881,000	102,150,000
Slaughtered animals	652,000	82,541,000	39,922,000
Rates of "offtake" (percent)	14	45	39

Source: Food and Agriculture Organization (FAO), Faostat Base, 2004.

I assume that most of these animals were raised by nomadic pastoralists and only a fraction by villagers, as the production costs of less mobile pastoralists are higher. In spite of the large number of animals produced, they did not satiate the region's demand for meat. It appears that the region's producers could satisfy the demand for camel meat, as indicated by the fact that 14 percent of the animals were sent to slaughter annually (this rate is called "offtake"). Offtakes of this magnitude are quite common. With regard to sheep and goats, the region is clearly not self-sufficient, for high offtakes such as 45 percent for sheep and 39 percent for goats have not been reported in the literature. In their exhaustive study of African pastoralists, Dahl and Hjort (1976: 208) consider an annual offtake of 25 percent for sheep or 21 percent for goats as feasible. Therefore, I must conclude that the figures in table 2 reflect a combination of offtake and import. I estimate that perhaps half the animals are imported live and slaughtered locally. Even so, the nomads clearly make an important contribution to the region's national economies: they are the most efficient, and usually also the largest, producers of meat and other animal products. If the states of the region were to encourage pastoral production instead of trying to suppress it, some of them could become nearly self-sufficient in animal products.

The data on animal sales in market towns do not give the full statistical picture. One reason is that animals are also sold to roving dealers in the desert. Unfortunately, in ethnographies of the region's pastoralists one looks in vain for the relevant data, even when sales must have taken place right in front of the anthropologist's eyes. Also, in some parts of the region the sale of other animal products, such as wool (Bradburd 1994) and hides, and sometimes also of milk products (Bates 1973), may become more important than the sale of meat.

Most "pastoral nomads" engage in a variety of economic pursuits, as Salzman (1972) was first to point out. Historically, the combination of pastoralism and cereal agriculture seems to have been most common, because they are so highly compatible: cultivation permits the herdsman to produce some of the cereals that are the mainstay of his diet. It also provides stubble pasture in early summer and some straw to tide the herds over during the hot late summer months (Marx 1967: 84). Another variant is orchard agriculture, as practiced in South Sinai, which provides Bedouin with fruit and vegetables and may leave over a surplus for sale in cities (Perevolotsky 1981). In this manner the pastoralists reduce their dependence on settled farmers, a dependence that, paradoxically, often led them to establish themselves as overlords of farming communities. Caravan trade has always been a major source of income that quite often supplanted the raising of animals in importance (Khazanov 1984: 202ff.; however, Albergoni [1990] disagrees). In recent times many cameleers became truck drivers, adapting relatively easily to the new situation, while continuing to raise pack and draft animals (Chatty 1980). Bedouin have for generations also engaged in labor migration. In the twentieth century labor migration became not only the most important source of cash income, but also led to a large-scale emigration of younger and productive households (see chapter 3). Soldiering is another time-honored occupation (Eph'al 1982: 99; Khazanov 1984: 212), and is a major source of income for Bedouin in Saudi Arabia (Cole 1975: 97; Fabietti 2000) and Jordan (Abu-Rabi'a 2001: 142–43). In the Arabian Gulf countries many pastoralists are absorbed in the civil service, without necessarily giving up their herds. Lastly, smuggling of drugs and other contraband has in recent generations been a significant source of income, particularly in Egypt (see chapter 5) and Morocco.

In exchange for their animals and animal products the nomads acquire more than simply cereals and other staples. Practically, all the commodities used in daily life, such as tent cloths, clothing, bedding, cooking utensils, coffee, tobacco, and soap, as well as weapons and jewelry, are bought in the market. The only items that may be manufactured in the nomadic community are tent cloths, some leather containers such as water skins and tobacco pouches, and—in some households in particular regions—woven rugs and embroidered women's dresses. They are produced for home consumption, but may also be sold. Thus, almost the entire material culture of pastoral nomads originates in the city (Boucheman 1935; Weir 1976). Even items specially made for nomadic customers, such as the ubiquitous sets of three or more copper coffeepots, porcelain cups, and tea glasses, are typical urban artifacts. They are not even particularly suited to the nomadic way of life, being too delicate to pack and transport.

Nomads depend on the settled regions even for pasture. Contrary to popular belief, pastoralists do not necessarily live in deserts; many of them exploit throughout the year regions well suited for cultivation (Marx 1980). Others may make use of the verdure and water available in the desert in the rainy season, rarely for more than six months, in order to save the well-watered areas until needed. Those who do not own summer pastures move in the height of the hot and dry summer into the cultivated areas where the animals feed on stubble and drink from perennial water sources, and they sell some of their animals there. The nomads benefit from cultivation, especially of cereals, which increases the plant cover. At the same time the flocks manure the villagers' fields, and the sale of pasture rights supplements the villagers' income (though sometimes pastoralists are paid for grazing on fallow land [Kavoori 1999: 111]). As the arrangement serves the interests of both parties, it often continues undisturbed for many seasons (Bates 1973; Shoup 1990: 206; see also Kavoori 1999: 139–46). The intensification of farming may thus go hand in hand with more intensive herding (Bencherifa and Johnson 1990: 396).

This does not mean that disputes between herders and peasants do not arise, and that herds do not occasionally damage crops and trees. This may happen after a dry winter and spring, when the starving herds move into settled regions before the villagers have harvested their crops (Lewis 2000: 37–38). Raswan (1936: 102ff.) vividly describes the havoc wrought by the famished camel herds of the Rwala during a drought. They swept like an avalanche through settled regions, devouring all the available herbage (see also Kavoori 1999: 138–46). Still, this is a far cry from the generalized notion of the battle of *The Desert and the Sown* (Bell 1907). Although the relationship between settlers and nomads may sometimes break down, it normally benefits both parties.

While the nomads are out in the desert, they may labor under the illusion that government is far away and cannot harm them, but during the summer sojourn in settled regions they are within easy reach of the authorities, who can then deal with offences committed in the desert. The nomads oscillate between the largely imaginary freedom of the desert and the regulated life of the settled areas. Obviously they behave more circumspectly in the summer quarters than during the spring migration. Only out in the desert did young men in the old days organize raids against distant tribes (Jarvis 1931: 27; Sweet 1965) in order to acquire the nucleus of their first herd and break away from their fathers. But at no time do the nomads escape from the total unilateral dependence on the market towns and the authorities.

Types of Tribe

Governments tend to subscribe to stereotyped images of the nomads and to treat them as a social problem. They do not appreciate the pastoralists' contribution to the economy and interpret their nomadic way of life as an attempt to evade civic obligations, such as military service and payment of taxes. In this respect there is hardly any difference between the Ottoman overlords and European colonial rulers and the modern nation-states and their development experts (Bocco 2000; Tapper 1991: 53). This prejudice is due, first, to the practical difficulties of regularly supervising a nomadic population without a fixed address. This mobility permits some nomads to shirk their obligations to the state, at least for a while. Bureaucratic discourse then magnifies these incidents into an ethnic stereotype: all Bedouin are bad citizens. A second and more important reason is that pastoral nomads occupy and use large areas of land that they cannot properly control. As the members of descent groups are at most times widely dispersed, they find it hard to concentrate the men needed to defend their land against the state and other powerful agencies. Their weakness almost invites predators on their land. It is precisely because the state authorities view the pastoralists as candidates for expropriation of land and therefore displacement that they consider them to be unproductive. That is why they firmly believe that the pastoralists produce animals mainly for their own subsistence, and not for sale on the market, a claim that is patently untrue (Gardner and Marx 2000: 21–22). For both reasons, the pastoralists are often treated as second-class citizens, and do not receive the full range of services provided by the state. In order to exploit the labor or fighting power of the nomads, or simply to make government easier and cheaper, the authorities often abdicate their civil responsibilities and treat the nomads as if they were independent groups. They imagine them as a closed society, as tribesmen who should be allowed to preserve their traditional culture and to run their affairs independently, with little government interference. They are allocated a territory, not necessarily their own patrimony, and are governed by a chief *(shaikh)* chosen from their midst. The pastoralists often call this man a "government chief" to distinguish him from other chiefs, elders who adjudicate their disputes and organize joint activities, such as tribal pilgrimages. The government chief mediates between the authorities and members of the tribe and, in certain critical matters such as control of land, tries to keep the authorities at arm's length. He may fulfill a variety of functions without being properly paid, and without being equipped with the necessary powers and resources (Marx 1967: 41–46).

This tribe is then an administrative division of the state (Fried 1975), and subject to its changing policies. The state may either turn the tribe into a deprived ethnic enclave or may gradually extend full citizenship to its members, or even abolish it altogether (Khoury and Kostiner 1991: 7). The tribesmen too develop divergent interests: some of them make every effort to become more fully integrated with the state, in order to gain access to its various services, while others benefit from the prevailing situation and wish it to continue.

Pastoral nomads offer a number of alternative theories about the constitution of their own society. One of these views the tribe as an overarching social formation, as the apex of a homologous series of more and more inclusive groups based on patrilineal descent. These groups, they say, are as a rule inactive. Only when aroused by external or internal stimuli, such as a threat to herding grounds or a dispute between neighbors, do these groups come alive and then join forces according to their genealogical closeness. This native theory was adopted by Evans-Pritchard (1940) and Fortes (1945) and their followers in preference to all others, perhaps because it obviated any kind of political analysis, and thus obscured the harsh reality of colonial rule. This "segmentary theory," as it was called, offered a mechanical model of political action, one that dealt only with "internal" tribal politics and totally ignored the forces at work in nomadic populations controlled by the state. In fact, mechanical segmentation does not even operate in "internal" tribal conflicts. In none of the numerous analyses of conflicts we possess, such as 'Arif (1934), Kressel (1982), and Shuqair (1916), did the disputing parties align according to their genealogical connections. While processes of fission and fusion did occur, they always aligned a number of corporate descent groups according to a variety of interests, and never according to their genealogical closeness. There is not a single documented instance in these studies of a whole tribe rallying around one leader (see also Lindner 1982: 697). Whenever a conflict broke out, the members of a tribe joined different protagonists.

While it is true that the "tribesmen" often put the tribe at the center of the image of their society, they do not do so because they view it as an autonomous social formation. The tribe they think of refers to their incorporation in the state and to the necessity to align every aspect of their lives to this reality. They do not consider the tribe to be a closed social system, but rather an indirectly ruled administrative division or dependency of the state.

The pastoralists are also members of another type of "tribe." This is an organization that protects a home base, a territory that assures members of a secure livelihood. It reserves for its members rights to cultivate land, to use water sources, and to control passage through the territory, as well as the right to extend some of these privileges to members of other tribes. In South Sinai every Bedouin belongs to two of these territorial tribes. One tribe gives him rights to cultivate land and build a house anywhere in the tribal territory, while the other gives him rights of passage and access to grazing throughout the southern half of the peninsula. As horticulturalist and labor migrant he belongs to one tribe, for example the Jabaliya, Muzena, or Sawalha, while as pastoralist and smuggler he belongs to the Tawara tribe, whose territory encompasses all of South Sinai. This territorial organization is run on a consensual basis by a network of respected elders, many of whom are also in demand as mediators in disputes. Ordinary tribesmen join into their deliberations as a matter of course, and to an outsider the discussions often seem to be tedious and inconclusive. Yet they work indefatigably toward a consensus, and once they agree on a course of action people tend to go along with it (Lavie 1990: 263ff.). While this organization operates openly, it deals largely with "internal" affairs, matters that the Bedouin prefer not to come to the knowledge of the authorities. The elders have few contacts with government agents, who therefore do not always realize that these men wield real power.

In no sense is either kind of tribe a total society or a focus of solidarity; it is merely one of a variety of organizations in which the nomad participates. The nomad's social round unfolds in numerous organizations that are neither hierarchically articulated nor centrally controlled. Every person belongs at each moment to a large number of corporate groups, such as trading and herding partnerships and descent groups, maintains networks of kinsmen and friends, participates in camps, and engages in various relationships with patrons and agents of the state. None of these formations is coextensive with the tribe, is part of it, or is controlled by it. Some of the activities of these groups, such as trading relations or migrant labor, may take place far beyond the tribe's territorial limits. These activities are partially coordinated by the fact that each member participates in a number of functionally related organizations whose activities may overlap. Thus, the activities of corporate groups, such as a collection of labor migrants employed in the same workplace, are affected by the recognition that some members are also kinsmen who are obliged to assist one another.

The state cannot ensure the safety of a population that is both mobile and, at least for part of the year, dispersed over large areas. Nomads rely on one another for the safe passage of individuals and small groups in the desert, and for sharing its scant resources equitably. How can one account for the fact that the far-ranging movements seem to take place in relative safety? The answer lies in the nomad's need to adapt to rapidly changing conditions, which requires him to maintain a complex and far-flung network of social relationships and to participate in a variety of groups. The interlocking networks and affiliations of all the nomads bring them together in a community of interests, which supports high standards of behavior among the members. They all recognize the need to adhere to a set of fundamental values, among which hospitality and chivalry rank high. These ensure safe travel and movement, respect for life and property, and honesty in commercial transactions. These values are not just abstract norms, for the nomads' indigenous law courts test their implementation in daily interaction. When Jarvis (1931: 25–26) observed that "litigation is the Arab pastime and sport, into which he enters with his whole heart," he unwittingly hit upon the most important institution governing the comportment of the pastoralists. Indigenous justice works as a system of social control respected and feared by every individual (Stewart 1988–90, 2003). Each person's activities are open to public scrutiny, as any infringement of the code of behavior, whether real or imagined, will without fail be brought before a court. He does not cherish the prospect of having his faults exposed in public. His fear is magnified by the knowledge that everyone takes an avid interest in the numerous cases brought before courts throughout the region, so that the information about his failings will spread fast and wide. He knows that his case will be discussed in intimate detail in every camp of the region, and will be recalled even after the lapse of many years. The fear of exposure to the critical gaze of the audience at a law session, of having to confess to deviations from the norm, suffices to keep most Bedouin on the straight and narrow path, and induces the offenders to hide their traces as best they can. Thus, the Bedouin are controlled and bound by their own detailed knowledge of the delicts of others. The constant and ubiquitous litigation then guarantees that people generally strive to conform to the norms. It enforces universal standards of comportment which, in the final analysis, allow the members of a widely spread population to maintain relations of trust. These may remain effective even when the state and its bureaucratic machinery break down, as in Somalia (Geshekter 2001: 10; Little 2003).

Adapting to Change

As the fate of specialized pastoral nomads is bound up with that of the urban economy in which they participate, they are obviously affected by every change in urban political and economic conditions. Their life is a continual adaptation to a changing world (Salzman 1980). Any change in the relative price of animals will lead to shifts in production. In a depression they will reduce the size of their herds and increase the agricultural component of their economic portfolio. Should the market economy collapse, they may even become subsistence cultivators. Therefore, the decline of a complex urban civilization may cause the disappearance of pastoral nomads, just as the growth of such a civilization allows them to reestablish themselves. Archaeological evidence for such a long-term correlation was found in the Negev in the Roman and Byzantine eras (Finkelstein and Perevolotsky 1989). Whenever urban civilizations were endangered, agricultural settlements sprang up in the desert. When the cities flourished, the small permanent settlements declined and almost disappeared, and were replaced by countless nomadic camps (Rosen 1988). A study of Morocco also shows that in a modern economy pastoralism may expand simultaneously with the expansion of sedentary agriculture; it becomes so profitable that even "merchants and bureaucrats commonly invest in animals" (Bencherifa and Johnson 1990: 399). Therefore, when we describe a particular population as "pastoral nomads," we must immediately specify the conditions that allow them to raise a herd. Thus, one can say that at a certain point in time a segment of the population raises animals for an urban market. Within months conditions may have changed, and that very same segment may have disbanded, some members becoming cultivators and others joining the ranks of the urban proletariat. Even that rare phenomenon, a group specializing in breeding animals, should not simply be categorized as pastoral nomads, for that epithet, if not used carefully, may give precedence to the pastoral pursuit over all other aspects of their economy, draw social boundaries where there are none, and impose a misplaced permanence on a temporary economic constellation.

Chapter Three

Oases in the Desert

⋖✶⭤⬤⭤✶⭢

Introduction

For its Bedouin inhabitants, South Sinai is not a desert *(sahra'),* an inhospitable region, but a country *(bilad)* with variegated features. While admitting that most of it is arid and mountainous, they see it as a complex and differentiated region, in which each site has special characteristics and possibilities. Thus, water can be tapped in many locations, and pockets of soil are found in numerous sites. The Bedouin know how to exploit these major resources. Most Bedouin, especially those living in the mountains, are expert gardeners, and some of them have specialized in well digging, in the grafting and pruning of deciduous fruit trees, and in the pollination of date palms. They know where to find pockets of fertile soil, which they do not necessarily exploit on site, but rather transport to their gardens. When Bedouin decide to develop a certain site, they take into account its physical characteristics, but these are always outweighed by various extraneous economic considerations, such as its proximity to a smuggling route or its inaccessibility to unwanted outsiders. The ethnographic data, as well as the scattered historical information, indicate that in Sinai oases are not simply concentrations of natural resources, but rather are human artifacts. An unpromising site can be turned into an oasis if it serves an ulterior purpose. Conversely, a potentially fertile site will remain derelict if it does not suit the Bedouin's interests. As these interests change over time, a seemingly thriving oasis may outlive its social usefulness. Its inhabitants then may become aware of its drawbacks and gradually abandon it.

It appears that oases are established for a variety of reasons. In South Sinai, five major types of oasis can be distinguished. First, there are the orchards, vegetable plots, and palm groves planted in the course of the centuries by the monks of Santa Katarina, oases that pointed the way for Bedouin who wished to emulate them. Second, there are the irregular clusters of orchards constructed by Bedouin in many parts of the mountains. Almost every Bedouin household owns one or more orchards in which they grow fruit, nuts, and vegetables. Third, there are the compact mountain hideouts developed by smugglers. The landscape is characterized by large numbers of fruit trees of many varieties, and some of them are difficult to access. Fourth, there are the large oases covered by extensive palm groves in which some Bedouin reside throughout the year, and on which many Bedouin households converge toward the end of summer. Finally, there is the unique village of Tarfat Qadren, where market gardeners cultivate irrigated vegetable plots and orchards year-round. Each oasis type has its particular pattern of settlement and vegetation, and imprints a distinctive mark on the landscape. See map 2 for the important oases.

These oases should not be viewed as permanent geographical features. Some of them have survived throughout the centuries, while adapting to changing conditions. Others have emerged quite rapidly, and shifted sites or disappeared almost as fast. Even during my fieldwork, which was spread out over ten years, I observed some rapid and quite radical changes. Thus, the Bedouin orchards in the mountains alternated between periods of neglect and periods of intensive cultivation. Their fate seemed to be inversely related to that of the "permanent" semiurban hamlets that grew up around the Israeli service centers: whenever the opportunities for wage labor declined, people tended to leave the solidly built houses in these hamlets and either repaired to their orchards and tried to produce fruit for the urban market, or increased their flock and moved with it from one pasture to the next. They thus entered a different, and less profitable, kind of market economy.

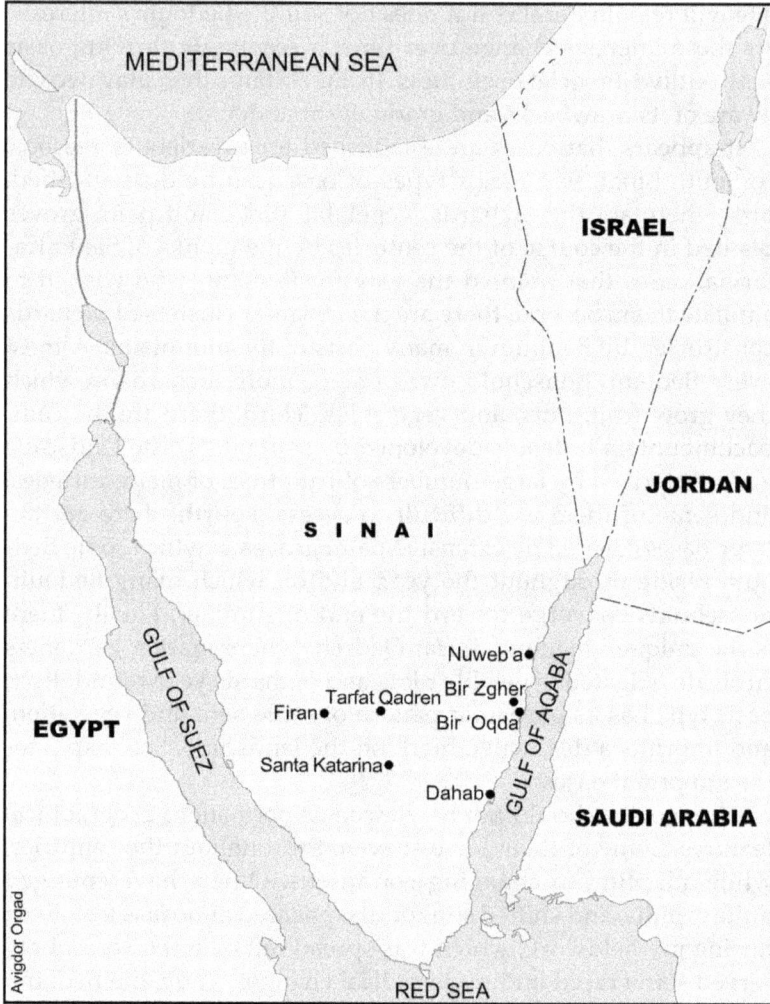

MAP 2. Oases

And conversely, whenever the wider economy flourished and migrant labor was plentiful, people moved back into the hamlets and tended to just keep their orchards going and to own only a handful of goats and sheep.

Land Uses

The peninsula of Sinai is situated in the Asian-African desert belt.
It receives scant rainfall and the vegetation is sparse. However, as
a land bridge between Asia and Africa and between Egypt and
Israel it has tremendous strategic significance (see Hamdan 1993;
for a contrasting viewpoint, see Bandman [1987]), and because of
its mineral wealth, oil fields, and deposits of gypsum and mag-
nesium, and no less for its tourist potential, it is a region of great
economic importance (Weissbrod 1987). While the Bedouin have
no share in its mineral wealth and only a small stake in tourism, the region's strategic location exposes them to the presence
of armed forces and the dangers of sporadic foreign occupation.
These and other users frequently contest even their land rights.
The most active and aggressive among the usurpers have always
been agencies of the state and, in recent years, economic entrepreneurs such as Israeli colonists or international hotel chains.
These organizations may pursue development agendas, which
totally ignore the existing land uses. Thus, when the Israeli occupation authorities sunk a well in a hitherto unclaimed location,
they caused a realignment of patterns of settlement over a large
area. When the authorities offered work outside the region, they
induced ever more Bedouin to settle in permanent locations. By
providing health and education services in such a site, they accelerated the growth of a permanent settlement. Some of these
sites, such as Dahab or Milqa, were inhabited by both Bedouin
and Israeli colonists living in separate hamlets. As the Israeli colonies expanded they began to displace the Bedouin neighbors. In
1975 the Israeli Nature Reserves Authority launched a plan to
set up a large nature reserve in the Santa Katarina region and
to evacuate the local Bedouin. The project was abandoned only
because the colonists departed following the Egyptian-Israeli
peace agreement. In short, wherever the authorities—be they Israeli or Egyptian—constructed military installations or ambitious
development projects, such as tourist villages and hotels, they
dislodged long-established local populations and deprived them
of their land (Gardner 1994: 297ff.).

The Bedouin Economy

From the beginning of the nineteenth century (and probably earlier) and up to the middle of the twentieth century, the Bedouin
obtained most of their income as migrant laborers in and outside
the region, and also engaged in the mobile way of life of cameleers and smugglers. However, they never ceased to cultivate
their gardens and to raise goats, sheep, and camels. The situation today has remained almost unchanged, except that camel
caravans have declined and given way to motor transport, while
drug smuggling has had its ups and downs. During my fieldwork
(1972–1982) many people claimed that their indigenous economy
no longer paid off. The mountain-dwelling Bedouin argued that
their gardens and orchards yielded little or no income. Most Bedouin households also claimed that they kept their flocks of goats
and sheep small because they only caused losses. While most
Bedouin owned date palms in the large oases on the coast, such as
Dahab, Nuweb'a, and al-Tur, and in the interior of the peninsula,
such as Wadi Firan, they did not consider dates a valuable food,
but rather a kind of sweet *(halawa)*. Nevertheless, they invested
prodigious amounts of labor and money in carving these small
oases out of the inhospitable environment (Perevolotsky 1981)
and in raising their small flocks. At first sight I was tempted to
dismiss these practices as a set of traditional sources of income
that had lost their economic significance. But a closer look showed
that the orchards, flocks, and palm groves played an important
role in the lives of the Bedouin. They were parts of a complex
system of social security, a way of life the Bedouin could fall back
on in an emergency. The system, as described in chapter 2, is composed of not only this alternative economy, which can be activated
at quite short notice, but also the protection of tribal territory, the
maintenance of networks of kinsmen and friends, the laying in
of stores of staple foods in caves or small secure buildings *(qerie)*,
and, lastly, the regular pilgrimages to the tombs of saints who can
mediate appeals to a provident God. It serves as a hedge against
the insecurity of wage labor, the inevitability of prolonged illness
and sudden death, the volatile political and economic conditions
in the region, the recurrent droughts and other ecological catas-

trophes. The Bedouin well know that such mishaps are bound to happen; they have observed them in daily life and personally experienced some of them. For instance, they well remember how in 1971 the Israeli occupation authorities expropriated farmland and palm groves owned by Bedouin in Nuweb'a oasis in order to settle Israeli colonists.

The proclaimed lack of income from horticulture and pastoralism is both a reflection of temporary conditions and a strategy of survival. During periods of abundant employment, when the men go abroad as migrant laborers, the members of their households stay behind in order to care for the orchards and flocks. As wage labor offers a much higher income than horticulture and pastoralism, the households of labor migrants tend to reduce the labor inputs in their home economy. They carry out the minimal amount of work needed to maintain them in working order. In these conditions the orchards and flocks do not yield an income; they are conceived of as an economic reserve. Whenever the need arises, Bedouin make a powerful effort to get them into shape and make them profitable. In the meantime, they consider it good policy not to attract the covetous eyes of the authorities, who may be tempted to tax the property or, worse still, to hand it over to colonists or hoteliers.

Sources of Information

At this point I must insert a methodological note. My argument relies partly on the Arabic and Turkish documents preserved in the archives of the Santa Katarina monastery, and the accounts of travelers and pilgrims who visited the area. The monastery as we know it today was founded in 563 CE, but the nun Etheria (or Egeria), who visited the site some thirty years earlier, reports that she stayed in a monastery (Eckenstein 1921: 116). It appears that this site has been continuously inhabited by Greek monks for at least 1,500 years, and another monastery at Raithu (today's al-Tur) is even older and also survives to this day (Shuqair 1916). The monks have preserved many old manuscripts, some of which go back to the thirteenth century; others were destroyed or lost over the centuries. The surviving documents have been copied and many of the Turkish and Arabic texts published and translated (see Bailey 1985; Stewart 1991: 98, 106). Hermits and pilgrims came to Sinai from around 250 CE, and their writings contain scraps of relevant information (Eckenstein 1921: 106ff.). The more informative travel accounts begin with Felix Fabri's 1483 journey (Prescott 1957), and culminate in the accounts of Niebuhr's visit of 1761 (Niebuhr [1774–78] 1968), Burckhardt's of 1816 (Burckhardt [1822] 1992), Robinson's of 1838 (Robinson 1867), and Palmer's of 1868 (Palmer 1871). It is only rarely that anthropologists encounter such a wealth of historical data, and it is even less common to find data spread out over such a long period. This unique opportunity to add a historical dimension to the argument could not be resisted. Indeed, without the support of these documents, the argument would have remained very tenuous. But the documents are very thinly and unevenly distributed and, furthermore, deal only incidentally with the subject of oases. The indirect references may, of course, lend the information greater credibility, and are often very enlightening. But this kind of material will, at least at first sight, appeal neither to historians used to continuous stories, nor to anthropological readers used to a full array of data, to "thick description." To these scholars the account may appear to be too sketchy, discontinuous, and uneven. However, this is a risk I must take. I should add that most anthropological studies of Middle Eastern oases address this historical variability and changeability only indirectly, for instance, when they refer to myths of foundation (Kilani 1992: 49), seek out the most ancient references (Boucheman 1939: 16), or piece together the scant historical information on an oasis (Altorki and Cole 1989: 15). Davis (1987: 12) noted that Kufra oasis was undergoing rapid change at the time of his fieldwork, but was mainly concerned with contemporary political developments. The exception is Rusch and Stein's (1988) careful study of two hundred years of change in Siwa, in the course of which the oasis economy went through cycles of growth and decline and—independently of the economic cycles—its main town fell into ruins and another was founded in a nearby location.

I now examine the special features of each type of oasis in greater detail, and show how they developed in response to pre-

vailing conditions. It will be seen that the various oases are inter-
dependent parts of a complex economic system.

Climate and Geography

South Sinai is the mountainous southern part of the Sinai Peninsula, bounded on the north by the escarpment of the Tih Pla-
teau. It covers an area of some 17,000 square kilometers. Most of
the interior of the peninsula is bare and rugged; the mountains
gradually ascend to the Mount Sinai massif, with peaks rising to
a height of 2,600 meters. The rocks are mainly red granite, which
holds water very well, but produces immature soils with only
small amounts of clay (Perevolotsky 1981: 335–36). Because water is the most critical economic resource, the Bedouin construct
orchards mostly in the granite mountains, even though the soil
there is not suitable for cultivation.

The region is arid, with small amounts of rainfall in the cool
winter months, between November and March. The average annual precipitation along the coast is between ten and twenty millimeters (Greenwood 1997: 57–58), rising in the high mountains
to about sixty millimeters (Ganor et al. 1973: 35). Rainfall is irregular, and all parts of Sinai, with the exception of the higher
mountains, experience two to three consecutive years without
any rain. The spatial distribution of rains is almost random, so
that pastures vary from season to season. Therefore, Bedouin consider the whole of South Sinai as one region, as far as pasture is
concerned. Any sizable rain results in flash floods (*fayadan*) in the
lower reaches of the valleys, causing serious losses of lives and
property. Occasionally most of a year's rainfall comes in a single
torrential downpour, sometimes outside the rainy season. A most
vivid description of a flood is that by F. W. Holland, of the Survey
of Sinai team:

> It was my good fortune, when traveling alone in the Peninsula in
> 1867, to witness … one of the most violent storms that had ever
> been known there. In the winter of 1867–68 I was encamped in
> Wady Feiran, on high ground, almost opposite the mouth of Wady
> Aleyat. There was no water to be found except in the wells, for the
> little stream had long been dry, and everything seemed parched

up by the long, rainless season. My Arabs, however, would never
permit me to pitch my tent in the bed of a wady. ... "There is fear of
a *seil*" they said ... on the 3rd of December [a storm] burst upon us.
A few heavy drops of rain began to fall at half past four ... at five
it commenced to rain in earnest, the Arabs quickly dispersed and I
had to gather all my goods together ... The rain fell in torrents, and
the roar of the thunder echoing from peak to peak, and the howl-
ing of the wind were quite deafening. ... In less than quarter of an
hour every ravine and gully in the mountains was pouring down a
foaming stream. ... Presently I heard a distant roaring behind us ...
and in a few minutes a tremendous torrent burst down ... carrying
with it a mass of *debris* into the Wady Feiran ... it seemed almost
impossible to believe that scarcely more than an hour's rain could
turn a desert wady, upwards of 300 yards broad, into a foaming
torrent from 8 to 10 feet deep ... carrying with it tangled masses
of tamarisks, and hundreds of beautiful palm trees. (Wilson and
Palmer 1869–71: 1:226–27).

Such disastrous floods occurred every few years. In May 1968 a
flood carried away hundreds of palm trees, houses, and gardens,
laying waste to most of a two-kilometer stretch of Wadi Firan
oasis. Other flash floods occurred in February 1975 and October
1979, with almost as disastrous results.

The cool season between December and March can be quite
cold, especially at night. In the mountains, temperatures occasionally fall to as low as –10°C (14°F). In summer, temperatures
are uniformly high. In the low-lying areas, such as Wadi Firan,
they often rise to over 40°C (105°F) during the day, and in the
mountains to around 30°C (86°F). Radiation is very high, and the
air extremely dry.

The natural vegetation is adapted to the harsh climate and relies largely on groundwater. During the long dry summer most
plants wither, and only the ubiquitous artemisia *(ba'tharan)*, anab-
asis *(ajram)*, retama *(ratam)*, and some other shrubs seem to with-
stand the heat successfully (see also Danin 1983: 69–73). But after
rains, colorful annuals spring out of the ground. The climate also
limits the varieties of trees that can be grown. Palms grow only
in sheltered, low-lying valleys where ground water is available,
and near the seashore. In the mountains, hardy varieties of deciduous fruits, such as apples, quinces, pears, and pomegranates
are grown. Almonds are a favorite crop because of their nutritive
value, but they are a little too delicate for the climate, and late

frosts often nip them in the bud. If these fruit trees are not watered regularly in summer they wilt and die.

Transportation and Accessibility

During the period of my fieldwork the only asphalt road on the peninsula ran close to the seashore. A number of dirt roads gave access to the interior. The main west-east route through the mountains leads from the port of al-Tur on the west coast to the oasis of Dahab on the east coast. This route was in those days only suitable for trucks and jeeps and other cross-country vehicles. From al-Tur it crosses the coastal plain and ascends the meandering Wadi Firan, passing through Firan, the largest palm grove in South Sinai, ten kilometers in length. From there the route, now called Wadi al-Sheikh, ascends the high mountains, passing Tarfat Qadren, a center of commercial gardening. It continues to the Nabi Saleh junction, where the descent to Wadi Nasb and Dahab begins. In the other direction, a short branch road leads up to the recently established Bedouin hamlets Milqa and Abu Silla, and the Santa Katarina monastery. A journey through the main thoroughfare of the Sinai, then, provides views of several types of oases, and also passes close by the major concentrations of cultivation.

Transportation in the interior is by car, and in the mountains by camel or donkey. There is no scheduled public transport, besides a daily flight between Lydda (Lod) and the Santa Katarina airfield, but over two hundred pickups and jeeps owned by Bedouin are available for hire.

The arid environment can sustain only a small population. There are about ten thousand Bedouin in South Sinai, giving a population density of one person for every two square kilometers. A considerable part of the population usually lives close to the main east-west passage through the mountainous interior, moving up into the mountains in spring and down to the seashore in late summer. Most of the permanent settlements were established in the early 1950s, when the smuggling of narcotics became widespread. The newly acquired wealth was invested in orchards, flocks, and gold. At that time numerous new wells were dug. This trend continued in the sixties and seventies, during which time more work, mostly in the form of wage labor, became available. Thus, the first houses of the Bedouin town Santa Katarina, which appears to have been standing since time immemorial, were in fact built in the 1950s.

Santa Katarina Monastery

Even before the Santa Katarina monastery was established, monks had been living in hermitages in South Sinai. In the sixth century they consolidated their hold when the Byzantine emperor Justinian built forts at Qulzum, today's Suez, and Raithu, today's al-Tur (Eutychius 1985: 89), and the fortified monastery of Mount Sinai (Procopius 1954: 357). Built around the year 550 CE (Nandris 1990: 49), the monastery has been inhabited almost continuously since 563 CE. Sometimes only a handful of Greek and Arab monks resided in it, and on two or three occasions the monks moved out for a short while (Labib 1961: 78, 97). In its heyday, the end of the fourteenth century, the monastery was inhabited by some two hundred monks (Labib 1961: 43), but in recent times the number of monks usually hovered between ten and twenty. The monks always cultivated orchards in and around the monastery and in several plantations in Wadi Firan and near al-Tur. This is documented in the monastery's rich archives, going back to the period of Mamluke and Ottoman rule (Ernst 1960; Schwarz 1970; Humbsch 1976). In numerous documents, extending from 1517 (Schwarz 1970: 25) to the middle of the nineteenth century, the Ottoman rulers constantly reaffirm the monastery's customary tax privileges with regard to their plantations. As early as 1518 one document refers to the monastery's "orchards, palm groves and cultivated lands in al-Tur and Firan," and ten years later another document mentions "vineyards, olive groves and palm groves in the Mountains, Wadi Firan and the coast of al-Tur" (Humbsch 1976: 175, 239). The monks apparently introduced numerous varieties of fruit trees and new horticultural techniques, which they had acquired in their Greek homeland; for example, an Arabic document from 1565 refers to the importation of olive saplings (Humbsch 1976: 356). The documents also show that the number of orchards and their locations varied over time.

The monks did not totally rely on their home-produced food. Apparently they never grew grain locally. With the income derived from their numerous possessions in Egypt and many other parts of the Ottoman Empire (Schwarz 1970: 15), they acquired all the grain they and their retainers needed, and often grew it on land leased in the Egyptian Delta; they also bought other foods in Egypt (see, e.g., Humbsch 1976: 308, 369, 512, 520).

The Bedouin employed by the monks gradually picked up the horticultural techniques and developed their own orchards, albeit on a smaller scale. There are major concentrations of orchards close to the main east-west thoroughfare, from Wadi Firan to the lower reaches of Wadi Nasb. Others are found in the high mountains, at an average altitude of two thousand meters, in Wadi Jibal and elsewhere. These are the territories of the Jabaliya and Awlad Sa'id tribes.

Uncertainty in the Bedouin Economy

Governments tend, in the best case, to pursue a laissez-faire policy in their relations with Bedouin. They often assume that Bedouin are economically self-sufficient, live on their garden produce and flocks, and only seek work in order to earn more spending money. This belief may serve as a convenient explanation for the exclusion of Bedouin from some types of work. Both under Egyptian rule and under Israeli occupation, most of the skilled government work available in the Sinai was done by outsiders, whether Egyptians or Israelis. Most Bedouin were employed in menial tasks, as waiters, watchmen, laborers, etc. Yet wage labor has for generations been, and still is, the Bedouin's main source of income. While lacking formal training, Bedouin are adepts in many specialized crafts. Before 1967, under Egyptian rule, many young unmarried men went out to work in Suez or Cairo, and sent home remittances to support their families. After spending three to five years abroad they returned home with their accumulated savings and got married. Then they would once more go out to work, but now for shorter periods, perhaps for six months or up to a year. Only when their sons were old enough to become wage laborers themselves could the fathers 'retire', i.e., stay at home and cultivate their orchards and partly rely on the son's remittances.

Under Israeli occupation a different work pattern developed. There was work for everyone, and practically the whole adult male population, irrespective of age and marital status, worked in Israeli towns and settlements in the Sinai and in southern Israel. The number of employed men rose from about 500 to 1,500, and remained at that level until the return of the region to Egyptian control in 1982. The only slack period followed the 1973 war between Egypt and Israel, and lasted less than a year. In the course of time transportation became easier and faster, and even men working in relatively distant towns like Eilat and Sharm al-Sheikh could return home every month or two. Men who worked closer to home, in government service or work projects, or building wells and houses for other Bedouin, could return home almost daily or at least weekly. In that time the standard of living rose about threefold, and Bedouin became accustomed to new foods, such as biscuits and canned meat and vegetables, as well as new manufactured goods. Produce from their orchards therefore played a smaller part in their economy. Only a handful of men went on working for the monks of Santa Katarina. Many of them had spent decades in the service of the monastery, and stayed on because work there seemed to remain secure for life, and therefore they grudgingly accepted the low wages.

Yet practically every Bedouin, no matter how large or secure his income, owned orchards and a small flock. Perevolotsky's (1981) survey of orchards in the mountains showed that 170 Jabaliya men owned 220 out of a total of 405 orchards. All the adult men encountered in the survey owned at least one orchard and over 40 percent owned two or more. Only some of the young men were still dependent on their fathers and did not yet own orchards. Some men had sold their orchards, but were about to construct or acquire new ones. My own inquiries show that almost every Bedouin owns a flock averaging six goats and a sheep or two. Only among the Jabaliya, there are a few men who rely mostly on orchards and do not raise animals.

Bedouin claim that they invest labor and money in orchards and flocks without getting an adequate return. Owners of flocks even argue that they lose money on them, because they have to feed them grain during four to six months every year. The owners of orchards, however, confirm that in the past, before the Israeli occupation, they obtained a considerable part of their grain from the sale of fruits, besides consuming some of the fruit themselves. They used to sell apples, almonds and pears, especially a late variety of pear called *shitwi,* in the markets at al-Tur, Suez and Cairo, and with the proceeds obtained a year's supply of grain. Niebuhr ([1774–78] 1968: 1: 241) reports the same practice in 1762: "the Arabs living on the western side of Jabal Musa every year bring many dates, grapes, apples, pears and other beautiful fruit to Suez and Cairo" (my translation). Similarly, Bedouin claim that in the past they led a more nomadic way of life, did not feed their animals on grain, and supported themselves by the sale of their animals. The flocks were larger in those times; fifty to sixty animals were the minimum required for subsistence.

The strategy adopted by the Bedouin is plain. They consider that they live in an insecure world, where work and income may disappear overnight, and in which they must prepare for such contingencies. Therefore, in times of plenty and security they cultivate orchards and raise flocks that can become alternative sources of livelihood. When the going is good they invest a limited amount of work in the orchards and keep only a small number of animals: that is, they maintain the alternative economy at idling speed. Should the need arise, they could cultivate their orchards more intensively and also grow more vegetables, and they could rapidly build up their flock. Within a year or two they could fully adjust to the new market conditions.

During my period of fieldwork there were two major occasions when such shifts in the economy actually took place. The first was in 1973, in the wake of the October (or Yom Kippur) war between Egypt and Israel. At the time most Bedouin men were employed in Israeli enterprises far from home. The war caught them unawares, and for some of them the first indications that something had gone wrong were Egyptian planes flying overhead and bombs exploding around them. All the Israelis left immediately, and the Bedouin working for them were left on their own and made their way home as best they could. As no transportation was available, they had to walk home. One man reported that he joined some other men, and walked for three days without sufficient food and water. Only when he was back in the mountains with his family did he feel safe.

Now that all the men were at home there was much visiting among relatives. The 'Araishieh, roving traders from al-'Arish on the Mediterranean coast who supply food and merchandise to the Bedouin and buy their animals, were no longer making their rounds. However, there was sufficient food for the present, for most Bedouin had stored food to last them for three months. There was a brisk trade in animals among the Bedouin, as many of them wished to increase their flock. Prices went up, and several Bedouin turned almost overnight into animal traders. Many Bedouin left the larger settlements, such as that near Santa Katarina, and pitched tents in small camps closer to pastures. People took a renewed interest in their orchards: they discussed their relative value and reminisced about how in the years before 1967 they had sold their fruit in the markets of al-Tur, Suez, and even Cairo. Numerous people started new orchards and made improvements to old ones. Some tried to acquire new gardens, but none were up for sale. It took several months before the food supply and services were fully restored and wage labor again became available. Only then did the Bedouin's concern with flocks and gardens become less intense.

The Bedouin reacted in the same manner to the Israeli evacuation, which proceeded in several stages from 1977 to 1982. But this time they also took care to ensure their continued possession of plots of land in the oases of Dahab and Nuweb'a. They assumed that the thriving vacationing centers set up there during Israeli rule would now be run by Egyptian entrepreneurs. Before the Israeli occupation, Bedouin had frequented these oases for the date harvest in late summer, and some had at those times engaged in fishing. The holiday villages set up by the Israelis provided opportunities to earn money, and more and more Bedouin settled permanently in the vicinity. As the population grew, land became scarce, and the occupants of sites became concerned about their rights. They marked boundaries with barbed wire fences or even stone walls, and created documents of ownership by arranging fictitious sales of plots to one another. In order to reinforce their claims of ownership before the Egyptian authorities came back, they hurriedly built houses or wooden huts on their plots. These activities accelerated as the date of evacuation approached. In the end, the Egyptian authorities did not contest the Bedouin's claims of ownership; for the time being they did not expand the holiday villages and therefore did not require the land. Many Bedouin left the oases, without relinquishing their claims of ownership, and returned periodically to inspect and maintain their houses. While returning to work in the alternative economy, they now claimed a stake in the conjectural economy that might once again flourish.

The Development of an Orchard

A Bedouin orchard is a man-made oasis. It is laboriously carved out of the desert, and its construction often extends over several years. First the Bedouin chooses a site, usually in a valley where members of his tribe and relatives have already laid out orchards. Any land in the tribal territory that is not already occupied is available to him. Bedouin do not claim ownership of the land itself, for there is plenty of it. Only cultivation bestows rights to the land: a well, walls, and trees belong to the individual who made or planted them and pass on to his male descendants. Only when the property is in ruins and completely abandoned can another person establish himself on the site. As an orchard deteriorates slowly, people may have doubts as to whether it has been relinquished or not. It may not have been worked for many years, but as soon as someone tries to take it over, old claims may be revived.

The next step is to dig a well. Bedouin have a good idea where groundwater can be tapped. They look out for the vertical dark stripes on rocks indicating geological dikes, for long, gradual slopes, and for patches of dense vegetation. They prefer to dig the wells near the margins of the valley, so as to prevent the silting up of the well by flash floods. The digging of wells is always a risky business. One may dig a few meters and reach the bedrock, or dig a deep pit without reaching water. Several attempts may be made before water is found. It is no wonder that this is considered the most expensive stage in the construction of an orchard. Sometimes the male members of a family will do the work collectively, especially when they hope to strike water at a shallow depth.

The construction of deep wells, often up to ten or twelve meters deep, is left to experts, who are invariably Jabaliya familiar with the local ground. The financial reserves of a family may well be exhausted by the time the well is completed, and they may wait several years before attempting the next steps.

The next stage is the construction of a rectangular enclosure around the future orchard and the well. Walls of dry stone construction are built to prevent animals from entering and to mark the boundaries of the property. Then the land is leveled, and the topsoil is mixed with clay from the mountainous slopes or soil from ancient habitations. A counterbalanced water hoist (*shaduf*) is built over the well. Only then can the garden be cultivated.

That is only the beginning. The trees and vegetable patches must be tended year-round. In summer they are watered twice a week, and in winter once every two weeks, on average. Any member of the household who can spare the time can do this work. The journey to the orchard up in the mountains may take anything from one to three hours. Watering may take an hour or more of energetic work, but it is usually done at a leisurely pace and connected with additional activities in the orchard. To this the long return journey must be added, so watering is a full day's work.

In the 1970s roving traders from al-'Arish introduced cheap plastic pipes, which revolutionized irrigation. Where before each Bedouin had dug his own well in his orchard, now several related households banded together and dug a well upstream. Alternatively, they developed new orchards downhill from existing ones. Irrigation by gravitation saved a great deal of work and expense (Katz 1983).

During the hot summer months many families stay in their orchards, in order to enjoy the cool breezes and to consume the homegrown fruit and vegetables. They do not consider these to be important items in their diet, but rather as tasty additions to it. Watering, of course, is at these times no longer a heavy chore. The stay in the orchards is viewed as a summer vacation, a treat to look forward to.

The orchards, then, are constructed and maintained at considerable expense and effort, but while wage labor is abundantly available, orchards are viewed as sources of enjoyment, and not as productive resources. They come into their own when conditions deteriorate and people are out of work. Then the returning men take over, cultivate them more intensively for food, and generally produce a surplus, which they sell in urban markets.

The Large Oases

Toward the end of summer, in August and September, there are no more deciduous fruit left in the orchards, but the dates in the large oases are ready for harvesting. Now people leave their orchards in the mountains, as well as their places of work, and congregate in large numbers in the major palm oases, in Wadi Firan, Dahab, and Nuweb'a. In each oasis three hundred households or more may gather. The migrant workers reunite with their families and visit their relatives and friends. Only a handful of families remain in the mountains to take care of the orchards.

All the members of a household, as well as relatives and neighbors, take part in the date harvest. Agile young men, followed by the critical eyes of elders, climb up to the treetops and cut down the clusters of dates. These are then caught in blankets held taut by the members of the household, in order to not bruise the delicate fruit. Most dates are taken down before they are ripe and ready for eating. The dates are spread out on an open-air drying floor *(masharr)* where in the hot, dry air they first turn sweet and soft and then dry out and shrivel. When wage labor is plentiful, the dates, like the produce of the orchards, are described as sweets *(halawa)*, and are not treated as a staple food. This tendency is perhaps reinforced by the patterns of ownership. Few people own complete palm groves; most people do not own more than a few trees. In addition, they hold shares in numerous palm trees in various parts of the peninsula. When a man dies his palm trees are divided up among his male heirs. When several persons have claims on the inheritance, rights in trees may be divided up among them. Each of them is then said to own a portion *(qarat)* of the tree. The portions are stated as fractions of twenty-four; the unit, i.e., a tree, is said to consist of twenty-four parts. Thus, most people own shares in palm trees in locations all over the peninsula, and do not consider it worth their while to invest much effort in tending the trees. Many do not bother to collect their share of the fruit, and donate it to relatives who happen to camp in the vicinity of their trees. They are satisfied with being served dates when visiting the relatives. Shared ownership thus turns the trees into foci for kinship links; the relationships are reaffirmed annually at the date harvest. The joint owners of palm trees tend to meet at harvest time. When inspecting the trees they own in various locations, they ipso facto make the rounds of relatives. While they may have seen the men only recently at work, here they meet them in their family circle, in the sociable atmosphere of mutual visiting and food sharing among the many relatives gathered in the oasis.

Some orchard and palm grove oases have in recent decades developed new features. Smuggling of narcotics has interested the Sinai Bedouin since the beginning of the century (Dumreicher 1931: 204; Russell 1949: 272), but became a really important part of their economy only in the 1950s. There were times when it provided about 30 percent of the aggregate income of the South Sinai Bedouin. At that time some of the orchards located in relatively inaccessible locations in the mountains became hideouts for bands of smugglers. This led to further investments in these oases. The entrepreneurs spent a great deal of money on diesel engines and pumps to make irrigation less arduous. Some of these retreats were created from scratch, even when ecological conditions were not ideal.

In between hauls, there would often be months of inactivity. The smugglers would spend them in their mountain retreats, away from prying eyes. The leaders of smuggling rings and their henchmen planted small but intensively cultivated orchards, which often included varieties not commonly found in the South Sinai mountains, such as mandarin, tangerine, plum, and avocado. They were keenly interested in introducing new varieties, in order to spread the supply of fruit over the longest possible period.

During the Israeli occupation there was a lull in drug smuggling. Today the South Sinai Bedouin are once again linked to the multinational network of drug distribution, especially hashish and opium. The drugs usually originate in Lebanon and are routed through Jordan and Saudi Arabia and across Sinai into the Nile Valley. On their way over the mountains, the drugs cross the territory of several tribes who either share in the transportation or collaborate in other ways. It is therefore in the Bedouin's interest to preserve peaceful relations between the tribes. It is no wonder that the Bedouin proudly declare themselves to be "peaceful people who never engage in fighting" (see chapter 4).

Bir 'Oqda and Bir Zgher are good examples of this type of oasis. In the early 1970s, the population in Bir 'Oqda rapidly declined, and most of the twenty-odd households moved to Dahab on the coast. In former years they had gone to Dahab in the late summer to enjoy the breeze, supplement their diet with seafood, and wait for the date harvest. Around October they would return to the mountain village. Now they simply stayed on in Dahab and delayed their departure from day to day. Only a few men made short trips to Bir 'Oqda, where the water pumps fell into disrepair and the fruit trees dried up. They explained the situation in ecological terms: the water sources in Bir 'Oqda were not as copious as they used to be, and therefore the yield of their fruit trees was dwindling. There simply was no point in cultivating the oasis. But another explanation may be more relevant. From 1970 onward, the smuggling of narcotics to Egypt had stopped almost completely. Therefore the hideout was no longer required and men saw no reason why they should invest more resources in the construction of new wells and in improving the orchards. The big operators were still hoping for conditions to change, and hanging on to their orchards. In the meantime, they lived on their often quite substantial hoarded savings. Other men could not hold out so long and became labor migrants like the rest of the male population. From time to time they returned to Bir 'Oqda to look after their orchards and to postpone what they considered to be the inevitable demise of the oasis.

The inhabitants of Bir Zgher responded differently to the changed situation. A new highway from Eilat to Sharm el-Sheikh, constructed by the Israeli administration, passed close to their village. They built a track to the main road, invested money in trucks and pickups, and became involved in transporting migrant workers and tourists. The population of the village actually grew.

The newfound wealth from smuggling also transformed the larger palm oases, especially the central oasis in Wadi Firan. Here, too, mechanical pumps were installed. More Bedouin now resided permanently in the oases; they cultivated the palms and grew vegetables under the trees. One outcome of the new situation was that the water level in the oasis gradually fell. In consequence the wells had to be sunk deeper and became more expensive to maintain. The shallower wells downstream dried up and only wealthy Bedouin could afford to carry out the required improvements. The poorer Bedouin moved out of the palm groves into the vicinity of perennial wells upstream. The trend of oasis society to become ever more exclusive ended, however, under the Israeli occupation, when wage labor became plentiful and almost all the men went to work and earned good wages. Now every owner of an orchard could afford a motor pump, and the downward spiral of declining ground water levels and ever deepening wells accelerated.

The increased flow of money from smuggling boosted the development of another type of oasis, where vegetables were grown commercially. The major example is Tarfat Qadren, a village on the main track from Wadi Firan to the Santa Katarina monastery. Until the middle of the twentieth century the site was uninhabited, although the existence of tamarisks *(tarfa)* indicated that groundwater ran close to the surface. E. H. Palmer describes it in 1868 as "a fine grove of tamarisk trees" (1871: 48). The first well was sunk in 1938 by a Jabaliya man (Ben-David 1981: 76), but only in the early 1950s, when smuggling was at its peak, did more people begin to grow vegetables. In the 1970s, when smuggling became impossible but the income from migrant labor increased rapidly, some Bedouin began to grow vegetables and tobacco in commercial quantities for Bedouin consumers. While the area of ordinary orchards ranged from one to two dunams (one quarter of an acre to half an acre), here the plots ranged from two to twenty dunams (half an acre to five acres), and most of the eighteen owners settled permanently in their gardens (Lida 1979: 28). There were few farmers elsewhere who grew produce for sale, and here too they could do so only as long as Bedouin earned enough money from wage labor. When this source of income dried up in the 1990s, Bedouin once more grew produce for home consumption and sold their surplus fruit in Santa Katarina City. Tarfat Qadren became a cluster of orchards like any other: only part of each garden was maintained as a reserve the owners can fall back on in time of need.

When Dahab and Nuweb'a and, to a lesser extent, Wadi Firan became permanently settled in the early 1970s and the scramble for privately owned plots of land began, people planted palm saplings on "their" land. Now they sought to grow their own palm trees, which were to supply them with a staple food. These trees, for a change, were carefully cultivated and watered regularly. They became part of the basic economy that was to sustain their owners in the event of an economic setback or political upheaval. In this sense, their function was similar to that of the orchards in the mountains.

In South Sinai, then, oases are tracts of land that are cultivated for a variety of reasons. They are man-made, in more than one sense. First, men select them for cultivation in preference to other tracts, which might have been equally suited for cultivation. The locations are chosen mainly on social grounds, and not so much on the basis of their natural endowments. Second, the choices become "rational" when viewed as elements in the Bedouin economy. The oases as such must not necessarily be profitable; but they play their part in the Bedouin's conception that they need an economy in reserve. As the oases do not in themselves provide sustenance, they do not attract a permanent settled population who might in the course of time be categorized as a separate "ethnic" category of oasis dwellers. And third, the oases are literally made and maintained by men. Countless abandoned sites, some dating back to prehistory and some to recent times, testify to the fact that whenever men cease to cultivate oases they revert to desert (Birks and Letts 1977). Land values are also determined by complex social conditions. Neither the amount of labor expended in the construction of orchards, palm groves, or dwellings nor the market price of the produce nor the natural qualities of a site determine the land values to the same extent as people's appraisals of political and economic conditions. The amount paid for an orchard is always based on its potential yield in an emergency, when it is cultivated intensively. Nevertheless, it is true that prices oscillate around this estimate. When conditions become unsafe and unstable, and labor migrants gravitate homeward, prices tend to go up; when the crisis is over and people return to work, they fall again.

Chapter Four

Labor Migrants

Balancing Income and Social Security

-<*≡○ ◯≡*>-

Introduction

This chapter deals with one variety of labor migration, the massive movement of unskilled Bedouin men from South Sinai to repeated spells of menial work in cities. "Labor migration" is a label attached to numerous social processes involving the periodic shuttling of workers between a "home" and a distant place of "work." Many labor migrants go abroad for a quite specific short-term purpose, such as to obtain money for taxes or a marriage payment. This can usually be accomplished on a single tour of work. Most labor migrants, however, go to work in the expectation of earning more money than they can make at home. These men and women return for further spells of migrant labor and, much against their wishes, end up working abroad for many years.

Most Bedouin men spend a considerable part of their working lives as labor migrants, although they rarely enjoy the periods of work abroad. This type of labor migration has intrinsic shortcomings that make it unattractive to candidates for work: it offers insecure employment, and is largely confined to the hardest and lowliest jobs in the economy. While the labor migrant often works in the company of fellow Bedouin and relatives, this does not make his job and his life in the city easier. Work keeps him apart from family and friends, and the low wages only rarely permit him to realize his cherished hopes. Therefore, most labor migrants go to work with great misgivings, and eagerly await the day they can return home. The women do not join the movement to work; they stay at home to manage the households and tend the flocks and orchards. I shall explain below why the men so regularly become migrant laborers and, a no less problematic issue, why the women do not participate in migrant labor.

Where labor migration affects a large segment of the population, as in South Sinai, it is liable to harm the economies of both the sending and the receiving communities. It withdraws the enterprising and skilled young men and women from the home economy, causing the older men and the women remaining at home to concentrate their efforts on conserving the locally available resources and reproducing the next generation of labor migrants. The people at home thus effectively subsidize the employers abroad by relieving them of the cost of reproduction. While the remittances sent by the labor migrants raise the standards of living at home, they do not enhance the economy, for in the absence of much of the skilled local labor force, the remittances are mostly spent on new homes and better food and clothing, and not on generating new productive resources.

An examination of the impact of labor migration on the Bedouin's political economy and their way of life reveals an even more surprising feature: in the long run, the cash income plays only a limited role in their economy. Due to the insecurity of labor migration and its damaging impact on the local economy, much of the cash income is dissipated in efforts to achieve greater social security and in preparing a viable economic alternative. Many efforts to achieve greater security are made at home, in the "tribal" area; others are made while at work. A close look at any particular instance of labor migration reveals that "work" for material gain is embedded in a variety of activities, both at home and at work, designed to promote the security of the worker and his dependents. These activities too are "economic" in the sense of providing an assured basic livelihood. Obviously, no economy is safe and stable, and people everywhere strive unceasingly, and often in vain, for greater security. But labor migration is a special case: it is an extreme instance of insecure employment. It takes people out of their accustomed surroundings, separates them for long periods from their families and friends, places them in the lowest and least secure ranks of the receiving economy, and exposes them to the whims of authorities and employers and to harsh living conditions. Therefore, only people living in especially unfavorable conditions will voluntarily leave home in order to work among strangers.

Labor migration is a situation people want to get out of at the earliest possible moment. Ironically, some people spend a great part of their adult life in vain attempts to escape. Others manage, sooner or later, to solve the problem, either by finding work nearer to home or by bringing their families to live near their place of work. People who can delegate others, such as their children, to work away from home often choose the former option. The latter option is open to those persons who have come to consider their employment secure and have established complex networks of relationships near their place of work, or those whose home base provides little security.

People seek to strike a balance between efforts to accumulate material resources and to bolster their security. The two aims may sometimes be incompatible and at other times may overlap, depending on the context. Where home is also the place of work and friends and relatives live and work nearby, there is no contradiction between the two aims. In a wage labor situation, and even more so in a migrant labor situation, the two aims are seemingly quite distinct: home stands for security, and work for cash income. Yet both at home and at work, people make many determined efforts to balance the two aims. This does not mean that people always try to invest a fixed proportion of their resources in security. Even where they are constantly reminded of the changeable nature of things, people sometimes feel more secure and sometimes less, and accordingly adjust their efforts to achieve social security. But even when employment is plentiful and appears to be steady, they never abandon the search for security.

This implies that the study of "work" and "home" cannot be separated. Case studies of labor migrants at work and with their families prove that point. When set in the social context, such case studies show that the rural background affects the labor migrant's behavior at work, and the work situation affects the people back home. Furthermore, both the rural and the industrial society and economy are shaped by the same political and economic forces. "Tribal" culture too is the net result of the working of complex contemporary forces, and is therefore totally "modern."

These considerations point the way to the method of studying labor migrants adopted here: I concentrated on a number of labor migrants and their households, followed their movements wherever they led, and explored their social interactions over an extended period. These events took place against a background of changing political, economic, and ecological conditions. In short, instead of dealing separately with people at home, at work, and in search of social security, I tried to embrace their "total" political economy (see Marx 1990). Before embarking on my case study of the Bedouin of Mount Sinai, I show how the analysis relates to the work of social anthropologists and political economists on the subject of labor migration.

The Study of Labor Migration

The argument that the labor migrant's life at home and at work can be understood only when viewed as belonging to a single social world is seemingly straightforward, almost trite. However, although the study of labor migration was a thriving concern between 1950 and 1980, especially among Africanist anthropologists, it took those early scholars some time to reach that conclusion. Although they knew that both home and place of work were affected by the political-economic environment, including the actions of colonial governments and capitalist entrepreneurs, and that "many cultural changes [were] taking place in [tribal] life" (Watson 1958: 7), they initially believed that the rural areas were less affected by change than the towns and that their indigenous traditions survived almost untouched. They did not always realize that the rural patterns of production, of domestic arrangements, and of local government, as well as the very tribe and its traditions, were part of the larger contemporary system. Instead, they noted, with some astonishment, that the tribal system "sur-

vived" or "persisted" into modern times. The failure to recognize
that home and work were all part of one and the same system led
them to see town and country as basically discontinuous. Thus,
Gluckman argues that "tribalism in urban areas is something
quite different from tribalism in the rural areas: in urban areas,
tribal ties link people in many forms of association, but are not an
organized system of relations involved in the bases of production
or in political authority" (1958: xi; see also Watson 1958: 6; Southall 1961: 35). Mayer (1963: 2) too was well aware that the Xhosa in
South Africa "have long been geared into a large-scale society of
'Western' type." Nevertheless, he was convinced that "this external system of 'wide-scale relations' … has been superimposed on
an internal system in which the tribal patterns and the small-scale
values have been left largely undisturbed."

The urban end of the system, the links between fellow tribesmen, or "home-boys," was sometimes interpreted as simply ties
between kinsmen who had "continuing series of rights and duties
towards [one another]" (Harries-Jones 1969: 04), as if kinship obligations were absolutely binding and could be treated in isolation
from other relationships. Others felt that tribalism in towns was
just "a category of interaction in casual social intercourse" (Mitchell 1956: 42). Anthropologists who thought that there was a dis-
continuity between towns and rural areas could not understand
that the village, the tribe, and the household were shaped by the
same forces as the town. Therefore, they could not fully appreciate that fellow tribesmen assured one another against risks in
town as part of the larger system of a market economy combined
with a system of social security anchored in the countryside.

Yet occasionally these same scholars also understood the part
the countryside played in the system. In a perceptive passage,
Gluckman shows that "though the [labor migrants] have profited materially from entry into a cash economy, the economy is
hazardous for them. They remember loss of work … they know
that sickness, or old age, will throw them back on the land …
the labor-centers do not provide places where they can rear their
families satisfactorily. Wages are not high and must be backed by
subsistence agriculture … tribal cohesion survives not despite
labor migration, but because of the conditions in which the [labor
migrants] participate in the cash economy" (1958: x).

This approach fully recognized the impact of the colonial state and its capitalist economy on rural society and, at the same time, drew attention to the conditions and pressures that brought about profound changes in African society. While early students of labor migration, such as Wilson (1941–42), Read (1942), and Schapera (1947), had believed that these pressures spelled the ruin of "tribal" society because they disrupted a traditional order, Gluckman (1958), Watson (1958), and Van Velsen (1961) found that migration "contributed to the 'cohesion' of African tribal life and to the perpetuation of certain forms of 'traditional' cultural values and practices" (Stichter 1985: 31). As Van Velsen (1961: 233) put it, those "working abroad look to the economic and social system of their tribal area for their ultimate security." Later students of labor migration have taken the position that "the capitalist mode of production has penetrated sufficiently into rural southern Africa to allow us to regard the rural population as part of the proletariat" (Spiegel 1980: 114). This is an interesting way to look at the situation that affords new insight into contemporary society. But Spiegel's assumption that the intrusion of the capitalist world happened recently burdens it with an earlier mode of interpretation that inevitably skews his reading of the past.

Newer anthropological studies have benefited from the work of neo-Marxists, such as Wolpe (1972), Meillassoux (1972), and Burawoy (1975), on the development of colonial capitalism in southern Africa. These scholars argue that labor migration was engineered by the colonial states and by capitalists in order to keep down the cost of labor. This was done chiefly by separating the functions of production from those of the reproduction of the labor force:

> The extended family in the Reserves is able to, and does, fulfill "social security" functions necessary for the reproduction of the migrant work force. By caring for the very young and very old, the sick, the migrant laborer in periods of rest, by educating the young, etc., the Reserve families relieve the capitalist sector and its state from the need to expend resources on these necessary functions. (Wolpe 1972: 435)

Formulations such as these give the impression that capitalists allied with the African state to profit from the exploitation of cheap black migrant laborers. In their preoccupation with domination and exploitation, these scholars did not fully appreciate the heavy price paid by the state and all its subjects. In its efforts to control the flow of cheap migrant labor, the state became increasingly repressive toward all its subjects; migrant laborers did not acquire the skills needed for the operation of complex industries; and the "tribal" population had the means neither to increase agricultural production nor to buy more industrial products, and thus held up the growth of the national economy. In addition, the state incurred special expenses in its pursuit of cheap labor: it paid for special services such as police surveillance, and subsidized the farms and mines of white colonists. In short, by preventing its black subjects from access to gainful work, the African state impoverished all its citizens. Poverty was thus not confined to rural reserves or urban slums, but became a characteristic of the state. The only beneficiaries of this situation were the small white capitalist elite.

In the 1980s the apartheid regime in South Africa began to realize that the system was bound to run into difficulties as the population in the "reserves" grew and productive resources there dwindled, as other employment opportunities became gradually available, and as the coercive measures that propped up the system became harder to enforce (Burawoy 1975: 1063–64). These were the conditions Sharp (1987) found in the South African Bantustan of Qwaqwa and Spiegel (1980) found among labor migrants from Lesotho. Thus, Spiegel writes:

> The migratory wage-labor system which prevails in southern Africa ... offers neither social security nor even a guarantee of continued employment. It breeds an insecurity which people attempt to counterbalance by viewing arable land and rural resources as being of greater significance than is promised by their potential. (1980: 115)

The inhabitants of these areas were irresistibly pulled toward their place of work, and no amount of coercion and repression could bring them back to the reserves. The men became urban proletarians, for whom the countryside held no promise of security. The greatest security they could hope for was to find long-term employment in town and settle there in spite of police harassment. In due course they hoped to bring their families to join them, so that home and work were reunited in town. In practice, they rarely took root in town, and often abandoned the members of the family left behind in the reserves (Sharp 1987: 141).

In contrast, the Bedouin of South Sinai still have a secure home base to which they return as long as they have not established a firm foothold in the urban economy. Unlike the southern Africans, the Bedouin are not coerced into becoming labor migrants. The state, in both its Egyptian and its Israeli incarnations, far from forcing the Bedouin to become labor migrants, rather tended to discourage them from moving to urban centers. The Bedouin needed no recruiting agents to persuade them to work; they were simply attracted by the economic rewards offered by work in towns and industrial plants and went out for a limited time to seek their fortune. One should also note that Bedouin always had other ways to earn a living. Although labor migration has for generations played a major role in their lives, they also engaged in horticulture, smuggling, commerce, trades, and crafts. In most of these occupations they still moved around a great deal, but stayed closer, and returned more frequently, to their homes. In these conditions, labor migrants who lost their jobs in town were soon fully integrated into less lucrative work at home, enjoying the warmth and security afforded by their families, kinsmen, business associates, and fellow tribesmen.

The literature shows that in all its many shapes and variants, labor migration deeply affects the lives of migrants and transforms their society. Their social practices, even those they dub as "traditions" and "customs," cannot be treated as relics of the past, but must be viewed as flowing out of volatile contemporary conditions. I shall now describe such a society, paying special attention to the economics of cash income and security and their impact on domestic relations.

Between 1971 and 1982, I spent a total of over twelve months in the mountainous regions of South Sinai. I succeeded in establishing close links with a few households whose members permitted me to accompany them on their round of activities. My main problem was to keep in step with the continuous peregrinations of these Bedouin men and women, which often led in different directions and more than once left me out of breath. The men took me along to their places of employment in various parts of Sinai or outside Sinai, to their orchards in the high mountains, on visits to relatives and friends, and on personal and tribal pilgrimages to the tombs of Muslim saints. Also, I often joined women and girls grazing their flocks in the vicinity of villages. All these activities turned out to be of a piece; they were all part of a way of life that took place in a modern context. They fitted together like pieces of an intricate jigsaw puzzle, and gradually began to make sense. Though Bedouin tended to speak of their activities in a traditional cultural idiom, they well knew that the activities were purposeful and essential to their well-being. The social worlds of these Bedouin took the form of networks of interaction, which spanned great distances and included membership in a variety of groups and relationships. The rapidly shifting interactions hardly heeded the boundaries of tribe, ethnic community, and religious affinity.

Conditions in South Sinai Generate Labor Migration

The southern part of the Sinai Peninsula extends over an area of 17,000 square kilometers. It is clearly separated from the larger northern part by an escarpment running roughly from east to west, which hinders movement between the two parts except along the littoral. Most of the country is made up of bare rugged mountains reaching a height of 2,600 meters. During fieldwork the asphalted main roads ran along the seashore, and the mountainous interior could be reached via dirt tracks running generally from east to west. Many parts in the interior are inaccessible by car and can only be reached by camel, donkey or on foot. Public transportation to places of employment, and for a growing number of tourist groups, was provided by a fleet of over a hundred American Jeeps, Russian military vehicles, and assorted pickups. These dilapidated vehicles were operated by individual Bedouin owner-drivers.

The arid climate of South Sinai produces little natural vegetation, and few trees and shrubs are able to survive the dry, hot summer. Horticulture is confined to the upper reaches of main valleys. The groundwater in these valleys is tapped by shallow wells. A Bedouin who wishes to set up a garden—usually no larger than two dunams (half an acre)—first excavates a well or hires the services of a professional well digger, and when he is lucky enough to strike water he builds the garden around the well. There also are several deep wells for drinking water that have been sunk by the government or by public-spirited Bedouin, to which all Bedouin have equal access.

South Sinai is inhabited by about ten thousand Bedouin, giving an average population density of one person to every two square kilometers. Permanent settlements were few until the 1950s. Up to that time the little port of al-Tur on the Gulf of Suez, where most of the residents were sailors and fishermen, was the main settlement. It had a quarantine station for Muslims returning from the annual pilgrimage to Mecca (see Bartheel 1943: 18–22). The other settlement was the Santa Katarina monastery of Mount Sinai, a venerable institution founded in the sixth century and continuously inhabited by Greek Orthodox monks since then. In recent years, ten to twenty monks, headed by an archbishop *(mutran)*, have lived in the monastery. Most of the monastery's menial work was, and still is, done by Jabaliya Bedouin encamped nearby.

In the 1950s Egypt established army camps and an airfield, built roads along the west coast of the peninsula, and exploited on a commercial scale the oil fields and gypsum and manganese deposits on the littoral of the Gulf of Suez. These enterprises employed relatively few Bedouin. Egypt has an almost infinite reservoir of men who had first claim on available work. Bedouin informants say that about four thousand Egyptian workers were employed in Sinai, not counting military personnel, compared to some three hundred Bedouin. Thus, the biggest industrial plant in Sinai, the gypsum factory at Ras Mal'ab, was reported to have employed nearly two thousand workers, of whom only sixty-five were local Bedouin. The Abu Rudes oil installations and the Umm Bogmah manganese mine together employed roughly one hundred and fifty Bedouin. Some twenty to thirty Bedouin were regularly employed by the Santa Katarina monastery, and a few men worked intermittently for government departments. Some of these men were well diggers and builders who also worked for Bedouin customers. During the annual pilgrimage season the quarantine station in al-Tur supplied work to as many as five hundred to six hundred men, but only for four to eight weeks.

The Bedouin never relied on wage labor alone. Many of them exploited the meager natural resources, raised goats and camels, and engaged in some gardening. Many of the younger men, up to one thousand at a time, sought employment as unskilled laborers and menials in Egyptian cities, staying away from home for months on end, and often for many years. Quite a few of these men eventually settled permanently with their families in Egypt, while others returned home when their children were old enough to replace them as laborers.

In the early 1950s the smuggling of hashish and opium, which had since the beginning of the twentieth century contributed to the economy of the Bedouin, became even more important. It brought more money into the region and created the incentive to raise standards of consumption (see chapter 5). As a result, ever more Bedouin sought employment, mostly as menial workers in the Egyptian cities Cairo and Suez. Labor migration further increased under Israeli rule, between 1967 and 1982. There were four main reasons for that: first, drug smuggling declined because it involved too many risks; second, work in the oil installations and in construction in Sinai, which had previously been mainly reserved for Egyptian laborers, now became available to Bedouin; third, Israeli colonist economic initiatives provided new jobs in Sinai; and fourth, there was no longer an Egyptian market for the Bedouin's garden produce and it thus became imperative for them to seek an alternative income. Although work was now found nearer to home, much of it was still at some distance from the tribal areas. A pattern of commuting developed, in which men remained at work for six to ten weeks and then spent between two to four weeks at home. When at home they might decide to stay on for a longer period, and often remained for as long as cash and provisions lasted.

The Bedouin of South Sinai possess a relatively secure home base because the state's agencies did not make the effort to provide the poor and widely dispersed inhabitants of the rather inaccessible region with services. This has allowed them to engage in a variety of locally based economic pursuits, such as growing fruit and vegetables, raising goats and camels, smuggling drugs, and plying various trades. Yet labor migration has at most times played a major role in the Bedouin economy. However, the successive rulers of the peninsula have never coerced them to go out and work for them. Egypt always suffers of an excess of labor, so that in most years it sends between 2.5 and 3 million men as labor migrants to the Gulf countries and elsewhere (Nassar 2008: 1). As

most migrants are skilled and educated (Nassar 2008: 4, 7), and
the unskilled tend to stay at home, there has never been a scarcity
of unskilled and illiterate workers such as the Bedouin in the Nile
Valley. The Egyptian authorities even offered the Bedouin certain
inducements, which proved inadequate, to remain at home: they
provided them with monthly food rations, usually supplied by
the American government. But Sinai offered very little paid employment, so that most young Bedouin spent some years working
in Egyptian cities or industrial installations. The Israeli occupation made migrant labor more attractive, although the Israeli authorities too made some short-lived attempts to fix low wages
for Bedouin labor and sought to prevent Bedouin from working
in Israel. However, the creeping colonization of Sinai that culminated in 1972 in the construction of an Israeli town, Ofira (now
Sharm al-Sheikh), near the southern tip of the peninsula offered
employment to Bedouin cooks, cleaners, and watchmen. The fast-
growing economy of Israel too needed more and more manual
laborers, and offered wages almost equal to those paid to Israeli
workers. Therefore, Bedouin laborers gradually infiltrated the
town of Eilat just beyond the then open border of Sinai, and some
of them found work further north.

Whatever the political regime, Bedouin never enjoyed job security and could be dismissed without notice. Therefore, Bedouin
always considered work to be temporary, and saved up for bad
times. They did not usually accumulate cash reserves; instead,
each household kept a stock of food sufficient to last it through
several months. Many Bedouin constructed storehouses in convenient locations or fitted natural caves with doors and locks (both
types of store are called *qeria*) in order to store their provisions.
Some of these sites later became the nuclei of hamlets.

As the Bedouin labor migrants constantly feared sudden loss
of employment due to economic change or political upheaval,
they wished to maintain their home base back in the mountains of
South Sinai in a state of readiness. They therefore left their families behind to take care of gardens and flocks and to keep in touch
with relatives and friends. Spatial proximity to other Bedouin was
most important. The children of migrants could be properly cared
for when they lived next door to other Bedouin. The migrants'
flocks were taken out to pasture in turn by the girls of neighbor-

ing households, and returned every evening to their pens. There was much cooperation between households in order to cope with the economic affairs of migrants. As none of the staple foodstuffs were produced locally, provisions were bought from a few stores dispersed in the countryside, and these became nuclei of Bedouin hamlets. When these hamlets grew in size they attracted government services and itinerant traders, and became starting points for motor transport. Thus, the establishment of some of the permanent settlements in South Sinai, such as Milqa, near the Santa Katarina monastery, can largely be attributed to the wage labor situation. Other Bedouin settlements, such as Bir Zgher and Bir 'Oqda, were founded as home bases for narcotics smugglers. In the recent past the sea beaches and lush palm groves of Dahab and Nuweb'a in the Gulf of Aqaba had served Bedouin fishermen as campsites during the summer months. When the Israeli authorities inserted Jewish colonies into that ecological niche in 1971 (Kliot and Albeck 1996: 56), these attracted a halo of year-round Bedouin settlers.

The growth of Bedouin hamlets could be very rapid. The hamlet of Milqa looks as if it had been in place since time immemorial, yet aerial photographs show that in 1950 there were only a few storage houses in the area, and not a single dwelling. By 1980 over eighty houses had been built, and in addition there were three to four stores, a coffeehouse, a school, a medical dispensary, a government service center, and a tourist center. Living in permanent hamlets had other far-reaching effects on the Bedouin, which will be explored below.

"Home" and "Work"

The Bedouin's "home" *(dar)* is the moral and spatial center of his basic security system and the economic alternative to labor migration. The upkeep of this system requires the cooperation of numerous persons and groups. There are first the members of the household, who maintain the flocks and gardens in readiness for activation. Then there are the spouses' close relatives, who assist the household in every possible way and whenever needed. The tribe and tribal confederation give the head of the family access

to land and pasture. The tribe protects the Bedouin's tribal territory *(dira)*, whereas the tribal confederation gives him access
to pasture and smuggling routes. Security is also provided by
flocks and orchards, which can always become sources of cash
income. The produce of the orchards can, furthermore, feed the
family for limited periods. Finally, the system of social security
includes the saints' tombs, which link the man and his family to
divine providence, to the world of Islam, and, during the annual
tribal pilgrimages, allow him to visualize the tribe as a living social entity and to form a coherent picture of his social world (see
chapter 7).

"Work" *(shughul)* is no less complex a concept, and is as relevant as home to the Bedouin's system of social security. To a
Bedouin man it denotes any productive activity that yields, or
could be made to yield, cash income. It is the man's duty to work,
and everything he does as a labor migrant belongs to the world
of work, even if it concerns the maintenance of links with fellow
Bedouin. While wage labor is available, the women's efforts in
tending gardens and grazing the small flocks are not considered
to be work, but are part of the complex maintenance operation going on at home. When a man returns home and devotes himself to
the same gardens and flocks, then he is doing "work." This argument conceals the very real contribution of women and girls to the
household, perhaps because its monetary value is insignificant in
periods of plentiful migrant work. Yet without the women's efforts, the system of social assurance would be unworkable.

The Jabaliya of South Sinai illustrate this argument. With
around 1,200 members, they are the second largest tribe in the region. The other Bedouin tribes often claim that they are the weak-
est and meekest tribe, perhaps because they inhabit a relatively
small area in the high mountains away from the main smuggling
routes. They live near the ancient Santa Katarina monastery and
have for many generations maintained a special historical link
with it. When the Byzantine emperor Justinian built the monastery in the sixth century, they say, he sent their Wallachian ancestors to serve the monks in perpetuity. The monks confirm this
ancient tradition. It is a myth underpinning ongoing complex relations between the Jabaliya and the monastery. In a world that is
all too insecure the monastery stands as a rock, and the tribesmen

rely on it in time of need. The monastery employs between twenty and thirty tribesmen (customarily only a few members of other tribes are employed) and while it pays low wages—less than half those currently obtainable elsewhere—most of them remain in its employ throughout their working life, and when they retire the monastery periodically supplies them with wheat rations. The monastery lays claim to the tribe's land, and thus helps to stem encroachment by the more powerful tribes. Until 1967 the monks collected an annual tithe from Jabaliya orchards and gardens located close by. During the Israeli occupation this practice was conveniently put aside, but not forgotten.

Gardens can provide some of the Jabaliya's requirements for fruit and vegetables. In the not too distant past they were the only source of fruit, nuts, and vegetables and still left some surplus. They used to sell part of their hardy pears and almonds in al-Tur, a three-day journey on camelback, and with the proceeds they were able to buy enough grain to last them through the year. In addition, they earned cash from working in the al-Tur quarantine station for pilgrims returning from Mecca. The pilgrimage season lasted several weeks, and with the money they earned they could buy some basic necessities such as tea, sugar, and clothing. The prevailing attitude of the Bedouin was then expressed by the saying, "The Bedouin loves freedom and hunger," for toward the end of summer they often ran short of grain, the basic food.

During periods of abundant employment, the Jabaliya view the gardens as summer retreats. Each family owns at least one garden (some men own several gardens in different locations) (Perevolotsky 1981: 339) and spends part of the hot summer months in the shade of the trees. The gardens are watered fairly regularly and in many some vegetables are grown in plots between the fruit trees. But the Bedouin consider neither the fruit nor the vegetables as valuable economic resources. They view them as delicious additions to their diet, not as staple food. Wage labor has brought them higher incomes and created new needs. Nowadays they buy more food, including a wide range of canned foodstuffs, and more and better clothing and household goods, as well as radios, pens, and watches. Since the days of the gardening economy expenditure on food has risen about three times, from an average of about $10 a month per household to $30 today.

Wherever one turns in South Sinai, one encounters women and girls herding flocks of black goats, with here and there a white sheep interspersed. These flocks vary in size, from a few heads to fifty or more. They are so ubiquitous that one may easily gain the impression that they are a major source of income for the Bedouin. In fact, the Jabaliya and the other tribe practice herding on a limited scale. The average family owns an estimated five to six goats and one camel. The women and girls of related or neighboring households take turns in herding, and every evening the animals return to their owner's home. As the Bedouin congregate in larger and more stable hamlets and the girl herders' range of movement is limited to a day's journey, the pasture is soon exhausted. The girls still take the animals out to pasture, in the vain hope that they might find some herbage here and there, and when they return home in the evening offer them a real meal. For about six months every year the animals are fed expensive, imported corn and sorghum. Bedouin claim that they spend more money each year on animal feed than the animals are worth. They try to keep their flocks quite small, in order to minimize their losses. But they do not abandon the flocks, because they are also a potential source of security. Should conditions change, they argue, the flock could be built up in two to three years. Then the household and the flock would move from pasture to pasture—and due to the irregularity of rainfall, all of South Sinai is one pastoral region to which all the tribesmen, the Tawara, have access—and supplementary feeding could be sharply reduced. The few nomadic Bedouin who keep larger flocks of fifty to sixty goats prove that in such conditions the flocks could become profitable.

As the able-bodied men are absent for extended periods, most of the work in the gardens and with the flocks is done by women and children. While it may often be hard and wearying work, Bedouin do not consider it to be productive. When compared to the income from wage labor, it is indeed not very profitable. From the men's viewpoint, the women's work is chiefly a maintenance operation. Should the men lose their jobs and return home, they would take over the management of the flocks and gardens and soon turn them into income-producing resources.

While the men work in towns they remain in constant communication with the people back home. They can do so because at work they maintain close links with fellow Bedouin, among them often close relatives. As this need to remain in touch is shared by all the migrant laborers, they tend to concentrate in certain parts of town, to enter the same places and types of employment, and to entrust each other with messages and errands on the periodic trips back home. This often leads to a castelike specialization of Bedouin from a particular area. Thus, if one or two members of a kinship network enter employment in an oil company, or become watchmen, others will soon follow them until they carve out a special economic niche.

Bedouin migrants do not set up house in order to be near their place of work. They prefer to remain close to kinsmen or neighbors from back home, so they stay with other men from their area, either in cheap lodgings or at their place of work. Often they do not possess so much as a corner where they can leave their few belongings. This is not a resurgence of "tribalism in town," but rather a network of relationships connected to the worker's need to maintain constant communication with the people back home (Ramphele [1993: 68] describes similar conditions in a hostel for labor migrants in Cape Town, South Africa).

The migrant labor situation has different effects on the social fields of Bedouin men and women, and their control of various resources. Men participate in a much larger social field than women. While the men maintain links with people from back home and these figure importantly in their social networks, in the course of their work they also establish important relationships about which the people back home know very little. Women see the city either when they are taken to hospital or when they visit relatives settled there. On these occasions they only get distant glimpses of the men's world. They obtain incoherent bits of information about city life, not enough to allow them to intervene in it through their menfolk.

The women's network of relationships may be more restricted than that of the men, but in terms of power and control of the networks at home the women are more than the men's equals. Although men are acquainted with practically all the members of their women's networks, they are not privy to all the detailed information about local affairs that the women share. This knowledge is a crucial resource; it permits the women to function as guardians of the home and the ideal of basic security it stands for. The migrant labor situation is thus reproduced in the family. Formally, each spouse should have his or her separate sphere of activity and control different resources. In reality, the man does not even fully control the spending of the money he has earned, because the day-to-day running of the household is done by his wife. While giving the man his due, the woman protects her sphere of influence by enveloping it in a cloak of modesty. The woman seemingly forfeits access to the outside world, but she participates and acts in a close-knit network of local relationships. The cloak and veil and the restrictions on public appearance that appear to the man to protect his wife's modesty restrict his own access to the relationships and information that she commands. Under the "veil of modesty," some of the more independent women may even engage in extramarital liaisons.

This may explain why it is women who enforce the "restrictions" on their freedom of movement. For instance, in Milqa, near the Santa Katarina monastery, women do not use the main road taken by motor traffic and by men. They walk on footpaths meandering behind and between the houses, so as not to be seen "in public." While controlling the family's spending money, women do not enter the village stores themselves, but send children to buy provisions. Even their appearance suggests that behind their veil there hides considerable power. They do their hair in a bun protruding from their forehead. While most of the hair is covered by a headcloth, this hornlike bun is carried openly. The veil covering their faces from below the eyes is gaily embroidered, with reds predominating, and embellished with coins. It projects the message that beneath a woman's cloak of modesty there is hidden strength and wealth. Even when the husband is at home between spells of work, he does not really get to control his wife. She is submissive and meek, but she keeps her information to herself.

It appears that there is little reason for married women to go into migrant labor. But why do young single women, divorcees, or women whose husbands are incapable of work not go out to work? The routinely advanced cultural explanation, that a tribal or Islamic code of honor and shame prevents women from entering the labor market, does not fit the case. The women of South Sinai are used to moving unaccompanied around the countryside, and engage as a matter of course in strenuous physical work. I argue that these women would go out to work if the labor market were ready to accept them. Before the Israeli occupation of Sinai, the chief work destination of Bedouin men was Cairo. There they became cheap replacements for the men of the Nile Valley who had gone in their masses to the Gulf countries. In the early 1980s Egyptian labor migration reached a climax of about three million workers abroad (Richards and Waterbury 1990: 378), practically all of them men. Egyptian women filled more and more of the vacant work positions, at the low wages paid in Egypt (Macleod 1992: 48–53), so that the men from South Sinai could only compete for the dregs of the job market. There was no point for women from South Sinai to enter such an unattractive labor situation. There were as yet no opportunities for them to work as maids or cooks in Egyptian homes, for only when the women in the receiving countries become well-paid professionals who spend long hours at work do they need female labor migrants to replace them at home, to love and raise their children and do the household chores (Sassen 2003: 258). This was a luxury that few Egyptian women could afford.

The opportunities for work greatly increased during the Israeli occupation, but so did the uncertainty about the future. While most Bedouin men went out to work, the women were therefore fully occupied in maintaining the system of security in readiness for the expected crisis. Perhaps, if the occupation had lasted longer and stabilized, Bedouin women too would in the end have joined the ranks of migrant workers.

Many men remain at work for several weeks at a time and then return home for a similar period. This shuttle movement is often interpreted by employers as laziness, or as lack of ambition. They consider the Bedouin worker to be unreliable, especially because he often fails to return to work at the stipulated time. But the returning migrant does not relax for long at home. He visits relatives, friends, and neighbors to reaffirm social links. He gives presents to each according to his degree of closeness. The members of his network of relationships may be widely dispersed, so that the visits are usually time-consuming, arduous, and costly. He returns to work only when he has completed his round of visits, knowing that he contributed his share to the maintenance of the system of security.

Tribal membership is still important for the Bedouin because it gives him the right to exploit certain resources within tribal territory, and other resources outside of it. The individual acquires membership of the tribe indirectly, by belonging to a patronymic group of agnates that is recognized as part of the tribe. The outward sign of a group's belonging is usually a place in the tribal genealogy. These groups, which were said to characterize pastoral nomads in the Middle East, have little work to do in today's conditions. There is no scarcity of land; no one will dispute a man's right to construct an orchard or palm grove anywhere on his tribe's territory. It is the tribe that controls rights to land and the tribal confederation—access to pasture—and not the descent group. Descent groups are not known to prosecute blood disputes or protect rights to land. Self-help and vengeance are frowned upon by the tribal elders, who do their best to keep the security forces out of their affairs. Thus the single remaining task of the agnatic descent group is to mediate the individual's membership of the tribe.

The tribe reserves for its members certain rights over the strategic resources found in its territory, such as water for the irrigation of gardens, house construction sites, and passage through, and employment opportunities in, the tribal area. Due to the extensive concern with wage labor some of these rights may not be fully exploited by tribesmen, but they devote considerable efforts to the preservation of the tribe, to make sure that the rights do not lapse. In the absence of joint activities they can do so chiefly by organizing gatherings, at which tribal solidarity is reaffirmed. These annual meetings are set to coincide with the date harvest or the ripening of other produce, so as to attract as many people as possible. Many of the labor migrants leave their employment at such times and return to the tribal area. In South Sinai hundreds of tribesmen congregate in the major oases of Dahab, Nuweb'a, and Wadi Firan, as well as in some smaller ones. At the end of the date harvest the gatherings culminate in tribal pilgrimages to the tombs of ancestral saints, at which people reanimate the tribe and reaffirm that they are still members in it (see chapter 7).

The "income and security" economy was put to the test repeatedly during the period of fieldwork. One such occasion was the short war between Egypt and Israel in October 1973, as a result of which all civilian Israeli activities in South Sinai were suspended for about five months. During that period all migrant laborers returned home. Most families had stored up basic foods, such as wheat, sugar, and oil, against such an eventuality. People who had large stores of food shared them with kinsmen. As everyone was back home, social relationships were intensified. There was a great deal of mutual visiting, especially by men. Work in the gardens was accelerated. Some men planned to acquire gardens; others built new gardens or improved existing ones. Men also bought goats and sheep and increased their flocks. Spatial mobility grew; some families left the settlements for their gardens, and others moved around with their flocks. The population in the "permanent" hamlets declined. Unusually large numbers of Bedouin attended the tribal pilgrimages in the following year. This flurry of activity was part of the Bedouin's efforts to reactivate their secure economic base. Not everyone had fully prepared for the sudden change, but all the Bedouin shared the benefits of this system of mutual assurance.

This is the foundation on which noncoercive labor migration is established. As it is deemed to provide an income over and beyond basic security, slight economic incentives are required for men to enter the labor market. They remain in it while the going is good, and willingly return to their mountains when economic and political conditions deteriorate. While the system is flexible and easily adapts to often unforeseeable changes in the Bedouin's social world, it does not allow them to accumulate great wealth or specialized knowledge, nor does it provide the coveted long-term security. However, the Bedouin are well aware that if they all came back home, they would not be able to make a living from their flocks and gardens. If every Bedouin decided to raise a larger flock, there would not be enough water and pasture for all the animals. Their gardens would supply only a fraction of the fruit and vegetables required by a larger population, and most necessities of life, and especially grain, would still have to be imported. Security is an elusive goal.

Chapter Five

Smuggling Drugs

Introduction

The Bedouin of South Sinai are a link in the international drug traffic delivering hashish and other narcotics to the inhabitants of the Nile Valley. In this chapter I examine the changing fortunes of their smuggling operations. The full-scale entry of the South Sinai Bedouin into drug smuggling began around 1950, and in less than two decades smuggling grew into a major industry. At its zenith it provided about 30 percent of the aggregate income of the Bedouin population. When Israel occupied Sinai in 1967, smuggling stopped almost immediately. During the fifteen years of Israeli occupation, from 1967 to 1982, the crossing from the Sinai Peninsula into mainland Egypt was too dangerous for the operators. At the time of my fieldwork in South Sinai, during the Israeli occupation, most Bedouin men had adapted to the new situation and made a living as migrant workers; others were employed locally in various trades, and a handful entered the budding local tourist industry. The loss of income from smuggling did not cause them economic hardship, and most of them were glad to adopt a less risky way of life.

But the leaders of the smuggling gangs did not go out to work. They remained at home in their mountain retreats, and kept open house for their many visitors. It was thus quite easy for me to meet them. While they appeared to be inactive in the economy, I soon realized that they were working hard to keep the smuggling organizations viable: they fostered the ties with their former associates and looked after the wells and orchards in their mountain retreats. They were convinced that the political and economic situation would sooner or later change, and that drug smuggling would once again become feasible.

Ordinary Bedouin too were concerned about the future, but dealt with it in a totally different way. They worked to forestall expected calamities, such as illness, death, and loss of income. For this purpose they built up a complex system of mutual assurance, whose main elements were the following: orchards and small flocks that they maintained as an economic reserve; close-knit networks of relationships with kin and corporate associates who would help them in time of need; and tribal bonds that gave them access to territorial resources. When migrant labor was plentiful, the Bedouin invested just the minimal effort needed to keep the system going. Whenever they could take time off from work, they maintained their networks by occasional visits to relatives and friends, and they maintained the tribe by attending the annual pilgrimage to the tombs of their ancestral patron saint. They herded their small flocks near their home hamlets, so that they had to be handfed at considerable expense, and invested only the necessary work in their orchards. When fate struck next, for instance, when migrant labor was no longer plentiful, they would fall back on these resources and turn them into useful and profitable assets.

These precautions were based on long experience. The Bedouin knew that conditions in Sinai could change dramatically, sometimes almost overnight. Thus, when the October 1973 war between Egypt and Israel broke out, most Bedouin men were engaged in migrant labor. They all lost their employment and were left stranded at their places of work, as there was no transport to take them home. Disaster struck again in 1982, when Sinai reverted to Egyptian rule and the Egyptian authorities developed hotel tourism as a major industry.

The tourist resorts on the shores of the Gulf of Aqaba catered to the requirements of an international and urban Egyptian clientele. The international hotel chains, and the government and commercial services that supported them, recruited most of their employees from among the dwellers of the Nile Valley. They hired only a small number of Bedouin men, and even the formerly thriving Bedouin guest lodges lost some of their customers. This resulted in a rapid deterioration of the Bedouin's economic situation. Many Bedouin returned to migrant labor. The hashish trade too revived very quickly, but this time with a difference: now the Bedouin smugglers not only conveyed drugs to the Nile Valley, but also sold them locally, both to the tourists and to fellow Bedouin. The drug dealers and other men were gradually becoming drug consumers.

Why did Bedouin Engage in Drug Smuggling?

How did hashish smuggling so rapidly become a major and seemingly permanent feature of the South Sinai Bedouin economy in the 1950s and 1960s, and again in the 1980s? The answer to this question is, I believe, related to three aspects of life in Sinai.

First, the Bedouin consider the smuggling of hashish and other drugs to be a legitimate economic enterprise, and not a criminal activity. Like many people the world over, they believe that the state and its laws "are only somewhat noticed, somewhat respected" (Nordstrom 2007: 207) and that it is therefore all right to engage in extralegal activities. But in their case the belief is solidly grounded, for every Bedouin man spends part of his life in Egyptian cities, where men of all classes indulge in the smoking of hashish. Although the habit is today illegal, Egyptians consider it a harmless habit. They had for centuries smoked locally grown hashish and the attitude toward the drug did not change when European imperialists outlawed it. Furthermore, the drug was in the 1960s still purveyed by powerful international organizations, and the Bedouin were proud to play a significant part in a great commercial enterprise. While the international drug trade mostly benefited big operators, in the Sinai leg of the operation, at least, the earnings were distributed widely among the many people who worked for it in various capacities, such as organizers, cameleers, truck drivers, boatmen, messengers, informers, and collaborators from the ranks of government (see Levi 1987: 373–74). The Bedouin respected and honored the chiefs of smuggling gangs as entrepreneurs who had brought them a higher standard of living. The Bedouin viewed the gang leaders as public benefactors who dug public wells, repaired saints' tombs, and improved dust tracks. They respected the smuggling chiefs as alert, experienced, and well-informed persons, not a few of whom composed widely circulated poems (Holes and Abu Athera 2009: 47, 97, 115). The Bedouin's attitude toward the drug trade was even tinged with defiance against the state that treated them as second-class citizens, whose agents suppressed and humiliated them, took over their land, and deprived them of their livelihood, and whose cooperation often had to be bought at great expense (see Kershaw [2006] for a similar situation in today's Native American reservations).

Even the illegality of the hashish trade did not deter the Bedouin. They knew that they were risking arrest and imprisonment, but did not see this in a different light from ordinary businessmen who routinely take calculated risks. As modern people with a cosmopolitan outlook, they treated smuggling as a strictly rational business matter and, just like other businessmen, they "silenced morality" (Bauman 2000: 29) as not being consistent with rational conduct. In the early days of smuggling, the prospect of higher earnings persuaded the smuggling chiefs to include in some consignments heavy drugs such as opium and heroin. From the 1980s onward this became a general trend. Smugglers became less selective about the goods they carried as long as they made a good profit. They included heavy drugs such as cocaine and heroin, and later on synthetic drugs and even weapons, in consignments.

Second, the Bedouin treated the drug trade as a windfall that had to be exploited while it lasted. They could do so because they had built up a system of mutual insurance that allowed them to overcome setbacks and calamities. Personal experience, further strengthened by frequent political and economic upheavals, had taught them that misfortunes such as death, illness, imprisonment, and impoverishment were part and parcel of life, bound to happen, and that one had to prepare for them. In order to cope with these expected events, they provided the members of their households with a comprehensive system of social assurance, and devoted much time and effort to its maintenance. This system gave the Bedouin not only the resilience to adapt to the rapidly changing circumstances of the drug trade, but also permitted them to accept with equanimity the cessation of smuggling in 1967. Smuggling has since 1982 again become important in the economy of the Sinai Bedouin, but its association with political insurgency has caused the Egyptian authorities to take extreme measures against smuggling organizations, such as rounding up and imprisoning hundreds of suspects and shooting smugglers on sight (Zambelis 2006). Today Bedouin smugglers are worried that smuggling may eventually become too risky and that they may once again have to fall back on their time-tested system of mutual assurance.

Third, the requirements of the smuggling trade fitted easily into the Bedouin's existing social realities and practices. These included an intimate knowledge of mountainous South Sinai acquired in pastoral migrations, based on the traditional right to free and unrestricted access of their flocks and herds to all parts of their country. Also relevant were their familiarity with life and work in cities, and their unceasing mobility over large distances to and from places of work. An added advantage was their reliance on dispersed networks of kinsmen and friends and the absence of small corporate agnatic groups that might be tempted to obstruct the free movement of the drug traffic through their territory. Even the 160-odd saints' tombs spread along the east-west passages through the peninsula facilitated the movement of smugglers, who could unobtrusively use the rest houses *(maq'ad)* attached to many saints' tombs. Before developing the argument, however, I must first sketch the historical background of the drug trade.

Drug Smuggling in Historical Context

Since the thirteenth century the smoking of hashish has been one of the favorite pleasures of the Islamic world (Levey 1971: 267; Rosenthal 1971). The practice was especially prevalent among Egyptians, who consumed large quantities of locally produced hashish. Thus, Lane reports in 1836 that "[t]he habit is now very common among the lower orders in the metropolis and other towns of Egypt" (1895: 347). Some 150 years later, in 1990, hashish is still "the most commonly used drug in Egypt" (Hussein 1990: v) and the circle of consumers has, if possible, broadened (see, e.g., Aswany 2004: 15, 51). But there is a fundamental difference between the two periods: although Indian hemp *(cannabis sativa),* the plant from which hashish is made, had for many years been grown locally and sold freely and cheaply, it became illegal as European involvement in Egypt increased. Under pressure from the European powers, Egypt outlawed hashish production in 1879, with the result that it was from then until the 1950s smuggled in from Morocco and Greece.

Over the years the Egyptian authorities resorted to ever-harsher measures against drug use; Law 182 of 1962 made the "cultivation, smuggling, sale and distribution of restricted drugs felonies punishable by life imprisonment" (Hussein 1990: v). The gradual criminalization of the drug trade may well be part of an encroaching Western imperialism. Agents of the state would ban the local drug hashish because of its predicated debilitating effect on the work and sexual prowess of users. At the same time they encouraged the use of the Western drug tobacco, which was in those days believed to be quite harmless. Interestingly, the French colonial authorities in Morocco adopted a similar policy of substituting tobacco for hashish at about the same time (Fournier 2002: 12). It is no coincidence that under the influence of the imperial British overlord tobacco, as well as salt, became government monopolies (Dumreicher 1931: ix). The Egyptian authorities considered both commodities to be basic necessities of life and therefore suitable for becoming a perpetual source of government revenue. Salt was quarried by Bedouin in the Eastern Desert and the Egyptian Treasury used every means to wrest the trade from their hands. Tobacco and tobacco products were imported from Europe through the customs station in the port of Alexandria. The drug hashish was liable to compete against this import, and was therefore outlawed under the pretext that it was harmful to people's health. Drug dealers were to be hunted down and put behind bars.

The Egyptian Coastguard Administration was set up in the 1880s to enforce the state monopoly on salt and tobacco, and restrict the free trade in narcotics. By the turn of the century the administration had branched out into three departments. One of these was the Desert Directorate, which became responsible not only for the prevention of drug smuggling, but also for public security in the Libyan, Eastern, and Southern deserts and the

Sinai Peninsula (Dumreicher 1931: xi). As the authorities knew that Egyptians did not consider hashish a harmful substance and might collaborate with the smugglers, they based the Desert Directorate chiefly on foreign personnel. European officers and Sudanese soldiers and noncommissioned officers carried out the policing operations, while "Egyptian sergeants … were responsible for the clerical work" (Dumreicher 1931: 6–7).

While the Egyptian Desert Directorate battled with the drug traffic, it also had a stake in maintaining the flow of drugs, so that it could continually make successful seizures. The smugglers, for their part, often assisted the law enforcement agencies in discovering small shipments (see Dumreicher 1931: 191), as it helped them to keep up the price of drugs. They also had a material interest in collaborating with the authorities, as this could assure safe passage for their goods. These parallel interests could easily develop into permanent or intermittent collaboration between law enforcement agents and smugglers. Several government officials recorded in their memoirs instances of such collusion (Dumreicher 1931: 191; Jarvis 1931: 199; Russell 1949: 275). In addition to this official collaboration, there were always law officers ready to enter into personal arrangements with smugglers in order to augment their low salaries.

The outlawing of the drug did not affect consumer demand, but rapidly reduced local production. Therefore, the price of the drug soon rose to the point where it became worthwhile for international businessmen to enter the lucrative trade. Most of the imports came overland or by sea from Morocco. Then Greek businessmen entered the fray. Their hashish was grown and produced in Greece and transported by boat to desolate spots on the Egyptian Mediterranean coast, where camel caravans took over and carried the merchandise into the Nile Valley. In 1932, however, Greece prohibited the cultivation of hashish, and its share in the trade declined rapidly. It was then that Syria and Lebanon took over the role of major suppliers of hashish (Russell 1949: 271), without ever displacing Morocco as the most important source of drugs for Egypt. Indeed, toward the end of the twentieth century Morocco became the world's biggest supplier of hashish (UNODC 2005: 83). It is an irony of history that western Europe has become the world's largest market for hashish and Middle Eastern coun-

tries, and especially Morocco, are again major producers and ex-
porters. According to a recent United Nations report, "[w]estern
Europe is the largest market for cannabis resin, responsible for
nearly 70 percent of global seizures in 2003, and 80 percent of this
hashish was produced in Morocco" (UNODC 2005: 81).

Needless to say, tobacco has not displaced hashish, just as it
has not reduced the use of qat and other local drugs in the Middle
East. The imported and the local drugs are used side by side,
sometimes simultaneously. Thus, each participant in a Yemeni qat
session provides his own bunch of leaves to suit his pocketbook,
while the host's tobacco pipe is passed around the circle of guests
in an egalitarian manner (Weir 1985: 119).

Smuggling of narcotics had interested the Sinai Bedouin since
the beginning of the twentieth century (Dumreicher 1931: 204;
Russell 1949: 272), but really took off in the 1930s, when the production of hashish in Syria and Lebanon accelerated. At first, the
traders sent the drugs through Palestine and North Sinai into the
Nile Valley. The Bedouin tribes on the Mediterranean coast of Sinai
between al-'Arish and Qantara organized the camel caravans that
carried the drugs. When the customs depot along the Palestinian
border became more effective and Egyptian law agents too ap-
prehended many shipments, the traders began to look around for
an alternative route. The Bedouin of North Sinai "resented [these]
measures which jeopardized a source of income as lucrative as
smuggling," but could express their anger only in powerful poetry (Bailey 1991: 369). Eventually the trade shifted to the longer
but safer route through Jordan (then the Emirate of Transjordan),
Saudi Arabia, and across the Gulf of Aqaba and South Sinai into
the Nile Valley. Only then did the Bedouin of South Sinai get seriously involved in the drug trade. After the establishment of Israel
in 1948 the North Sinai border became too dangerous, and the
route through South Sinai became, for nearly twenty years (until
the Israeli occupation of Sinai in 1967), a major import channel of
hashish into Egypt. At its height, the drug trade provided about
30 percent of the income of the Bedouin population. In retrospect,
it is astonishing to see how in just two decades it became such a
major, and seemingly primordial, component of the economy of
South Sinai.

During the Israeli occupation smuggling was at low ebb, because the Israeli and Egyptian forces were facing each other along

the land and sea frontiers. Smuggling became very risky in these conditions, except in the first years of the occupation when the Israeli army permitted informers to take small quantities of hashish on the vessel that plied the route between Abu Znema in Sinai and the Egyptian mainland. At the same time, there was abundant work for labor migrants, so most of the male adults were generally away at work. Some of the men who stayed at home were former smugglers who were now living in what Lavie (1990: 157) describes as semiretirement. Among them were some of the most prominent and interesting people I met during my fieldwork in Sinai. As their businesses were inactive at the time, they reluctantly agreed to talk about them. These men entertained a stream of visitors, maintained links with numerous kin and former associates, established contacts with the military and civilian authorities, and took care of the oases that had served them as hideouts (see chapter 3). When the Israeli authorities permitted the inhabitants of Sinai in 1976 to attend the Mecca pilgrimage, the smuggling chiefs were among the first pilgrims. Presumably, they were eager to refresh their links with leaders of the international hashish trade.

The smugglers were not simply waiting for Israel to evacuate Sinai. They sought for ways and means to resume their activities under the watchful eyes of the occupying forces. Here is a somewhat morbid example: one of the chiefs of the Muzaina tribe, formerly a prominent organizer of smuggling gangs, received a visit from the Israeli military governor of South Sinai. During their conversation, to which I was privy, the chief expressed concern for the burial of Bedouin who had died in Israel. The problem was acute: the Israeli administration used to fly seriously ill and wounded Bedouin for treatment at the Tel Hashomer Hospital near Tel Aviv. Several Bedouin had died in this and other hospitals, but the military had neither buried the bodies nor found a way to return them to Sinai. The chief now made a most humane offer: he would convert a light truck into a hearse and from time to time pick up the cadavers and bring them back for burial in Sinai. He volunteered to make all the necessary arrangements and cover all the expenses. I understood intuitively that the chief had devised an ingenious way of importing drugs from Israel, as no customs officer would search a decomposing body. I assume the military governor too knew that he was being asked to connive at a renewal of drug smuggling, but with diplomatic adroitness he assured the chief that he would consider the request favorably.

The Organization of Drug Smuggling

The running battle between the smugglers and the law enforcement agents brought about continuous changes in the composition of the smuggling organizations and in the routes and methods of operation. There were five to six prominent men who led the larger and relatively permanent organizations, as well as a number of smaller ephemeral smuggling groups. Each group recruited some members on a kinship basis and others according to the services they could provide. The nuclei of such enterprises were often sets of brothers, whose abodes were spaced out along a west-east axis, presumably to facilitate the movement of goods. As each member also brought in maternal and affinal relatives, as well as unrelated persons who fulfilled useful functions as boatmen or truck drivers, or because they had useful ties with government agents, eventually many members of smuggling organizations were not related by kinship. This was not unlike the chain migration of laborers in which each man, in his turn, joins a relative or friend who is already established in a particular place of work. Such an arrangement assured both the loyalty of the members and the relatively wide and even distribution of the group's earnings. As the smuggling operations traversed the territories of several tribes and the members of smuggling groups were recruited from various tribes, there was no point in enforcing tribal territorial claims. The arrangements were thus analogous to the customary herding practices: as rain might fall quite unpredictably anywhere in the peninsula, herd owners from all tribes had the right to graze their flock anywhere in the South Sinai (Perevolotsky 1987: 156–57). In the same manner, smuggling caravans moved all over the region. But that does not imply that they did not take precautions against prying eyes. Thus, they kept away from villages and tent camps, where they ran the risk of exposure. Instead, they varied the routes and made special arrangements for each consignment. They tended to travel by night and to take breaks at saints' tombs. Many of the 160 or so saints' tombs (see a list and a map in Levi

[1980: 139–48]) are conveniently strung out along the main routes that cross the mountainous interior from east to west. The sanctuaries are located close to water sources, and provide a lodge for pilgrims who wish to stay overnight. These huts are equipped with cooking utensils and a small stock of food that each visitor is welcome to use and expected to replenish. As all the tombs are frequented by bona fide pilgrims throughout the year, they provide a suitable cover for smugglers.

Each smuggling haul was planned months ahead, in order to assure the smooth passage and minimize the risks of discovery. Three points were of particular importance in planning. First, caravans should not encounter military patrols. For this purpose the smugglers collected detailed information about their movements. Second, the paths of the various smuggling caravans should never cross. While the operations of the various organizations were not coordinated, they collected information about each other's plans and movements. And third, as the slow camel caravans were likely to be detected at the point of entry into mainland Egypt, the cargoes were transferred, usually in the Firan oasis, to motorcars or trucks. This last link was mostly provided by truckers from the Qararsha tribe or taxi drivers from the port of al-Tur. A man from al-Tur told me that he had regularly delivered consignments of hashish to Suez, hidden in the doors of his taxi.

The earnings from drug smuggling filtered down from the organizers to the rank and file of their employees. Smuggling thus made an important contribution to the economy of South Sinai. It was the driving force behind the development of orchards, the digging of new wells, and the installation of motorized water pumps, and contributed to the development of new oases, which served as hideouts for smuggling gangs.

Due to the irregularity of drug transports, there would often be months of inactivity between hauls. The smugglers would spend them in their inaccessible mountain retreats, tending their small but intensively cultivated orchards. They were keenly interested in introducing new varieties, as they aimed to spread the supply of fresh fruit over the longest possible period. As a result of such intensive cultivation, the retreats turned into lush oases. Inaccessibility was desired to prevent the unwelcome attentions of government agents. Therefore the retreats were set up in locations where ecological conditions were not ideal. In the 1950s, when smuggling became a major source of income for the South Sinai Bedouin, the entrepreneurs made further investments in these oases. They spent a great deal of money on diesel engines and pumps, in order to make irrigation less arduous. They also built sturdy houses for their families, on the expectation that they would often be absent on drug hauls. When the drug traffic ceased during the Israeli occupation, the oases rapidly fell into desuetude but were never abandoned.

Bir 'Oqda and Bir Zgher are good examples of this type of oasis. When I first visited Bir 'Oqda in 1972, the population was rapidly declining. Most of the twenty-odd households had moved to Dahab, on the coast. In former years they had gone to Dahab in the late summer, to enjoy the breeze and supplement their diet with seafood, and to wait for the date harvest at the end of August. Around October they would return to the mountain village of Bir 'Oqda. Now they simply stayed on in Dahab and delayed their departure from day to day. Only a few men made short trips to Bir 'Oqda, where the water pumps fell into disrepair and the fruit trees dried up. They explained the situation in ecological terms: the water sources in Bir 'Oqda were not as copious as they used to be, and therefore the yield of the fruit trees was dwindling. There simply was no point in cultivating the oasis. But another explanation may be more relevant: during the Israeli occupation, the smuggling of narcotics to Egypt stopped almost completely. Therefore, many former smugglers felt that the hideout was no longer required; they saw no reason why they should invest more resources in the construction of new wells and in improving the orchards. Some men became labor migrants like the rest of the male population. Others resolved to stay on in Dahab, where they developed tourist facilities or worked in the Israeli colony. Still, from time to time they returned to Bir 'Oqda to look after their orchards. They often argued that they wished to postpone the inevitable decline of the oasis, and as often thought that they had to maintain it in a state of readiness for a possible revival of the drug traffic.

The big operators looked at the situation quite differently. They hoped and expected conditions to change and had the resources to hold out until that day came. Therefore, they spent much of

their time in the oasis and hung on to their orchards. In the meantime, they lived on their often quite substantial hoarded savings
and regularly entertained guests, among them many associates
from their smuggling days.

The inhabitants of Bir Zgher responded differently to the
changed situation. A new highway from Eilat to Sharm al-Sheikh,
constructed by the Israeli administration, passed close to their village. They built a track to the main road, invested money in trucks
and pickups, and became involved in transporting migrant workers and tourists. The population of the village actually grew. Today, the people of Bir Zgher depend heavily on the unpredictable
flow of adventurous young Israeli and Egyptian tourists. This
does not mean that they discarded the smuggling option. If ever
the tourist traffic should decline or if they are pushed out by the
big hotels, they will once more resort to a combination of trucking
and smuggling.

The newfound wealth from smuggling also transformed the
larger palm oases, especially the central oasis in Wadi Firan. It
has always been on the major east-west thoroughfare, and almost
all traffic, including some smuggling caravans, passed through it.
Members of the various tribes owned shares in its palm trees and
in their shade built permanent huts and set up vegetable plots.
The oasis has for generations been exterritorial, but preserved
along its length are clusters of plots belonging to a particular tribe.
For instance, Qararsha tribesmen were concentrated in the lower
reaches of the wadi, and Jabaliya could be found upstream.

In Wadi Firan too many cultivators installed mechanical
pumps. One outcome of the new situation was that the water level
in the oasis gradually fell. In consequence, the wells had to be
deepened and became more expensive to maintain. The shallower
wells downstream dried up, and only wealthy Bedouin could afford to carry out the repeated excavations. The poorer Bedouin
moved out of the palm groves into the vicinity of perennial wells
upstream. The trend of oasis society to become ever more exclusive ended, however, under the Israeli occupation, when wage
labor became plentiful and almost all the men took part in it and
earned good wages. Now every plot owner could afford a motor
pump, and installed plastic pipes that delivered water by gravity
to several gardens downstream. The result was that the down-

ward spiral of declining groundwater levels and ever deepening wells accelerated.

Another outcome of drug smuggling was the self-declared peacefulness of the South Sinai Bedouin. Men would often say that "we Bedouin are a peace-loving people who never engage in fighting. In fifty years there has not been a single case of murder." They also pointed out that, in contrast to Bedouin in other regions, Sinai men did not carry weapons. These categorical statements referred to the need to maintain the public peace throughout the peninsula, as a precondition for large-scale smuggling. On their way over the mountains, the drugs crossed the territories of several tribes. The safe passage of drugs could be assured only if they all agreed to drop their differences and collaborate for a common good. This became possible because so many members of the various tribes participated in the drug trade, and the whole population benefited from the wealth it created.

In a sense, the peaceful atmosphere continued during the period of my fieldwork, a time when smuggling had almost ceased. South Sinai was very tranquil and safe, and Bedouin men and women, as well as tourists, moved freely and without hindrance throughout the countryside. The few violent incidents that did occur involved former smugglers. For instance, a prominent smuggler who had spent more than a decade in Egyptian prisons was shot at by an old competitor and lost the fingers of one hand. Now that smuggling was in abeyance, the men could settle outstanding accounts. However, it appears that when the hashish trade resumed in 1982 the smugglers put all their disputes aside in order to present a united front to the security forces, their common enemy. Peace was to reign once again in Sinai.

Recent Developments and Future Prospects

From the 1980s onward South Sinai became an important tourist center. Numerous international hotels line the east coast of Sinai, from Taba, just south of the Israeli border, to the tourist towns of Nuweb'a and Dahab, and down to Sharm al-Sheikh, the major tourist center near the southern tip of the peninsula. In between the larger tourist centers there are smaller tourist camps, mostly run by Egyptian entrepreneurs, some of whom collaborate with local Bedouin partners. Other tourist hotels and camps were established in the mountainous Santa Katarina region. The hotels in the Santa Katarina, Dahab, and Nuweb'a regions were built on land that Bedouin had considered their own, parts of which they had cultivated. The hotels squandered the limited water supply that had served the Bedouin for drinking and irrigation, and which they had husbanded carefully. The hotels tended to monopolize their guests, and thus put many of the simple Bedouin tourist camps and guides out of business. Only the backpackers and the younger and less affluent tourists still patronize Bedouin camping sites. Some of the adventurous tourists in Dahab may now even take a camel tour to the old smuggler's hideout Bir 'Oqda (Smadar Lavie, personal communication), and tourists from Santa Katarina hire Bedouin guides for treks to the Bedouin orchards in the high mountains. These tourists provide some income to the local Bedouin population. The hotels, however, recruit most of their staff in mainland Egypt, or even in places as far away as Sudan, and employ only a small number of Bedouin men in menial jobs. Modesty keeps women away from the hotels and the camping sites on the beaches, but some children earn petty cash by selling homemade clothing and trinkets to tourists (Aziz 2000: 38).

The international drug organizations have resumed operations in Sinai, now with a broader list of goods. The transportation of drugs through South Sinai into mainland Egypt has also regained its place in the Bedouin economy. In addition to hashish, the old staple, the Bedouin now deal in a wide range of addictive drugs, such as ecstasy, cocaine, and heroin (Smadar Lavie, personal communication). They have also added homegrown and imported marijuana and opium to their merchandise. A major change is that they now sell drugs to tourists. Some of the drug dealers, as well as ordinary Bedouin, have themselves become consumers.

As to the future, one may safely predict that the smuggling rings will sooner or later add to their inventory even more profitable heavily taxed or illicit commodities, such as diamonds and weapons. Ultimately, this may lead to a situation in which the smugglers operate quite openly, work hand in glove with some local and national authorities, employ the most technically advanced means of transportation and communication, and trade in a wide and variable range of contraband commodities, just as they do in the Sahara today (Claudot-Hawad 2006: 673–74; see Nordstrom [2007: 8] for a wider discussion).

The local haulage organizers will seek to benefit from this growing wealth. They will no longer be satisfied with conveying the drugs to mainland Egypt, but will sell increasing quantities of drugs to tourists and fellow Bedouin. These local agents may eventually become so wealthy and powerful that they dispense with the moral approval of their fellow citizens. At first they will carry them along on the expectation of higher rewards, and later they will coerce them, as well as the government's agents, into submission.

But not only government agencies may become involved in the trade. Militant political groups may set up their own smuggling organizations, or gain control over existing ones, in order to finance their activities, which may include acts of terror. Such was the case in the Sicily of the 1970s (J. C. Schneider and P. T. Schneider 2003: 68–69), and that seems to have happened recently in Sinai, where Bedouin have been involved in terrorist attacks on hotels in Taba (October 2004), Sharm al-Sheikh (July 2005), and Dahab (April 2006). In each case, the assailants included Bedouin from North Sinai, mainly from the Sawarka and Malalha tribes (Aljazeera TV 6 June 2006; Zambelis 2006; and see Tayib [1993] for details of the Bedouin groups), precisely those that had in the past engaged in drug smuggling and were displaced when the trade moved to South Sinai. The North Sinai Bedouin probably still resent both the Egyptian authorities who destroyed their source of livelihood, and the South Sinai Bedouin who took over from where they left off. Yet the terrorist attacks could not have succeeded without the approval and logistic support of some of those local Bedouin.

The discontent of two groups, the oppressed North Sinai Bedouin and their abettors among the South Sinai Bedouin, converges in these terrorist acts. The North Sinai Bedouin militants have been branded by the government and the media as "Muslim fundamentalists," a term that overlooks the fact that their aims are essentially political. They are out to attack the state that has in the past deprived them of their income from smuggling and today controls their every movement, including their efforts to renew smuggling activities—the North Sinai Bedouin began in recent years to supply arms to the Gaza Strip and to guide African refugees and Eastern European women to Israel. They hope these activities will gradually lead to a resumption of the even more lucrative drug smuggling.

The Bedouin of North Sinai felt that the state was taking away their livelihood, while not doing enough for their economic and social welfare. On a higher level of ideology this translated into a concern with social justice and equity. Members of similar militant Islamist organizations firmly believe that "it is the responsibility of the ruler ... to see to it that justice and equity are observed" (Ibrahim 1980: 433). Where these are perverted, they have a duty to reform the state, even at the cost of their lives. They are "fearless of death, and even eager for martyrdom," reports Ibrahim (1980: 436). The North Sinai militants were no different; most of them blew themselves up in the assaults. They attacked the state at the point where it hurt most, for each assault on foreign tourists interrupted the flow of tourists for many months, causing irreparable loss of revenue. They did not hate the tourists and did not enquire into their nationalities. The sheer fact that the tourists patronized international hotels was enough for them to be classified as foreigners, even when they were Egyptians and Muslims. The tourists were simply the incidental victims of attacks directed at the state (Aziz 1995: 94).

The story has an additional angle. By directing their attacks against the tourist industry in South Sinai, far from home, the North Sinai Bedouin militants hoped to turn the local Bedouin into prime suspects. The South Sinai Bedouin may not even be aware that the attackers were thus both settling old accounts with them for having usurped the drug trade half a century earlier, and also trying to wrest the trade from their hands. The protest of the South Sinai Bedouin, on the other hand, was directed at the state that handed over their water and land to the hotel chains, and against the hotels that monopolized tourism and employed Egyptians from the Nile Valley instead of Bedouin. But their protest was muted and restricted to a few hotheads, for they feared that the Egyptian authorities would respond by mounting a major campaign against the drug trade.

There is no easy way to end the traffic in drugs. As long as South Sinai remains the safest route into Egypt, it will retain its attraction to the international business world, and the traffic of contraband goods will continue. Even if the state were to legalize the production and consumption of hashish and provide the Bedouin with regular employment, this state of affairs would persist (see Bovenkerk 2004). Smuggling would continue unabated, punctuated by recurrent waves of terrorism. Drug trafficking would probably become decentralized and flexible, as is the case with the Dutch cocaine trade (Zaitch 2003: 13–14). The state could, of course, declare war on the drug traffic in Sinai, and cause it to be diverted to safer routes. Such a course of action would deeply affect the economy of the Sinai Bedouin, but would not stem the flow of hashish and other contraband into Egypt.

Chapter Six

Roving Traders Are the Bedouin's Lifeline

Introduction

Traders play a vital role among the Bedouin in South Sinai, for they supply them with most of their essential food and consumer goods. The most crucial imported commodity is grain, as the limited availability of soil and water has never permitted local grain production. Without a steady supply of the staple foodstuffs of wheat and corn, neither man nor flock could survive in this arid region. Most other foods and condiments, clothing, tools and technological appliances, and building materials are also imported. Documents from the Santa Katarina monastery, some of which go back to the eleventh century, and the reports of travelers throughout the ages indicate that the trade was usually in the hands of the Bedouin themselves. But from the early 1970s until the mid-1980s it was taken over by roving merchants from the town of al-'Arish in North Sinai. This chapter explores the relations of these strangers with their Bedouin customers and attempts to explain why the merchants from al-'Arish supplanted the Bedouin traders at that particular juncture. This will require another look at Simmel's concept of the stranger. I argue that in his *Soziologie* (originally published in 1908; I use the excerpts translated in Simmel 1950)

Simmel used the word in two distinct senses, only one of which has been adopted by anthropologists, but is not especially relevant to our case. This is "the stranger [as] the outsider who has come to stay" (Simmel 1950b: 403). The other sense is that in the modern cosmopolitan world every individual becomes a stranger (1950a: 409), an idea that reemerges in the work of Lofland (1973), Bauman (1995), Lipman (1997), and others. This idea neatly fits the case of the traders from al-'Arish and their Bedouin customers, as they are members of a complex modern civilization.

As the preceding sentence may surprise some readers, let me reiterate a proposition that has in recent years become widely accepted, namely, that Bedouin everywhere are citizens of the modern world, that they are integrated in urban civilization, and that they participate in the market economy in numerous ways (see chapter 1). That applies in even greater degree to the Bedouin of South Sinai, whose sheer survival depends on urban markets. The men are either migrant laborers working mostly outside the region, or they make a living close to home, as horticulturalists and herders, smugglers, drivers, storekeepers, traders, artisans such as builders, well diggers and basket weavers, healers, employees of the monastery and the administration, tourist guides, and so forth. The smuggling of narcotics, in particular, has often been an important branch of the economy, second only to migrant labor. During my fieldwork smuggling was at low ebb, but continued to play an important role in the thoughts and actions of the Bedouin, who knew that it would sooner or later reemerge as a major source of income. Only a handful of Bedouin engage in full-time nomadic animal husbandry, raising flocks of fifty or more goats. As they cannot easily leave the flock they do not attend urban markets regularly and instead sell goats and the occasional sheep or camel to the roving traders. Most Bedouin households raise small flocks of around six sheep and goats and a camel or two and maintain orchards in the mountains. Bedouin consider this to be a reserve economy, to take care of expected contingencies, such as the loss of employment chances for labor migrants. While they intend to expand the flocks and orchards when needed, they are sometimes forced to sell an animal or two.

All the Bedouin's economic transactions are made in cash. Those who are involved in the drug traffic, a large-scale international operation, are involved in complex financial transactions and stay abreast of the exact exchange rates of several currencies. Those who become migrant laborers know the rates of pay in various jobs and the current market prices of the commodities they consume. They receive their wages and other types of income in cash, and the people at home spend the money on imported goods. Most values are translated into terms of money. Even the bride-price is, in contrast to Bedouin practice elsewhere, quoted in cash and not in numbers of animals, although here too it is mostly paid off in several instalments.

South Sinai

The southern half of the Sinai Peninsula is a huge triangle whose tip points south, lapped by the deep waters of the Gulf of Suez and the Gulf of Aqaba. It covers an area of 17,000 square kilometers. At the time of my fieldwork, the only paved highway hugged the seashore. The mountainous interior, with pinnacles rising to a height of 2,600 meters, was reached by rough motor tracks, generally running on an east-west axis. Toward the end of the Israeli occupation another asphalted road was completed. It led from the main road running along the east coast up to Santa Katarina and down to Wadi Firan and the west coast, and considerably improved access to the mountain regions.

My fieldwork period in South Sinai largely coincided with the Israeli occupation, which lasted from 1967 to 1982. The Santa Katarina region had reverted to Egyptian rule already in 1979. The indigenous civilian population of South Sinai consisted of about 10,000 Bedouin. Many of the men were labor migrants, who spent months on end away from home. The Israelis set up army camps, and established a new town, Sharm al-Sheikh, and other villages for Jewish colonists, thus more than doubling the population. The Israelis developed the oil fields in the region and built roads, tourist villages, and military installations, which provided employment for hundreds of workers. The skilled jobs went to highly paid Israelis, while the badly paid Bedouin did the menial and semiskilled work. Although the Israeli authorities tried at first to regulate the wages of Bedouin workers, they gradually relented and allowed the market forces free rein. While the wages of the Bedouin were always lower than those of Israeli workers, they were higher than the wages paid by the former Egyptian administration and the monks of Santa Katarina. Work opportunities increased constantly and wages rose accordingly, so that in the end most men became migrant laborers. The trend was temporarily interrupted by the October 1973 war between Egypt and Israel, but it resumed and even accelerated from 1974 onward. It was to be disturbed once again in 1976, when US Secretary of State Henry Kissinger tried to bring about a peace agreement between Egypt and Israel and the Bedouin feared that the Egyptians would soon return and employment opportunities decline.

Due to the unsettled political and economic conditions and a harsh and fickle climate, most of the Bedouin alternate between two types of market economy, both of which comprise nomadic and sedentary activities. When employment is scarce, the men stay at home and become pastoralists and gardeners. At such times the search for water and pasture through the cycle of seasons and the necessity to irrigate the orchards and oases in which they grow fruit and vegetables compels the Bedouin households to move between the desert pastures and the mountain valleys. In the decades before the Israeli occupation, there were times when jobs in the cities were scarce, and many Bedouin remained in Sinai, either living in tents and moving around with their flocks or residing for months in the mountains cultivating their gardens, or alternating between the two economic modes. Flock owners with grown-up sons would adopt this nomadic way of life routinely. Those Bedouin who owned only small flocks resided during the long summer months in their orchards in the mountains and consumed some of their own produce. The annual movement cycle of both herders and cultivators generally culminated in one or more visits to the city markets in al-Tur, Suez, and even distant Cairo. There they sold their animals, fruits, and nuts, for which there was a ready demand, and bought their annual supply of grain, as well as all the other necessities of life. The visits to town did not exhaust the Bedouin's contacts with markets. Throughout their annual movement cycle, and even while camping out in the desert, they relied on the services of itinerant traders and artisans.

During the greater part of the twentieth century, however, labor migration was the Bedouin's chief source of income. Every able-bodied Bedouin male in South Sinai spent the best years of manhood as migrant laborer, starting as a young unmarried adult and continuing for many years after marriage, expecting eventually to send out his teenage sons to take their turn as labor migrants. At that stage, he returned home to become a full-time petty pastoralist and horticulturalist, and if his ambitions ran high he would join a smuggling gang. He could also engage in one of the many trades and occupations plied by the Bedouin.

During the Israeli occupation of Sinai the pattern of labor migration changed. Due to Israeli colonization and intensive exploitation of Sinai's oil fields, work opportunities in the region and its periphery multiplied. Now every man, whether young or old, had access to regular work in Eilat or the new town of Sharm al-Sheikh (Ofira), as well as the colonies set up by the Israelis on the Gulf of Aqaba and in the Santa Katarina area. The workers in the Israeli towns and colonies did not settle their families near their place of work, mainly because they knew from experience that they might lose their jobs almost overnight. Therefore, the older men and the women and children remained at home and maintained the alternative economy of orchards and flocks. The spatial segregation of the Bedouin and the lack of privacy at their work places, as well as the often arbitrary demands of Israeli military personnel and colonists, were other reasons why workers did not bring their families with them.

Those who stayed at home soon began to congregate in permanent hamlets. The foundations of the hamlets were laid by enterprising Bedouin, who established transport terminals and trading posts for the labor migrants and their families. The health clinics and employment services of the Israeli administration then gravitated to these locations, which gradually became service centers for Bedouin and Israelis. Around these centers more and more Bedouin households settled, to make use of the shops, schools, medical clinics, and transport services. In these settlements relatives were within easy reach and could be relied on to lend a helping hand. Soon people began to build solid houses around the service centers. At Milqa and Abu Silla near the Santa Katarina monastery houses were constructed of local stone, and at Dahab and Nuweb'a on the Gulf of Aqaba they were constructed of reeds, or of concrete, mud bricks, and slabs of coral. These settlements rapidly grew into regular villages. The Bedouin houses, in contrast to those built by the Jewish colonists, fitted so snugly into the landscape that one was tempted to believe they had been there since time immemorial, yet aerial photographs up to the early 1960s show no permanent houses in those locations.

The women ran the households, raised the families, and maintained relationships with neighbors and kin. They also made weekly trips into the mountains to cultivate and irrigate the orchards. They put limited efforts into the orchards, watering the trees and vegetable patches in order to just keep them alive. Herding practices also changed. The Bedouin tended to raise fewer animals and to replace camels with sheep and goats, and instead of moving between pastures they now sent young women and girls to graze the small flocks of six to eight animals on the periphery of the village. The animals rapidly devoured all the available vegetation, and when they returned to the village in the evening they had to be given supplementary feed. It was also up to the women to maintain the vital networks of relations with kin, friends, and neighbors, and in the settlements they could meet and entertain them at leisure.

The rising standard of living was expressed in new consumption patterns. In each village there were several stores that stocked not only the traditional staples, such as wheat and corn, sugar, oil, and tea, but also tinned foods, biscuits, sweets, dresses, shoes, knives, electric torches, plastic piping, baby foods, and medicines. The labor migrants brought home a taste for fresh vegetables and spices that they had acquired in town. The new needs made the Bedouin even more dependent on the external world than before. Hardly any of these varied goods, with the exception of fresh fruit, vegetables, tobacco, and wickerwork baskets, were produced locally. The traders thus did more than simply provide an essential link between the village and the urban supply centers. They were the Bedouin's lifeline; without their services the Bedouin would not survive for long.

Transportation became almost neatly segmented. One segment was a fleet of over a hundred American and Russian light army vehicles and assorted pickups, mostly in run-down condition and owned by individual Bedouin, which transported passengers to areas of employment in Israeli settlements in Sinai, the town of Sharm al-Sheikh (Ofira), and smaller colonies at Dahab (Di Zahav), Nuweb'a (Neviot), and al-Tur, as well as Eilat and other towns in southern Israel. The other segment, a dozen or so well-maintained heavy trucks owned by entrepreneurs from the town of al-'Arish in North Sinai, carried the bulky commercial goods. These mobile traders traveled all over the mountain ranges and supplied both the Bedouin stores and the camps encountered along the route. This division of tasks was caused by the market conditions. The Bedouin labor migrants found employment in centers of economic growth, where wages were decent but the price of goods was high. Therefore, they brought home only small gifts for family, relatives, and friends, and did not buy great quantities of food and everyday clothing. The roving traders from al-'Arish, on the other hand, obtained their merchandise in the economically depressed, Israeli-occupied Gaza Strip, and were therefore able to sell it relatively cheaply, in spite of the high cost of transportation. They also had access to garages and spare parts, which did not exist in South Sinai.

The Traders

As the old market town of al-Tur was deserted in the wake of the Israeli occupation, and Suez and Cairo were no longer accessible, most goods were now supplied by roving traders from the town of al-'Arish in North Sinai, whose trucks called on the new villages and the scattered nomadic camps. These traders supplied both the village stores and the mobile camps with grains and other staples, as well as with a rapidly growing range of groceries, clothing, household goods, and agricultural implements. They also took orders for special deliveries, such as spare parts for water pumps or cars, or plastic pipes, which revolutionized gardening practice (Katz 1983: 39ff.), and they even brought in circumcisers for the boys. These traders provided the Bedouin with basic foods and essential goods and services, which enabled the women, children, and flocks to survive while their men worked outside the region. But the Israeli authorities, unlike the preceding colonial and Egyptian governments, which had adopted a laissez-faire attitude, never saw eye to eye with the traders. As they did not realize how crucial they were for the Bedouin's existence, they frequently sought to curb their activities or to dispense with their services altogether. As far as they were concerned, the traders were strangers who could not be trusted: they overcharged the Bedouin, their activities and movements were not easily regulated, and, furthermore, they opened a window to the wider Arab world, and that could become dangerous.

In my field trips to South Sinai I observed how the changing political and economic conditions affected the Bedouin's economic pursuits, gender relations, and patterns of consumption. At first, I did not pay much attention to the 'Arishi traders, who appeared at roughly monthly intervals in the Santa Katarina area. They usually arrived in the afternoon, transacted business with the storekeepers and with other persons, and left early the following morning. They were not very friendly and talkative, and they kept their own counsel. They did not stay overnight with shopkeepers, but slept on or under their trucks. Only when I realized how precarious the local economy was, and how much people relied on goods brought in from outside the region, did I begin to appreciate the central role of the traders.

Wheat and corn, the staple foods of humans and animals, are not grown in Sinai. From the documents preserved in the Santa Katarina monastery we learn that grain has always been imported (Humbsch 1976: documents 29, 41, 46, 66, 69). The documents, dated between 1567 and 1790, show that the monks regularly imported large quantities of wheat from the Egyptian Delta to Sinai. Shuqair (1916: 127) reports that in the beginning of the twentieth century the South Sinai Bedouin (the Tawara tribe that all belong to and allows them to range over the entire pasture area) bought from traders in Suez some 4,500 ardeb (an ardeb contains 198 liters) of grain annually, which accounted for two-thirds of their food consumption.

Labor migration led to a strict sexual division of labor: most adult men left to work away from home, while the women remained behind and maintained the household and the gardens and small flocks that served as an economic security net. There was no need for them to move around with flocks or to spend long periods in their orchards up in the mountains. All they had to do was to keep these economic ventures going. The men were earning good wages, which they remitted to their wives' care. The women controlled the spending of these relatively large amounts of money. They used the money mainly for daily consumption, but also managed to put aside savings. Women never went to the stores in person. Instead, they sent children with instructions for what to buy. For while women acquired much power, they knew it was temporary. Even during the height of the migrant labor market, most men interrupted work every six to eight weeks to return home for short visits, during which they maintained and strengthened their social networks. Sooner or later the men would return home for good and take over the management of the household.

The advent of the 'Arishi traders was a relatively recent development. In preindependence Egypt, in the early twentieth century, Bedouin obtained most of their grain from one or two wholesalers in Suez (Shuqair 1916: 127), although some Muzaina tribesmen brought their grain from the Negev, where they hired themselves out as reapers. Those Bedouin who owned orchards in the mountains sold apples, pears, quinces, and almonds in al-Tur or Suez, and bought grain with the proceeds. Some informants claimed that with the money they could acquire enough grain to last them for a year. Under Egyptian rule, before 1967, Bedouin had operated some twenty-six trucks. Qararsha tribesmen of Wadi Firan owned twenty-one of these; it appears that they had specialized in the business of importing food and exporting drugs. The Sawalha owned three trucks and the Jabaliya two. These had hauled minerals from the Umm Bogma and Abu Zneima mines, which employed over two thousand workers from mainland Egypt, and also a handful of Bedouin, and they also carried food and supplies for the Bedouin and the mineworkers. The supply base of all the truckers had been Suez, and most of the business had been conducted with one store owner, Mahmud al-Masri. "We used to sit and drink a cup of coffee, while he took care of our list of requirements," recounted one Qararsha chief. Al-Masri extended credit to his customers, and also obtained for them the shop licenses required to get through "customs" (*jumruk*). In order to combat smuggling, the Egyptian police had set up a checkpoint on the road from Abu Zneima to Suez, where all cars were searched for contraband and travelers questioned about their destination. This procedure was popularly called "customs." The Bedouin truck owners and the merchant from Suez jointly almost monopolized the wholesale trade. The truck owners not only acted as wholesalers for practically the whole of South Sinai, but also acted as agents for the government's food aid to the Bedouin (sadaqa), periodical rations of wheat flour, sugar, and oil. They set up a commercial center in Faranja, an exposed hilltop on the main east-west thoroughfare near Nabi Saleh, the central pilgrimage site of several tribes. This supply center served the Bedouin living in the mountains and the eastern reaches of South Sinai. The truck owners owned or controlled the sixteen stores. They sold their wares on the spot to individual customers and distributed them by truck all over the region. Jum'a Ghanem, a public-spirited truck owner who was also one of the biggest smugglers in Sinai, dug a well on the site, which permitted the storekeepers to live comfortably in the place. Soon tracks and footpaths branched out in every direction.

This arrangement broke down immediately after the Israeli occupation. By the time I worked in Sinai, there were no stores left in Faranja. The occupation cut off Sinai from its regular sources of supply in Egypt, and all commodities had to be brought from Israel and the Israeli-occupied Gaza Strip. Mining operations and industrial production in the occupied areas ceased entirely, so that truckers had to look for alternative employment. While the Bedouin population still depended on imported grains and other foods and goods, the Bedouin truckers could no longer supply them at competitive prices. The merchants from al-'Arish were in a much better position: they could obtain goods at the lowest prices in the Gaza area, close to home, where the rate of taxation and the cost of labor were lower than in Israel. The merchandise had to be cheap because transportation costs were high; goods had to travel over a long distance and rough terrain. The traders from al-'Arish drove powerful new trucks, but the rocky mountain tracks took a heavy toll on them. However, they had at their disposal an infrastructure of garages, spare parts, and trained mechanics, all of which were lacking in Sinai.

The military administration was concerned about the displacement of the Bedouin truckers. It worked out a plan that would, so it hoped, gradually phase out the 'Arishi traders: they would be allowed to proceed as far as Gharandal, a crossroads located some thirty kilometers north of Abu Zneima. This small way station on the road from Suez to Mount Sinai never attained the status of an oasis. It was visited by Niebuhr ([1774–78] 1968: 227) in 1762 and Burckhardt ([1822] 1992: 473) in 1816. Both travelers describe its clusters of palm trees and copious supply of water. It now became the boundary between the military districts of North Sinai and South Sinai. The 'Arishis and other traders would be permitted to bring their goods as far as Gharandal; from there the Bedouin truck owners would take over and distribute the goods among the tribes. The Bedouin truck owners were to be subsidized, so that they would be able to compete with the 'Arishi traders. The administration also sought, unsuccessfully, to reopen a garage in Abu Zneima.

One major element in this arrangement worked for approximately five years: from 1968 until 1973 Gharandal became the exclusive supply center for South Sinai. Despite the authorities' good intentions, the Bedouin truck owners never stood a chance. Having no sources of supply, lacking garages and spare parts, and saddled with an incompetent administration located in distant Tel Aviv that attended to their affairs only sporadically, they were no match for the 'Arishi traders.

When I visited Gharandal in August 1972, there were five stores and a coffeehouse, all of which were branches of 'Arishi firms. Each store consisted of a booth, which remained open day and night, and a locked storeroom just behind it. The stores were owned by two or three partners, each of whom stayed about fourteen days and nights in Gharandal and was then relieved by a partner. The traders worked, ate, and slept in their booths. The biggest trader was Matar, who claimed that his partnership owned eleven trucks, all working in Sinai. Another trader, Suliman Musallam, had formerly owned a store in Qusaima, now a deserted town on the route to Gharandal. They all belonged to the large Fawakhriya clan of al-'Arish.

The traders sold wheat, corn, rice, lentils, and sugar by the bag, paraffin by the barrel, and cooking oil in tin cans. They also stocked potatoes, tea, coffee, cigarettes and rice paper for home-made cigarettes, bottled soft drinks, and chewing gum. Although

the transportation costs were quite high, prices seemed to be similar to those charged elsewhere in Israel, and lower than the prices
in the village stores elsewhere in Sinai. The traders made a profit
by buying goods in the cheap markets of the Gaza Strip, as well
as by supplying inferior quality goods. For instance, they sub-
stituted rigid plastic pipes used for electric wiring for the more
expensive elastic irrigation pipes demanded by the Bedouin. They
adulterated foods by adding water to sugar, sold rancid oil (letter
from Shefer to Fish, 25 September 1975, in my possession), and
mixed corn and wheat flour. The traders also bought animals for
slaughter. I was told that an average of twenty camels changed
hands monthly in Gharandal.

At that time most of the trade in South Sinai passed through
the hands of the traders of Gharandal, so that the figures obtained
from them allow us to make a rough estimate of the Bedouin's
'national accounts', i.e. of the total imports, which equal the total
consumption of the Bedouin population less small quantities of
home-produced fruit and vegetables. Every month some thirty
trucks left al-'Arish for Gharandal, carrying a payload of approximately 6,000 Israeli pounds. Assuming that most of the supplies passed through Gharandal, the annual imports amounted
to 2,160,000 Israeli pounds, or 216 Israeli pounds per capita. In
addition, the traders distributed on behalf of the Israeli authorities, who carried over a practice from the Egyptian administration
of supplying the Bedouin with monthly food rations (sadaqa) of
flour, oil, and sugar. The total annual value of this assistance was
372,000 Israeli pounds, or 37.2 Israeli pounds per capita. Each
Bedouin then spent 253.2 Israeli pounds on food annually, which
indicates that in 1972 the standard of living was very low (for
most of the period from the 1970s to the 2010s the USD aver-
aged 3.51 Israeli pounds or shekels). The number of jobs in Sinai
was still limited, and smuggling had ceased altogether in 1970,
as the smugglers were finding it too dangerous to cross the lines
between two powerful armies facing each other. The Bedouin
were tending their orchards in the mountains in order to increase
their food supply. However, they could no longer sell their fruit
in town: al-Tur was deserted and Suez had become inaccessible.
They also tried to develop their herds of camels and their flocks,
as animals could be sold to the traders in Gharandal. One chief

described the situation in these terms: "Today there is no income from smuggling or from trade [which is controlled by the traders from al-'Arish]; there is only employment for menial workers. The days of Gamal ['Abd al-Nasser] were much better."

The Bedouin truck owners of Wadi Firan were in no position to compete with the al-'Arish traders. The mines that had provided a large part of their business had closed down. In addition, they were cut off from both sources of supply and maintenance facilities. There was not one car repair shop or trained mechanic in South Sinai. The trucks were turning into scrap metal before their very eyes. The trade had moved to the eastern reaches of Sinai, where the owners of pickups served not only the migrant workers, but also the international tourists who flocked to the beaches and coral reefs of the Gulf of Aqaba in large numbers. These car owners had access to garages in Eilat and elsewhere.

All that changed abruptly in October 1973, when Egyptian and Syrian armies carried out a coordinated attack on Israel. The Israeli positions on the Suez Canal succumbed to the first onslaught, and the Israeli army was hard pressed to repel the attack. Israeli government and civilian activities in Sinai stopped completely, and were not resumed for about six months. There was not even enough transport to take the Bedouin migrant workers back to their homes. Most of them walked two to three days over the mountains to return to their families. As all sources of employment had dried up, the Bedouin made great efforts to develop their gardens and build up their flocks, but in the meantime, they dug into their hoards of food. Every Bedouin household maintains a storehouse (qerie), usually a cave secured by a door and a heavy padlock or a small building, for just such an expected eventuality. They lay in a food stock that should suffice for about three months. The first supplies of grain and other foods were brought in by the al-'Arish traders two months later, when food stocks were running low. If they had not arrived in time, the Bedouin population would have starved. The traders retained their near-monopoly on supplying South Sinai after the Israelis returned to the region, and in return for providing an essential service they made a good profit.

That is not how the officials of the Israeli Sinai Development Authority in Tel Aviv viewed the situation. Just a month before the war broke out, in September 1973, the councilor for trade demanded in a memoir that "[t]he traders from al-'Arish ... be restricted. In this critical civilian matter the Police must be involved" (letter from Fish to Aloni, 6 September 1973, in my possession). The same official pursued this idea after the war, and again claimed that the traders overcharged the Bedouin and demanded, this time explicitly, that they be banned. These recommendations were not implemented, as Egypt and Israel began negotiations for the restoration of Sinai to Egypt.

The traders from al-'Arish carved out a new, but probably temporary, economic niche, which helped them to survive the loss of work caused by the Israeli occupation. They managed to achieve this because they provided a vital service to the Bedouin of South Sinai at a time when the latter could no longer supply their own food and other necessities.

A Historical Dimension

The literature on Middle Eastern pastoralists is very extensive, but only a handful of authors pay much attention to the traders (Ferdinand 1962; Lancaster and Lancaster 1987; Musil 1928; Stein 1967). Khazanov (1984: 212) discusses the role of traders among nomads through the ages in some detail, and reaches the seemingly paradoxical conclusion that "as a whole trade with the sedentary agricultural and urban world was not something from which the nomads profited, but it was vitally necessary from the economic point of view." He may imply that the nomads viewed the merchants as unscrupulous exploiters, but could not survive without them. The salient point to emerge from the literature and from experience in the field is that most traders are based in cities, and that only they have the funds to finance the buying up of large numbers of animals. They maintain long-term links with their potential consumers. A famous example is the house of Ibn Bassam, which had by the beginning of the twentieth century established branches in Basra, Bombay, Cairo, Damascus, and Taif (Musil 1928: 278–79). Its agents, the so-called 'Aqelis, went out to the nomads' camps, bought the animals with money advanced by Ibn Bassam, and were responsible for driving the animals to the market at the right times (see also Stein 1967: 84–89). These dealers released the Bedouin from making frequent visits to the market and permitted them to devote themselves to the demanding routine of nomadic animal husbandry. Other traders, also based in cities, supplied the Bedouin with the necessities of daily life. They would move from one camp to the next, selling goods mostly on credit. As they were providing a vital service to the Bedouin, their safe passage and the payment of debts was assured (Musil 1928: 269).

This trade could become the mainstay of the ephemeral states set up by Bedouin chiefs in the Arabian Peninsula. It could, as Rosenfeld (1965: 80–85) has shown, even become the reason for Bedouin chiefs to impose their rule on desert cities, such as Ha'il. The ruler made it his aim to provide safe passage for traders. Safe trading provided him with a steady source of income, and the Bedouin with a secure market town.

Trade among the Bedouin of South Sinai followed a dynamic pattern: prior to the Israeli occupation of Sinai in 1967 the traders came from their midst. There was no need for big animal buyers, as the Sinai Bedouin raised sheep and goats only in a small way. The Bedouin truckers could fulfill both the functions of animal dealers and of itinerant traders. Their limited capital sufficed for local needs. The new conditions created by the Israeli occupation cut off the Bedouin truckers from their sources of supply and from their regular animal markets, and ruined their livelihood. This vacuum was filled, very efficiently, by the traders from al-'Arish who, in turn, were after 1982 once more replaced by roving Bedouin traders.

There was yet another reason for the displacement of the Bedouin traders. Members of tribes could engage in mobile trade during periods of intensive smuggling, for smuggling caravans crossed all tribal boundaries and the big smugglers saw to it that the roads remained open and that peace reigned between the tribes. When smuggling was no longer possible on a large scale, labor migration became the only important source of income. Most of the men stayed for months on end at their workplaces outside the tribe, and worried about maintaining links with home. Therefore, most men made a point of returning periodically to their homes. They also became concerned for the tribe, and returned home especially for the annual tribal pilgrimage, a main purpose of which was to reaffirm the tribe as a living reality. In this manner they wished to remind themselves and others of their exclusive rights to tribal resources, such as the trade routes crossing tribal territory and sites suitable for the development of orchards. All these people carried goods destined for people at home and in consequence the Bedouin traders' business declined in volume. They could no longer maintain heavy trucks with their high overhead costs. Therefore, each Bedouin trader now sought to monopolize business in his own tribe. This was the time for the traders from al-'Arish to appear on the scene. As strangers who supplied a basic service, they could freely cross tribal boundaries and move among the tribes. Soon they became wholesalers for the entire Bedouin population.

Traders as Strangers

While the traders from al-'Arish are strangers, they are unlike the "stranger" described in much of the anthropological literature. The anthropological concept is derived from Simmel (1950b: 402), who taught us to perceive the stranger not "as the wanderer who comes today and goes tomorrow, but rather as the person who comes today and stays tomorrow." He is both integrated in his adopted community and knows a great deal about it, and is more at liberty to act and move around than his fellow men. As Bodemann (1998: 126) has pointed out, he is an integral functioning element of the community, and only conceived by other members as external to it. Because of his ambiguous position in society, conventions and social pressures are less binding on him than on ordinary members of the community. Simmel's insight has influenced several generations of social scientists. In anthropology, the stranger first appeared as the Nuer "leopard skin chief" (Evans-Pritchard 1940), the archetypal mediator and peacemaker. Almost forty years later, Shack and Skinner (1979), while still relying on Simmel's seminal essay, sought to apply the concept to groups of strangers in the new African nations, such as white colonialists, Lebanese traders, and groups of labor migrants from neighboring countries. In the following generation, Berland and Rao (2004) offer another crop of essays based on Simmel's fertile idea. Clearly, Simmel suggested a most interesting way to look at the stranger.

The popularity of this idea has obscured Simmel's other contribution to the understanding of the stranger, namely, that modern man, overburdened as he is with sensual stimulations, reduces them to the minimum by eliminating all individuality, all relationships that "cannot be exhausted with logical operations" (Simmel 1950a: 411). Therefore, "metropolitan man reckons with his merchants and customers … and often even with persons with whom he is obliged to have social intercourse" (1950a: 411). In this formulation, everyone who is beyond the small circle of a person's intimate relationships becomes a stranger. For in the city, he argues, people depend on one another to the extent that "without the strictest punctuality in promises and services the whole structure would break down into an inextricable chaos" (1950a: 412). Their relations must therefore be, or be made to be, impersonal.

The Bedouin in South Sinai are wholly integrated in a cosmopolitan world, on which they rely for most of their income as well as their supply of food and other goods. Their dependence on a regular food supply is so great that the relations with the traders of al-'Arish must be rational and regulated, based on the commercial interest of both sides, and not on friendship or other diffuse ties.

In the same vein, Bauman argues that "the movements of the [strangers] being not fully predictable … navigating contains always an element of risk and adventure and is always plagued by the paucity of reliable signposts and in need of more routine" (1995: 126). One way of coping with this contingency is to ignore it: by blending "the movement of strangers into the background one need neither notice nor care about [them]" (1995: 128). This common but self-defeating tactic appears to be the one adopted by the Bedouin. Now we can better understand why traders were not invited into Bedouin homes, and why some Bedouin even spoke of getting rid of the rapacious traders, words that could never be translated into action.

Chapter Seven

Personal and Tribal Pilgrimages

Imagining an Orderly Social World

-‹›⇌◯◯⇌‹›-

Introduction

There are about one hundred and thirty saints' tombs in South Sinai, twenty of which serve as pilgrimage centers of tribes and subtribes (see map 3). Most of the tombs are strung out along the main east-west passage of the region. They are usually located at major crossroads and not far from water sources. Some are found close to centers of population, while others are far from habitation. Bedouin men and women visit tombs in various parts of South Sinai every few months, in order to keep in touch with God or to beg the saints to intercede with God on their behalf. Some of these tombs are also centers of annual tribal pilgrimages, which take place toward the end of summer. As the personal pilgrimages provide the belief and institutional infrastructure of the tribal gatherings, I shall first examine them, and then go on to deal with tribal pilgrimages. I intend to look closely at the annual pilgrimages of three tribes. First, I examine the Muzaina, who used to meet for three consecutive days and make the round of three holy tombs—from the tomb of their founding ancestor Faraj they moved to that of the prophet (nabi) Saleh, and thence to the tomb

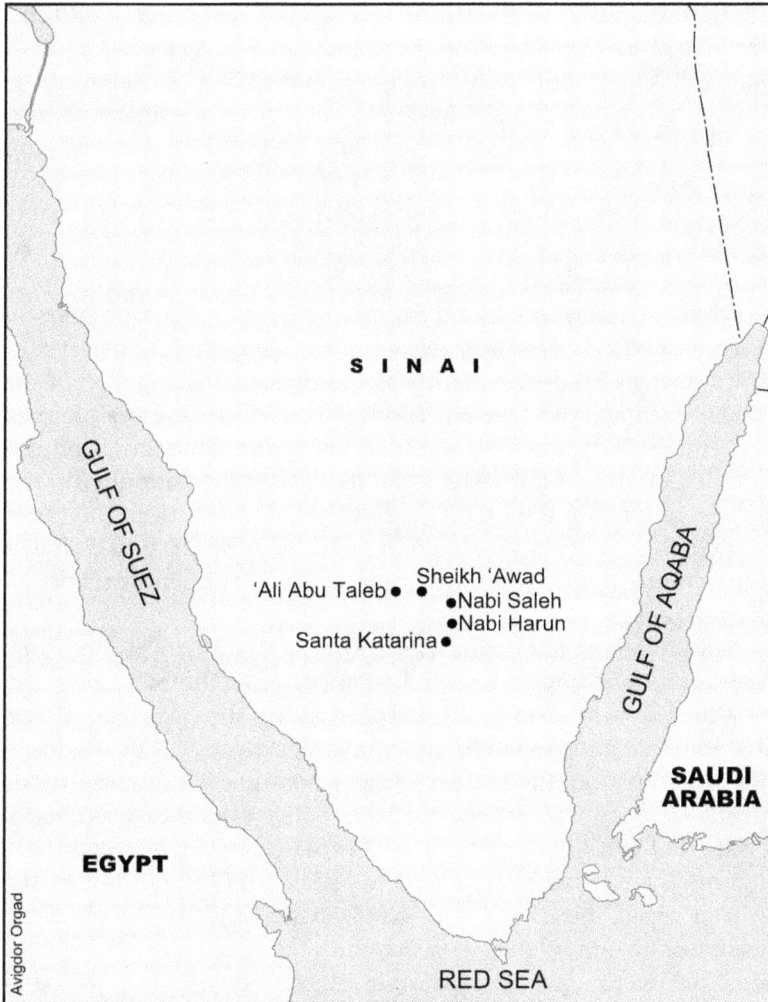

MAP 3. Pilgrimage sites

of Nabi Harun (identified as Aaron, the brother of Moses). Nowadays they visit only Nabi Saleh. Second, I study the Awlad Sa'id, who gather once a year at a tomb named after 'Ali Abu Taleb, the fourth Khalif. And third, I investigate the Jabaliya, sections of whom gather on separate occasions at the tomb of Sheikh 'Awad, a holy man whose antecedents are unclear, but according to the Bedouin "may have been a member of the tribe."

The mountainous interior of South Sinai is endowed with impressive landscapes and historical sites, but cannot offer its Bedouin inhabitants much gainful employment and social security. There is too little soil and water for extensive pastoralism and horticulture. In order to sustain their families, most men are obliged to spend a great part of their working lives outside the region. They find mostly unrewarding and insecure jobs, and are liable to be dismissed at a day's notice. At home too they are exposed to endless natural, economic, and political tribulations. They protect themselves against these expected blows by a comprehensive system of social assurance (as set out in chapter 4). The apex of this system is an open channel of communication, by way of the saints, with a provident but distant God. This God maintains a just and orderly world, and if anything has gone amiss he can put it right. By regular visits to saints' tombs, the Bedouin foster a good relationship with God, just as they do with other members of their social networks. When in need they can pray to God at a saint's tomb, hoping for the saint to support and lend urgency to their requests.

Nabi Saleh is the acknowledged major saint in South Sinai. Although he is often identified as ancestor of the Sawalha tribe, he has also been claimed as patron saint by the Muzaina, Qararsha, Jabaliya and Awlad Sa'id, and, generally, by all the Bedouin of the peninsula, the Tawara. Until recently, each of these tribes arranged its own pilgrimage to Nabi Saleh, taking care to choose a date that would not overlap with other pilgrimages. Other sites that attracted tribal pilgrimages were Sheikh Qra'i visited by the 'Aleqat tribe, Sheikh Suliman Nfe'i, visited by the Qararsha, al-Hashash, visited by the small Hamada tribe, and the female saint Sheikha Swerha, patron of another pilgrimage center of the Sawalha. Bedouin classify all these major shrines as *maqam* (literally, a site or place), a term widely used in the Islamic world to denote an important holy place mostly, but not always, associated with a saint's tomb. The most famous *maqam* is, of course, *maqam Ibrahim* in the Mecca mosque, which is not a tomb but "a place of prayer" (Kister 1991: 104–5). Interestingly, it is not invoked by Muslim scholars in discussions of the worship of saints. To the Sinai Bedouin too a *maqam* is "a place of prayer," and they insist that the shrine's patron saint is definitely not buried in it. It is contrasted with the *turba,* a lesser shrine supposed to enclose the remains of a holy man. Cemeteries surround the shrines, for it is assumed that the deceased are thus nearer to their God. Some of the tombs at two major shrines, Nabi Saleh and Nabi Harun, and elsewhere, have themselves become shrines of a kind. The ancestors of some Muzaina descent groups buried at Nabi Saleh, and of Jabaliya groups at Nabi Harun, are visited by their descendants on *'id al-adha,* the Feast of Sacrifices, one of the two major holy days of Islam. All the major shrines are square stone buildings surmounted by a cupola crowned with a crescent, the emblem of Islam. Near each shrine, an assembly hut has been erected, which throughout the year serves as a rest house for weary travelers. It is always equipped with cooking utensils, and each traveler leaves a small supply of tea and sugar for the next guest.

Tribesmen attend these gatherings for a number of reasons. They intend to meet friends, relatives, and business associates from their own and other tribes, to fulfill a religious duty, and to reaffirm their membership in the tribe and their right to use its territorial resources. For the greater part of the year they are dispersed in small groups, and many men work for long periods outside their tribal area and even outside South Sinai. The tribal reunions are the culmination of their ceaseless efforts to maintain ties with other Bedouin. The variations in the reunions of the three tribes I examine here are connected to their different habitats and economies. Attendance at the tribal gatherings also fluctuates from year to year. But why should tribes celebrate an annual reunion, why should such tribal gatherings take place at saints' tombs, why do the reunions of each tribe follow a different pattern, and why does the attendance vary? Some of these questions were raised over a century ago in W. Robertson Smith's *Lectures on the Religion of the Semites* (1894) and in Goldziher's essays on the cult of saints (1967, 1971). Most of their arguments have withstood the rigors of time remarkably well, but certain points require revision.

The Cult of Saints

The cult of saints is common to Islam, Judaism, and many Christian confessions. In a study of saints' cults in Spain, William A.

Christian argues that saints respond to the unrequited needs of people. One of his informants put this very eloquently, when explaining why people visit a famous image of the Virgin Mary: "God is simply not involved in our everyday activities, either because he chooses not to be involved, or because he does not have the power to act … [but the Virgin] actively helps us, whether this be by intervention with God, or whatever. She is closer to us, does things for us in this world" (Christian 1972: 147–48). This man's God is so distant that he even doubts his power to intervene in the concerns of individuals. But most adherents of the world religions believe in a middle range God, who is close enough to care for humanity, but not sufficiently close to concern himself with the humdrum affairs of men. He is too distant to be approached by living human beings, distinguished and saintly as they may be, but not too distant to become inaccessible. Therefore men take recourse to the mediation of saints, whose proximity to God is assured, and who continue to maintain an interest in the people whose life they shared in the past.

Saints' cults are prevalent in many parts of Islam (Levy 1962: 258). Although the cult of saints is widespread, there are some Bedouin who do not practice it. As Musil states:

> The Bedouins know of no communion with the saints. In the whole inner desert there is not a single holy grave or shrine erected in honor of a saint. In fact they have no saints whatsoever. When they make their short sojourns in the settled territory, where by every village the dome of a shrine rises above the real or imaginary grave of some man or woman whom public opinion considers to be a saint, they never pay attention to these domes. (Musil 1928: 417–18)

The Bedouin he refers to are the great camel-raising Rwala of Syria. But among the Bedouin of South Sinai and, incidentally, those of Cyrenaica (Evans-Pritchard 1949: 66–67; Peters 1976), Morocco (Berque 1955: 268ff.; Eickelman 1976; Gellner 1969), and the Negev (Bar-Zvi, Abu-Rabi'a, and Kressel 1998), the visiting of shrines and pilgrimages are an important feature of social life. By gaining some insight into the cult of saints in Sinai we may improve our understanding of such cults elsewhere and, perhaps, explain their absence among the Rwala and some other nomadic pastoralists.

Islamic leaders and scholars of Islam disagree about whether the cult of saints is a legitimate part of Islam or just an aberration or accretion (see Meri [1999: 273–86] for a balanced discussion). Some scholars approve wholeheartedly of the practice. For instance, Linant de Bellefonds (1978: 355) claims that "the permissibility of visiting tombs was admitted very early on by *ijma'* [consensual canonical law]: all the [law] schools ... even went so far as to recommend the practice." Other scholars reject the practice as opposed to the pure monotheism of Islam. Goldziher may serve as an instructive example. He utterly disapproves of "the veneration of the dead," and views it as a pagan survival. He claims that "in ancient Islam an insurmountable barrier divides an infinite and unapproachable Godhead from weak and finite humanity" (Goldziher 1971: 255). But then he admits that "shortly after the spread of the new religion" saints were already venerated (1971: 259) and, more importantly, he clearly perceives their mediatory role: "The believers sought to create, through the concept of saints, mediators between themselves and an omnipotent Godhead in order to satisfy the need which was served by the gods and masters of their old tradition" (1971: 259). Many writers have followed Goldziher's lead and rejected the cult, sometimes without understanding that it fulfils a vital function. Thus Grunebaum (1951: 67) views the cult of saints as simply "a striking deviation from the genuine prophetic tradition," and Lazarus-Jaffé (1976: 223) describes even the pilgrimage to Mecca as a "pagan heritage." Geertz (1968: 48) too interprets the worship of saints as an "expression of that necessity ... for a world religion to come to terms with ... a multiplicity of local forms of faith and yet maintain the essence of its own identity." Other authors treat the cults as a more or less legitimate alternative or complement to official Islam. Thus Waardenburg argues that the worship of saints is part of popular Islam, which has local currency, as distinct from "normative," universally recognized Islam (1979: 363). When Gellner claims that the cult of saints is practiced in regions where "two ... forces were present only in a minimal form, or not at all: (a) official, genuinely literate Islam, and (b) central government" (1973: 59), he views the cult as a nonauthentic but acceptable form of Islam. At the same time, he makes the important point that it appears where central government is absent.

All these critical evaluations start out from the position that
genuine Islam is a strictly monotheistic religion. Accordingly,
they treat the cult of saints as either a pagan survival, an aberration from orthodox religion, or as a local custom, a small tradition.
They seem to forget that the cult of saints is found throughout
Islam, and takes the same form everywhere. It emerges not only
in places that are off the beaten track, but is also practiced in cities, villages, and even associated with mosques (Canaan 1927: 2;
Eickelman 1976: 112). Therefore, one must view orthodox Islam
and the cult of saints as the two sides of a coin: the cult of a distant omnipotent God and the cult of saints simply complement
each other. A distant God can be approached only through holy
mediators. Individuals in need, who are unable to obtain the aid
of their fellow men, whose wishes cannot be satisfied by human
agents, or whose problems are beyond remedy, commune with
God through the saint. This is the practice among Muslims everywhere, although it is sometimes and in some regions suppressed
by zealous civil or religious authorities who may view it as an
infringement of their monopoly on temporal or spiritual power.

It is easy to be taken in by the opinions of orthodox Islamic
scholars and the equally strictly monotheistic Western interpret-
ers of Islam who treat the cult of saints as a deviation from the
true "religion." For them religion is coterminous with *din,* which
can be translated as a combination of "(a) the contents of the faith
(iman), (b) the practice of *islam,* (c) *ihsan* or interiorization of the
faith" (Gardet 1965: 294). It requires the believers to submit meekly
and unquestioningly to the laws and regulations handed down
by religious leaders, and it measures the submission (the original
meaning of the concept *islam*) of these people not so much by their
moral standards, but by the strict observation of the various rules.
The Prophet of Islam himself adopted this authoritative viewpoint on numerous occasions. Here is one such passage: "The
Bedouins say, 'we believe.' Say: 'You do not believe'; rather say,
'We surrender'; for belief has not yet entered your hearts" (Quran,
sura 49, verse 14). Most anthropological definitions of religion
take the same position: that religion is a system of symbols and
regulations, which should guide the behavior of man (see Geertz
1966). That these standards of behavior are often formulated by
political leaders, who then supervise their implementation and

punish transgressors, is usually glossed over. This "religion" is a system of control, the responses to which may range from internalization to contestation (see Bax 1995: xvi). As we find that pilgrimage is partly a response to the distance and ineffectiveness of the state, such authority-conscious definitions of religion cannot help in its analysis.

We need a different definition of religion, one that can help us understand the realities of pilgrimage to saints' tombs. The following facets may be relevant: The individual Muslim believes in the efficacy of saintly mediation. This faith also underlies the communal pilgrimage. People perform the pilgrimage to a saint's tomb or a tribal sanctuary both as individuals and as members of a larger entity, whenever they face a series of problems that the authorities of this world either caused or cannot remedy, such as the men's extended absences from their homes and the failure of the authorities to provide even a modicum of social security. The tribal gatherings are designed to revitalize the tribe and to reinforce other relationships supporting the Bedouin's basic security. Pilgrimages thus play an important role in the Bedouin's strategy of dealing with the expected and inevitable misfortunes of human existence, such as loss of livelihood, accidents, sickness and death. We may therefore formulate the following working definition: *religion is the ensemble of beliefs and practices through which people cope with the expected adversities of life.* The analysis of pilgrimage in South Sinai will proceed with this definition in mind.

A Bedouin Conceives the Tribe in Three Different Ways

When the Bedouin of South Sinai talk about the tribe, they may refer to three separate, partly overlapping conceptions. First, they consider the tribe a territorial organization, whose members control certain resources in that territory, and obtain rights to exploit resources in a larger area of subsistence. Membership of the tribe confers the following rights: "building a house" or orchard anywhere in the tribal territory, which in practice means in oases or valleys where water can be tapped; preferential access to pastures and employment in the territory; and participation in caravans passing through it. This last is a recent transformation of the

former monopoly on conducting travelers through the territory
(Niebuhr 1799: 1: 141,153). The tribe claims not so much to control
a clearly bounded territory, but defined points in it and paths
leading through it. When asked to describe their tribal territory,
Bedouin come up with a list of salient points, such as oases, wells,
and pastures, but there is much disagreement between their statements about boundaries and even considerable overlap between
tribal territories. This is to be expected in a country whose practical value to the Bedouin is located in particular tracts and where
the population is very mobile. At any moment a considerable proportion of the men may be working outside the territory, and their
flocks herding in the grounds of other tribes. Of course, this never
deterred administrators and travelers from sketching tribal maps,
which neatly apportion all of South Sinai to the various tribes (see
Murray 1935: 247; Israel Army 1962: map 3; Glassner 1974: 35;
Bailey 1985: 23). The joint ownership of territorial resources unites
the tribesmen, and when necessary some of them join forces to
prevent outsiders from encroaching on their land. Thus, I was
told that some years ago an Awlad Sa'id man had constructed a
stone house near a route that the Jabaliya claimed as their own.
One of the Jabaliya elders warned him that he was welcome to
set up a tent in that place, but not a house. The Awlad Sa'id man
moved away, and the house was then torn down.

Bedouin claim that membership of the tribe also gives them access to all the pastures of South Sinai. They consider their tribes to
belong to an alliance, which until World War I elected a common
leader and moderator (Murray 1935: 259), and together they are
called the people of Mount Sinai *(tawara,* s. *turi),* the Tawara. The
tribal confederation is not represented in the Bedouin's genealogies by an apical ancestor. The authorities occasionally appointed
one of the tribal chiefs as paramount chief, but this appointment
was mainly ceremonial and the chief never exercised control over
the whole population. Members of several tribes frequently share
pastures; whenever this happens, the herdsmen may camp together, irrespective of their tribal affiliation. Without this sharing
of pastures, pastoralism in South Sinai would be unthinkable. Six
tribes are usually considered members of the alliance of Tawara:
the Muzaina and 'Aleqat, who together constitute one moiety; the
Sawalha, Qararsha and Awlad Sa'id, who constitute the other;

and the Jabaliya, whom the other tribes treat as slightly inferior members of the alliance. The Bedouin view the two other small tribes, the Hamada and the Bani Wasil, as remnants of the ancient inhabitants of the country who lost their land, but tacitly accept them as belonging to the Tawara. Only the Huwetat tribesmen are thought to be intruders without right to land; and indeed, most of them appear to have entered the area as late as after World War I. They only do not perform an annual tribal pilgrimage.

Second, the Bedouin view the tribe as a political organization, as an alliance of numerous patrilineal descent groups whose purpose is to defend individual members and to protect the territory and its resources against intruders. The political tribe is made up in this manner: each Bedouin is born into a noncorporate patronymic group. The group is called a family (*'eleh*), and is named after an ancestor who lived two to four generations ago. The group name may be either the ancestor's first name or his nickname (*naqbah* or *nabadh*). Some people cannot trace the details of their connection to this ancestor. Members of the descent group do not necessarily camp together or own joint property, or obey a formal leader. Some of them, often close paternal kin may, in company with other relatives or even nonrelatives, engage in joint economic ventures such as smuggling partnerships. Others, and even the members of the economic partnership themselves, may then consider this as an activity of the agnatic descent group, oblivious to the fact that not all its members participate in the joint activity and that some nonmembers are involved.

Several patronymic groups are affiliated with a large unit, which is at one and the same time considered a large descent group and a subunit of the tribe. It is believed to be associated with a not too clearly defined part of the tribal territory. This unit is called a quarter (*ruba'*, pl. *rubu'*) or branch (*fara'*, pl. *furu'*), both terms implying that it is a subdivision of a larger unit, the tribe. Tribesmen freely admit that their patronyms are not necessarily descendants of the ancestors of the *ruba'* and that some tribesmen originated outside the tribe and joined the *ruba'* within living memory. The members of the *ruba'* do not all reside in the territory associated with their ancestor. A respected member of one of the constituent groups—not necessarily a large or wealthy one—is elected as elder, and his home becomes a meeting place for members. This man distributes resources allocated to the group by external agencies, such as work supplied by the state, and in this context acts as representative of the tribal chief. He also makes the arrangements for periodical reunions of the group. The tribe is conceptualized as a group founded by a single eponym, whose sons—and as the term *ruba'* implies, there are often four—are the ancestors of the *ruba'*. This tribe, as distinct from the administrative tribe headed by a chief, exists exclusively as an organization for the control of territory and beyond that initiates few joint political or economic activities. Bedouin often argue that the tribe as a whole pays blood compensation *(diya)*, but no one can recall any concrete instance. A few respected old men, who are usually not in the limelight, and often not known to the authorities, do act as mediators in disputes and, when working in concert, exert great influence. It is they who make the arrangements for the tribal pilgrimage. They may also make other important decisions, such as the decision in the 1990s to prohibit Bedouin from grazing their flocks in Wadi Firan as long as the natural vegetation had not recovered from overgrazing.

And third, the Bedouin endorse the authorities' conception of the tribe as an administrative unit, headed by a chief and by *ruba'* headmen. These men are chosen by the tribesmen, and confirmed in office by the authorities, who deal with the tribe through these representatives. The chiefs provide the authorities with well-sifted information, often taking into consideration their personal interest, and distribute the limited resources allocated by the authorities as they see fit. In an economy based largely on wage labor outside the tribe, and with government services few and far between, the Bedouin do not attach great importance to these chiefs. They do, however, realize that the chiefs act as liaison officers between the authorities—and in the case of the Jabaliya also between the monks of Santa Katarina—and the tribesmen, and that their potential for causing harm is considerable. Bedouin usually describe them as "government chiefs, who really represent only their personal interest," and treat them with caution.

Bedouin are well aware that the term tribe refers to different things, but often consider these to be several aspects of the same social entity. They do so by conceptualizing the tribe as a segmentary political organization flowing out of joint descent, and summarized in genealogies. In this manner they subsume under one heading a number of totally different organizations, namely the territorial tribe, the descent groups, political alliances, and the government chief and his links with the administration. As distinct from the belief of anthropologists of an earlier generation that there is such a thing as a segmentary political organization (see Peters [1990: chap. 4, 5] for an incisive critique), Bedouin use the theory for ad hoc explanations of social behavior. But these are not the only sociological theories they entertain. They possess theories on various aspects of social life, such as relations with the authorities, the nature of leadership, cooperation between members of different tribes in such matters as tourism, the uses of far-flung networks of kinship ties, and the organization of wage labor in towns.

In the annual tribal pilgrimage the three kinds of tribe merge and, what is more, for once the "tribe" becomes a living reality. Its various aspects are represented in the ebb and flow of gatherings at the pilgrimage site, in the detail of the ritual, and in the form of the saint's tomb itself. It reflects not only aspects of social life covered by the theory of segmentary organization, but also other aspects of Bedouin life. Especially salient are the perennial problems of uncertain political conditions, the changing employment situation, and the hazards of life in a desert where drought and natural disasters are common occurrences.

I shall now briefly introduce the three tribes whose pilgrimages will be discussed, the Muzaina, Awlad Sa'id, and Jabaliya. The tribes differ in size, territorial resources, and economic activities. Table 3 lists all the Bedouin tribes of South Sinai by size. The figures are based on Nir (1987: 810), who compared a census carried out by the Israeli military authorities in 1975 to data he collected in 1979.

The Muzaina are the largest tribe and also occupy the largest territory. Murray (1935: 265) describes them as camel and sheep breeders, many of whom "have lately taken to fishing." Their control of the east coast and part of the west coast puts them in an ideal position for receiving consignments of narcotics from Saudi Arabia and passing them on to other middlemen in Wadi Firan and along the west coast, from whence they were sent on to the Nile Valley. Smuggling thrived until about 1970, when the Israeli

TABLE 3. Bedouin tribes of South Sinai

Tribe	Territory	Population
Muzaina	East, center, and southwest	3,500
Jabaliya	High mountains	1,400
'Aleqat	West coast	2,150
Qararsha	From Wadi Firan to west coast	1,200
Awlad Sa'id	High mountains	850
Hamada	Northwest	500
Huwetat	Lower reaches of Wadi Firan	400
Sawalha	Northwest	400
Bani Wasil	Around al-Tur	60
Total Bedouin population		*10,460*

authorities stopped it almost completely. Some of the best-known organizers of smuggling bands stem from this tribe, and Muzaina estimate that until the early 1970s about one-third of their income was derived from smuggling. In the 1980s smuggling of narcotics was resumed, probably on an even larger scale.

Most Muzaina households live on the wages of one or more migrant workers, who earn 40 Israeli Pounds (about US$ 10) a day or more. Several Muzaina owned flocks of goats and sheep large enough for making a decent living. Bedouin claim that fifty to sixty animals are the minimum needed. One of the few men I encountered who owned a flock of that size claimed that he obtained on average a monthly revenue of 400 Israeli Pounds, in addition to which the Israeli National Insurance paid him 200 Israeli Pounds. His monthly income thus amounted to 600 Israeli Pounds (approximately US$ 150). While almost every household raises five to six goats or sheep, most people claim that they do not expect to make a profit on animals. For part of the dry season the animals are fed millet or corn, imported from outside Sinai. Women and girls herd the small flocks. This seems to have been the situation for a long time, since Henry S. Palmer (1906: 69–72) found in 1869 that girls exclusively tended flocks. The men earned their living away from home (not so much as wage laborers, but as cameleers), and bought grain with the money earned (see also E. H. Palmer 1871: 81–82; Keller 1900: 26). A few Muzaina men owned orchards and had a share in palm groves. In addition, there were fishermen and sailors. Before the Israeli occupation the Muzaina owned dozens of rowing boats for offshore fishing, which at night also doubled as drug haulers. The Israeli administration first prohibited fishing by boat and later destroyed most of the boats. Instead, teams of fishermen cast large nylon nets from the coral reefs.

The Awlad Sa'id reside in the mountains west of the Santa Katarina monastery. Their territory surrounds the much smaller territory of the Jabaliya and encompasses some of the best pasture in the high mountains, leaving only a small area to the Jabaliya. They rely to a much greater extent than the Muzaina on flocks, and not a few of them possess small and relatively neglected orchards in the mountains. In past generations their camels had carried pilgrims from Egypt and supplies from al-Tur to the monastery which also customarily employs some members of the tribe. As their territory straddles all the east-west routes across the mountains, they also engaged in drug smuggling. During the Israeli occupation they too depended largely on wage labor.

The habitat of the Jabaliya is the high mountains of South Sinai. Their flocks were smaller than those of the other two tribes, and some households did not raise any animals. As their small territory includes no major mountain pass, they were more or less excluded from drug smuggling. They invested in horticulture more than other tribes. Almost every family owns one or more orchards in the high mountains, which it irrigates and cultivates regularly, even when it resides elsewhere. Before the Israeli occupation the Jabaliya used to market pears, quinces and almonds in al-Tur, a three-day journey on camel, and with the proceeds they bought a year's supply of grain. That did not leave enough money for other items, such as tea, sugar and clothing, so the men sought employment wherever available, whether in Sinai or in the Nile Valley. The Santa Katarina monastery traditionally employs between twenty to thirty Jabaliya men and also a few Awlad Sa'id. While it pays its workers much lower wages than the open labor market, it can offer them two advantages: work close to home and relatively secure employment. The monastery's employees often remain in their jobs throughout their working life, and even after retirement the monastery supplies them with small but regular food rations. Tribesmen complain about the meager pay, but remain in their jobs, for they know that the future is uncertain. The Jabaliya also used to supply guides for pilgrims who wished to visit the many legendary sites associated with Moses in the vicinity of the monastery.

Jabaliya explain that their close ties with the monastery go far back in history. They claim that their ancestor Constantine was one of a number of Greek slaves sent out to serve the monks when the monastery was established in the sixth century. Procopius, the Byzantine chronicler, indeed reports that the emperor Justinian supplied the monastery with Vlach slaves (Procopius 1954: 357). The story both supports the Jabaliya's claim for a special link to the monastery and their assertion that the tribal territory "is owned by the monastery," and cannot therefore be touched by the authorities. On the other hand, when I asked individual tribesmen about their origins, they claimed to come from the Arabian Peninsula, Egypt, and even Palestine, and no one ever claimed to be of Vlach or other Balkanic descent. It is their attachment to one of the tribe's four sections, whose ancestors were linked either to the mythical Constantine or belonged to another group of servants of the monastery imported from Egypt, that underpins the Jabaliya's right to enjoy the advantages of being "children of the monastery" (subyan al-der), an epithet often used by the monks that they have adopted.

As their territory was too small for herding large flocks, and the monastery could employ only a handful of men, the Jabaliya were among the first Bedouin to engage in wage labor. Most men worked regularly in the towns of Sinai or in the Abu Rudes oil field. Thirty to fifty men were employed by the Israeli administration. Other Jabaliya men became skilled builders and well diggers whose services were in demand all over Sinai.

Jabaliya households alternated as a rule between two locations: for most of the year, and especially during the cooler months, they stayed in the "low-lying" areas at an elevation of about 1,600 meters; during the hot summer months they moved to their orchards situated another 300 to 400 meters up, in order to enjoy the cool mountain air and harvest the fruit. The Awlad Sa'id tribesmen observed a similar transhumance, but it took place at lower altitudes. Their cool summer sites were at about the same elevation as the "sheltered" winter sites of the Jabaliya.

All three tribes, then, depended on unskilled and semiskilled wage labor for their living, and most men stayed for long periods away from home. At the same time, they tended their orchards and flocks of goats and sheep, while admitting that they either made little money, or even incurred losses, on their flocks and gardens. Why, then, did the Bedouin behave as if they were gardeners and herdsmen, and did not move their families nearer to their places of work? The answer is twofold. First, when Bedouin obtained secure jobs, they often did settle in the towns and cities of Egypt, and were then followed by their households and by other kin. Many 'Aleqat and Qararsha, and some members of other tribes, have become townsmen. I would hazard a guess that in each generation about half the Bedouin inhabitants of South Sinai ended up living in the Nile Valley. While these people rarely returned to live in South Sinai, they insisted that they are always drawn back to their homeland. They did not allow kinship ties to lapse and some of them still owned orchards in the mountains. Second, the majority of Bedouin, especially those who stayed in South Sinai, keep a secure foothold in the mountains of South Sinai because their employment is insecure. While most of their income is derived from wage labor, they know this to be of limited duration. They could lose their work at any time, through political upheavals and economic fluctuations, or because of illness, accident, or death. They expect these mishaps to occur and know they must prepare for them. Therefore they maintain an alternative, if less lucrative, market economy (I use the term "economy" in the most inclusive sense), which they can fall back on in time of need. In order to maintain their orchards and herd the small flocks, they leave their families behind. By some serious effort they can increase their garden produce, and migrate with their flocks so as to make the best use of the available pasture. They also keep the tribe intact by protecting territorial rights and organizing an annual tribal reunion. In addition, they foster kinship and other social networks, and they pray, sacrifice animals, and go on pilgrimages in order to keep in touch with God. If anything should go wrong, they can always fall back on these resources.

But the Bedouin's first line of defense is their country. Without control of the land they would enjoy neither the various employment opportunities nor social security. They often express this utilitarian behavior as a sentimental attachment to their land. A Jabaliya man put it thus:

> Our country is arid, nothing grows in it. Last night the dew froze and burnt [sic] my tomato plants. The same happens to the almond and apple blossoms. It is not even a good country for goats, for you always have to supplement their food and you lose money on them. Only the landscapes are beautiful and in summer the climate is good, but we obtain our livelihood (rizq) outside the country. Yet I always return to it, because my family lives here. And I do not leave because my country is dear to me. I am tied to it by my navel-string. For when a child is born, the father buries the navel-string and the placenta deep in the ground.

Attachment to the land thus symbolizes both the secure base established on the ground and the social security provided by the people living on it. It indicates that the system is all of one piece, and that it is well worth preserving.

While the going is good, Bedouin do not balance the two economies very carefully. They feel relatively secure, and put less work into their orchards and flocks. But they never neglect or abandon the second economy. When they feel threatened, they increase their efforts. Thus the input of work and effort varies with the news. This became evident in the 1973 war between Egypt and Israel, in 1975 during the negotiations between Egypt and Israel over an "interim agreement" in Sinai, and a third time in 1979 when it became clear that Israel would evacuate the Mount Sinai region. On each occasion there was a sudden flourish of activity in the alternative economy. Bedouin stopped the sale of animals and showed a renewed interest in gardens. Some people acquired existing gardens; others dug wells and planted new gardens. These arrangements, they hoped, would enable them to compensate for the expected loss of employment.

Smuggling is to be viewed as a secondary accommodation to prevailing conditions. This wild and mountainous country is well suited to clandestine activities. The inhabitants eke out a bare living, and are therefore ready to do any gainful work that offers itself. In spite of high risks and the not extravagant pay, numerous people viewed smuggling as a business just like any other, as an accepted and respectable way of making a living, one that furthermore had many advantages over migrant labor. While only a handful of entrepreneurs made fortunes out of smuggling, it permitted the rank and file smugglers to stay at home for much longer periods, and did not expose them to the humiliating conditions of work in the city. Smuggling reinforces tribal allegiance, as control over routes is a precondition for entering the game. It is also predicated on peaceful relations between the tribes located along the smuggling routes. Therefore the Bedouin of South Sinai shun violent disputes and, quite justly, refer to themselves as "peaceful people."

The Pilgrimage

Wage labor was the main source of the Bedouin's income. It took many men away from their families and kin and out of the tribal area for months on end. The families they left behind converged on the relatively large villages, where services and shops were located, and did not give the flocks and gardens all the attention they merit. Although the men often work in the company of relatives, most of the people on whom they depend for mutual assistance and reassurance are located in the tribal area. Relationships with these people require maintenance, for if one does not interact regularly with them, the relationship can no longer be relied upon. One cannot be certain whether it will hold in time of need. Therefore each Bedouin strives to visit his relatives and friends, whenever he takes time off from work. The opportunity to see many relatives at once presents itself in late summer, when the Bedouin congregate in the oases for the date harvest. These large concentrations, in turn, form the basis for the organization of the even more encompassing tribal gatherings.

Those Muzaina and Awlad Sa'id who do not become labor migrants go through annual migrations. Their pastoral year begins in *rabi'a* (spring), the season when the weather becomes a little warmer and verdure springs up. This usually happens around February. In the mountains spring comes round every year, but in the lower areas only if there has been some rain in winter. Then

the Bedouin leave their winter quarters, relatively large station-
ary hamlets of tin shacks and tents, and some of them divide
up into small camps of two to three tents in order to exploit the
pasture wherever it is available. These movements are largely
determined by the requirements of the larger flocks, but even
households owning few animals may join in because they wish
to stay close to relatives. Spring pasture does not last long, and
once it is exhausted the flocks move into the few reliable early
summer pastures, such as Wadi Rahaba and Wadi Slaf. Some of
the larger encampments remain almost immobile. They are made
up of households whose income depends on wage labor, and who
put little emphasis on herding. In spring these camps just move a
short distance from the sheltered winter camping site to one that
allows in refreshing breezes.

The annual migratory cycle reaches the point of maximum concentration in summer, when the pasture is exhausted and water
sources dry up. Then people converge on the remaining wells in
the oases or on the seashore and harvest their dates or, in the case
of the Jabaliya, repair to their gardens in the mountains. Here
people gather in larger concentrations; some of the men have already returned from work in order to enjoy the conviviality and
to exchange visits. On moonlit nights the young, unmarried Muzaina men organize dances. After the fruit have been picked and
the time comes to move, the elders of the tribe call for a tribal
gathering. The gathering not only fits into the seasonal pattern of
maximum concentration of tribesmen, but also enhances it. It is
the only occasion when the "tribe" visibly becomes a group. At
other times it does not operate as a united political group. People
can plant gardens, build houses, engage in smuggling, and even
work in towns only because they are tribesmen, but in all these
activities they meet only as associates and not as the tribe. There
are no constant reminders of its existence, such as tribal identifica-
tion marks. Even the tribal camel brands (wasm) are rarely applied
these days.

What is it that makes a considerable number of tribesmen participate in the pilgrimage? There is very little persuasion involved;
the organizers of the pilgrimage are respected elders, who exert a
strong hold on people precisely because their decisions always ac-
commodate various conflicting interests. There is no tribal chief or

economic entrepreneur among them. Their main duties are to fix the date of the pilgrimage and to collect from their neighbors contributions for the tribal sacrifice, which are eventually returned to the donors as portions of boiled meat. A basic attraction of the pilgrimage is that each individual considers it as a beneficial activity. All the people of South Sinai, and not only those in whose territory the shrines are located, acknowledge the reputations of the major shrines all over the region. Each saint attracts individual pilgrims from all over the region, and the fame of some shrines has spread beyond the borders of South Sinai. Monday and Friday eves are considered as propitious for pilgrimage. On these days, throughout most of the year, individual households make their way to a shrine of their choice. In most instances this will be a saint's tomb, but there are also a few other pilgrimage sites. One of these, and the one most venerated, is the summit of Jabal Musa (where Moses is said to have received the Tablets of the Law). Others are Jabal Muneja' in Wadi Firan (Levi 1980: 150), and the uninhabited monastery of the Forty Martyrs in Wadi Leja, near Santa Katarina. In these pilgrimages people either redeem vows made in times of trouble or request the saint's intercession. As the saint only mediates requests to almighty God, and he himself cannot grant wishes, a visit to any holy tomb, perhaps the one closest to home, should do. Yet people are slightly skeptical, and trust their own and their relatives' experience, which shows that some saints intercede more effectively, while others are more efficacious in some matters than in others. While individual experience varies widely, some specialization has developed among the saints. Therefore, each holy tomb attracts visitors from all parts of South Sinai, often coming from distant places. Thus members of one patronymic group of the Jabaliya visited at various times during a five-year period the following sites: a woman who had not conceived for two years ascended Jabal Musa with her family; a man wished to protect the well-being of his family by taking them on an outing to Sheikh 'Awad; two men took their flocks by car to Sheikh Habus in order to safeguard their health; a man who had just recovered from an illness carried his family by camel to Nabi Saleh; and an old lady had her wish to make the expensive pilgrimage to Mecca granted. In similar fashion, people from all over South Sinai visited close and distant shrines, thus covering the whole region with a dense network of pilgrimage sites, and reaffirming their respect for, and recognition of, all the saints of the region.

This situation affects tribal gatherings in two ways. First, the commonly shared belief in saints' tombs, and in saints as intercessors with God, is one of the foundations of the tribal pilgrimage. Each of the individuals who participate in the gathering believes that he or she obtains a spiritual benefit. It must be added, however, that he may also expect material advantages, such as encountering a debtor or getting an opportunity to offer a car or a camel for sale. Bedouin see nothing incongruous in seeking spiritual and material benefits at the same time. They do not conceive of purely spiritual occasions, or purely material exchanges, that are so typical of societies with centralized governments and more diversified economies. In contrast, the Christians who made the arduous pilgrimage to Santa Katarina's shrine over the centuries sought only to heal their souls (Hobbs 1995: chap. 8), as do the Christian pilgrims who visit holy places such as Lourdes. While both the journey and the site are run just like other businesses, the pilgrims expect purely spiritual benefits (Dahlberg 1991: 43).

Second, all the participants in the gathering, whether belonging to the celebrating tribe or not, respect the saint's tomb, and consider it the equal of the saints' tombs of other tribes. Even Nabi Saleh, whose tomb is the recognized center of the tribal gatherings, is not considered superior to the others. Individual pilgrims do not prefer him in any way to other saints, and there are weeks when no one visits the site. This equality among saints expresses an important facet of the gatherings: they are not held exclusively for the members of one tribe, and people from other tribes can also attend. Indeed, people say explicitly that the gatherings are expected to attract visitors from other tribes. Thus the meeting place of the Bedouin of South Sinai shifts periodically from one site to another. At each gathering one tribe slightly dominates because of its numerical preponderance, but never becomes superior to the others. Still, until recently the tribes preferred to gather at one particular site. People say that up to 1965, at least five tribes, the Sawalha, Awlad Sa'id, Qararsha, Muzaina, and Jabaliya, held their separate annual tribal gatherings at Nabi Saleh. I surmise that the location turned this tomb into the central meeting place of the Mount Sinai Bedouin: it is situated at the intersection of the major east-west and north-south mountain passes, close to the main pastures, in an area frequented by Muzaina, Awlad Sa'id and Jabaliya. In view of the great importance of smuggling in those days, and of caravan traffic in earlier times, each tribe attached great significance to its rights of passage through the mountains, as well as to the coordination of activities and the maintenance of peaceful relations with other tribes. Today each tribe has its own pilgrimage site in its tribal territory. There are two clusters of such sites. In the west, not far from the sea, are the pilgrimage centers of the 'Aleqat, Qararsha, and Hamada tribes. They are located close to the main concentrations of the homes of labor migrants employed in the towns in and around Sinai. Before the Israeli occupation, some men were employed in the mines and industries of the region, but the majority worked year-round as migrant laborers, and approximately half of them eventually settled in Egypt proper. For these geographically mobile people, the saint's tomb must be located close to home, as it refers to their attachment to the territory. The other cluster of pilgrimage centers, those of the Muzaina, Awlad Sa'id, and Jabaliya, are located in the mountains. The tomb of the Muzaina patron saint is located at the center of the tribe's large territory. Those of the other two tribes are on the outskirts of their territories. Here pilgrimage requires most people to leave their homes and to travel some distance. They go through a rite of passage, "beginning in a Familiar Place, going to a Far Place, and returning, ideally 'changed,' to a Familiar Place" (Turner 1973: 213). These tribesmen are intimately tied to the land, where their basic economy lies. Here the attachment to the land is a given, and Bedouin use their pilgrimages to maintain relationships and forge new ones, in and outside the tribe. The individual is drawn away from his round of daily life and its circumscribed field of relationships, and brought to another place where he meets people from a wider region.

The elders who set the date of the tribal gathering take into account all the relevant factors. A Bedouin explained what these are: "The date of the gathering is fixed perhaps two months in advance, so that the news will get around to all tribesmen. Conditions of work are taken into account, as well as the end of the date harvest (*masif*) in Wadi Firan, where the dates ripen later than in other oases. The position of the stars is important. Only after Canopus *(thraiya)* and other stars rise to the firmament, the mutton becomes suitable for eating. Before that the goats are too lean and their meat is hard to digest." To complicate matters further, the feasts are held on Thursday afternoons, the eve of the Muslim weekend, and at full moon. The dates of the tribal gatherings vary but little over the years. The earliest reported date is the end of July (Burckhardt [1822] 1992: 489). The gatherings I attended, or for which I obtained the dates, all took place between the end of June and the beginning of September. In this respect there was no difference between the Muzaina, Awlad Sa'id and Jabaliya.

My data on attendance are incomplete, but they do show that in recent years it varied considerably. Bedouin gave me only figures for the attendance of men and, for comparative purposes, I followed their example, but it should be remembered that whole families make the pilgrimage, so that the real figures are more than double. Thus, for the Muzaina gathering at Nabi Saleh in 1970, one hundred to one hundred and fifty men are reported (Meshel 1971: 95). In following years the numbers declined sharply, until in 1973 only fifty men were reported to be present. In 1975 the figure again rose to nearly two hundred men.

The Awlad Sa'id attended their tribal meeting at Abu Taleb more regularly. In July 1973 I attended a meeting of about seventy men, gathered in the rectangular open-sided hut opposite the saint's tomb. A year later Kapara (1975: 193) reports forty to fifty men in the big hut, while others were still arriving. In contrast to the Muzaina, whose attendance declined up to 1973 and went up again in the following year, the Awlad Sa'id pattern was stable. Most of the men attended year after year.

The Jabaliya's pattern of attendance differed again. Tribesmen claimed that in the past the annual tribal gatherings had lasted three days. They used to start at Nabi Saleh, the major site for tribal gatherings, moved on to Nabi Harun (the reputed tomb of Aaron, the high priest and brother of Moses), near the Santa Katarina monastery, and from there on to the monastery itself. This gathering was held for the last time in 1965. After that there were no more gatherings of the whole tribe, but in August 1973 I attended a gathering of about sixty-five to seventy men of the Awlad Jindi subtribe of the Jabaliya at Sheikh 'Awad, and in August

1975 another one at the same place attended by nearly all Awlad Jindi men. A month later another subtribe of the Jabaliya, the
Wuhebat, held a gathering of their own at Sheikh 'Awad. While
I was told that previously they had not had such gatherings, the
pilgrimages of subtribes now became a regular annual feature.

A clear pattern emerges here: though the gatherings never
ceased, attendance declined when plenty of work was available
and when it was expected that the favorable economic and political conditions would continue. This was particularly true for
the Muzaina and Jabaliya, who largely depended on wage labor. People who regularly turned up at the gatherings were those
who had a predominant interest in herding, as well as the former
smugglers, who presented themselves as keepers of tradition:
they were waiting for better times, when they would be able to
resume operations. When I asked why others did not participate,
I was often told that they were away working and would not jeopardize their jobs. The men who had an interest in maintaining the
tribe showed up at all the meetings, while those whose employment was secure did not. After 1973, the employed people also
took part in the gatherings. This was the result of a new kind of
uncertainty. At that time work was plentiful and well paid, but the
political future of Sinai was uncertain. The Egyptians and Israelis
were negotiating under the aegis of the American Secretary of
State Henry Kissinger, the Israelis were giving up territory in Sinai, and no one knew where it was going to end. While elsewhere
in the Middle East the extended negotiations raised hopes that
peace would come to the region, they only spelled doubts and
insecurity for the Bedouin. As an example, an Awlad Jindi man
employed as driver by the Israeli administration had often told
me that he never attended tribal gatherings. These were suited for
old people, he thought. In 1975 he attended for the first time, explaining that his wife had begged him to go and that he could not
refuse her wish. He did not admit, perhaps not even to himself,
that the future was uncertain and that he might have to rely to a
larger extent than hitherto on the help of agnates and tribesmen.
At the time he was toying with the idea of setting up a repair shop
for cars. Relatives and neighbors could thus become more important, even if only as customers. He has attended the pilgrimage
every year since.

The two levels of the individual's involvement in the pilgrimage are shown in the arrangements for the communal meal that is part of every tribal gathering. Several sheep or a young camel are slaughtered and all the men who contributed to the collection attend the meal. The animals are bought, and cooking arrangements made, by an elder of the group. In the late afternoon or early evening all the men gather for a festive meal. They pray together and then sit down in a large circle for a meal. Each man's name is announced for all to hear, as a tribesman who contributed to the tribal sacrifice. Then his portion of meat, wrapped in a flap of flat bread, is passed along a chain of servers up to the announcer, who hands it to the man. There is no visible leader at these functions; no speeches and announcements are made. Visitors from other tribes are welcome. Their names are announced, and the epithet "guest" added. They too are given portions of meat. At a meal I attended, I was announced as a "nameless guest," and also given meat. At the gatherings, chiefs and notables mingle with other men and no special area is reserved for them. At one of the Muzaina gatherings the paramount chief of the tribe put in a short appearance, to pay respect to a gathering at which he did not preside. At the Awlad Sa'id gatherings the two tribal chiefs were present all the time and moved among the people. The Jabaliya chief did not attend the Awlad Jindi meetings at all, but he was present at those of his own subtribe, the Wuhebat.

The chiefs' participation in the proceedings was largely determined by their position in the tribe. While all chiefs are considered to be the representatives of the administration, this does not count much where government is as distant and inactive as in South Sinai. The saint is treated as a mediator between the tribe and divine authority precisely because government is so distant and does not assure the Bedouin's basic requirements. Therefore there was no place for the "government" chiefs in the ceremonies. Some of these men were, however, important in their own right, as organizers of smuggling rings and other economic activities, as powerful leaders of large groups of men, and as mediators in disputes between tribesmen. Such were the chiefs of the Awlad Sa'id and the headmen of the Muzaina subtribes, and they took their rightful place in the ceremonies. Others, like the chiefs of the

Jabaliya and the Muzaina, played less important internal roles and did not need to be present.

The participants in the tribal gathering were at the same time individual pilgrims. All round the saint's tomb related families gathered in small circles. The women began to prepare food for a festive meal. In the late afternoon each man led his family and a sacrificial goat round the tomb, bearing a pan with burning incense and repeating the phrase *"twakkal allah"* (rely on God). He then recited the *fatiha,* the opening chapter of the Quran, dedicating it to the saint, and offered a prayer for the health, well-being and livelihood of his family. Thereupon he slaughtered the animal, and while he prepared the meat, the women and children returned to their own family circle. The family and its guests, men, women and children, shared in a joint meal of meat and other dishes. For once, the order of precedence was dropped and all the members of the household ate together. The women in particular wore their finest dresses, embroidered with silver and gold thread. The atmosphere was relaxed and the women spoke up freely, even making jokes with sexual innuendoes. There was much mutual visiting. The men spent most of their time making the rounds of friends, now and again returning to spend a few minutes with their families. At these gatherings people reaffirmed their friendly relations and, incidentally, settled debts and disputes and initiated commercial dealings, such as the sale of animals and cars, and other joint activities. Shopkeepers too had arrived and made brisk sales of cola bottles and sweets.

The significance of the tribal pilgrimages has gradually emerged. People attend them for their material and spiritual well-being. They hope to meet their relatives and friends, to reaffirm old ties and forge new ones. Throughout most of the year they do not meet many of these people. By participating in the annual tribal muster, and sharing the tribal sacrificial meal, they renew bonds with the tribe and its members, and assure themselves of access to territorial resources. The attendance of guests from other tribes emphasizes solidarity with the people of South Sinai for the preservation of peace, a precondition for access to pastures throughout the peninsula and for joint smuggling operations. Lastly, they supplicate the saint to forward their prayers to a distant God, in whom they put their trust. Without his help they could not survive in the wider world, on which they depend in so many ways and over which they exert no influence.

Pilgrimage as Symbolic Activity

The symbolism of the tribal pilgrimages must now be examined. I take a "symbol" to be a sign replete with many interrelated meanings. In this working definition, which resembles Sapir's (1934: 493) characterization of the "condensation symbol," I wish to stress the richness of meaning as the identifying mark of the symbol, as opposed to the mechanical multiplication of mental associations that may attach to a particular sign. The meanings of the condensation symbol express, as Sapir pointed out, "a condensation of energy, its actual significance being out of all proportion to the apparent triviality of meaning suggested by its mere form" (1934: 493). To this I would add that much of the emotional impact of condensation symbols derives from the fact that they evoke numerous, often contested and contradictory, meanings simultaneously. The secret of this immediate impact probably lies in the symbol's full integration in the daily routine of its users. Because of this, many students of society today agree that an external observer can tap the multiple meanings of symbols only through intimate knowledge of both native conceptions of society and of the social contexts in which the symbols are invoked. The whole gamut of a symbol's contextual uses, as well as the associated symbols and contexts, must be explored before it can be properly understood. But once this is done, one may find that each element of a symbol's meaning has a precise referent and thus appeals directly to communicants.

Bedouin clearly distinguish between the meaning of the Mecca pilgrimage, which every Muslim should ideally make at least once in a lifetime, and the repetitive and regular pilgrimages to saints' tombs. The symbolism of the pilgrimage to Mecca centers no less on the journey than on the holy site itself. The route is often seen as a staging of the life course; it offers the pilgrim an opportunity to reflect on his or her past life, to make a clean break, and to formulate a plan for the future. The journey to Mecca is divided into stages of ever-growing sanctity, culminating in the pilgrim's donning of two lengths of white cloth *(ihram)* on the outskirts of Mecca. The *ihram* is also the shroud he will be buried in, a reminder that his whole life is under review. Even in the sacred city, the pilgrim is obliged to continue the journey from one site to the next. He must thus consider the pilgrimage as a turning point in life and a preparation for death. By the time he reaches the Mecca sanctuary the journey has been completed and he is on his own. The anthropologist Hammoudi describes his encounter with the Kaaba in Mecca in these words: "Each of us was alone, our solitude reflected back at us by the black cube" (2006: 153). The outstanding example of those who take part in such a sacred journey are the Nigerian Muslims described by Yamba (1995: 181ff.), whose pilgrimage may last a whole lifetime. Many pilgrims interrupt the journey in Sudan, in order to collect money for the onward journey. They may spend many years in Sudan, raise a family and die there. But no matter how long the sojourn in Sudan, they will at all times view it as a way station on the road to Mecca.

This is emphatically not the case in the personal pilgrimage to saints' tombs, a repetitive performance whose main purpose is to maintain a useful relationship with God. Here the journey becomes less important and attention centers on the saint's tomb. The Bedouin even use different terms for the pilgrimage to Mecca and the pilgrimage to saints' tombs. For both the tribal gatherings and the personal pilgrimages to saints' tombs, they employ the term used for visiting among friends and acquaintances (*ziyara*, locally pronounced *zuwara*). This usage is common in most Islamic regions. Only the pilgrimage to Mecca is called *hajj* (meaning precisely a "sacred journey"). While Sinai Bedouin often compare the ascent to the summit of Jabal Musa to a pilgrimage to Mecca, they nevertheless call it a *zuwara*. There is only one place to which a Muslim pilgrimage is made, and that is Mecca. Every year a number of Bedouin men and women make the arduous and costly journey there.

I shall now attempt to unravel the major strands in the mesh of meanings attached to the saint's tomb, concentrating on three major elements: the significance of the building erected over the tomb, the tomb itself, and the saint's person. I argue that the building symbolizes the Bedouin's conception of the tribe's territorial rights, whose essence is the tribesman's exclusive right to build a house on tribal land. Geertz's (1968: 49) concise description of the Moroccan shrine fits that of South Sinai too: "It is a squat, white, usually domed block-like stone building set under a tree, on a hilltop, or isolated, like an abandoned pillbox, in the middle of an open plain" (see also Canaan 1927: 11; Westermarck 1926: 151–52). One might add that each shrine has a door, and usually also a small window. Only the dome *(kubba)*, often crowned with a crescent, and sometimes embellished with a prayer niche facing in the direction of Mecca, distinguish the shrine from an ordinary house, and indicate that it serves a religious purpose. We already know that Bedouin consider the building of a house as the exclusive right of tribesmen and do not permit outsiders to build houses on tribal territory. The shrine represents, among other things, the territorial claims of the tribe on whose land it is located. Besides the local tribesmen, there are other Bedouin who visit the shrine; the rights of each category are clearly defined. While the owners of the land exercise exclusive rights to the construction of wells, orchards and houses, the members of other tribes possess rights of pasture and of passage through the territory of the local tribe. On another level, the use of the saint's tomb as a symbol of tribal ownership indicates that territorial rights are protected by supernatural sanctions, and not necessarily by the might of the whole tribe. Bedouin store property, such as tents and farming implements, inside or near saints' tombs, secure in the belief that the saint protects them. They recount stories about misfortunes that befell men who stole such property, until they restored it. Construction or repair of a saint's tomb is a meritorious act that gains the donors the respect of the community. They are also political acts: when Ghanem Jum'a, a wealthy Muzaina, built the shrine of Faraj, the tribe's ancestor, in the 1960s, he reasserted the tribe's sovereignty over an area that was at the time becoming the main supply center in South Sinai. The mobile merchants from al-'Arish, who then controlled nearly all the commerce in the region, had set up a dozen shops there. On similar grounds, Jabaliya elders invite their tribesmen every few years to subscribe money for repairs to the shrine of Sheikh 'Awad. This building activity publicly announces that a tribe owns the holy tomb, that it is part of the tribal territory. Incidentally, in this manner all the shrines are kept in a good state of repair.

The saint's tomb occupies the center of the building, thus allowing visitors to circumambulate. The tomb rises to a height of about three feet. It is covered by a shroud made of white or green cloth, on which the Islamic creed and the saint's name are sometimes embroidered. There are usually several layers of shrouds, for each time a shroud is worn out and torn it remains in place and a new one is placed on top of it. The old one is too sacred to be simply disposed of.

It is always doubtful whether the holy tomb actually contains a human body. While the tomb of Nabi Saleh is solidly built and one cannot therefore know whether anyone is buried beneath it, the tomb of 'Ali Abu Taleb consists of a flimsy wooden frame, just sufficient to carry several layers of embroidered shrouds. Canaan (1927: 22) remarks, with regard to Palestinian sanctuaries, that "the tomb is often not in the shrine, but outside of it ... it is not at all necessary that there should be a tomb ... connected with the place to make it a shrine." In South Sinai the Bedouin have gone a step further: they insist that no person is buried in a *maqam*. As proof they cite the "well-known fact that Nabi Saleh is buried in Ramlah, in Israel, and has another tomb in Mada'in Saleh in Saudi Arabia, and that even the Sheikhs Habus and Abu Shabib have two holy tombs each. Only one of these holds a grave *(turba)*, while the other is a place for gatherings of men *(maq'ad)*. This, incidentally, is true for many Islamic regions. Landau-Tasseron (1997: 52), for instance, discusses a North African saint who is said to have at least five different tombs. The shrines at which tribes gather could not contain a body, even if the saint had been buried there, for it is common knowledge among Bedouin that the remains of good men dissolve into air *(hawa)* after some time, and only the bodies of ordinary persons remain in their tombs. This belief releases the saint from his earthly vestiges; he is removed from this world, and is therefore closer to the distant deity. He may be close enough to approach the deity and intercede on behalf of the Bedouin he associated with in life. By the same token, the living saints of North Africa and elsewhere cannot get close to the deity. In order to be a useful mediator, the saint must be dead. Indeed, Colonna (1980: 644) has pointed out that the living saints of North African Islam do not mediate requests to God. Instead, they are experts on such matters as scriptural learning, irrigation and law.

While people often believe that the tribe's patron saint may be an ancestor, they are never certain about his antecedents. Most people cannot say anything definite about his person, except that he was a holy man during his lifetime, as proven by instances in which he helped individuals from various tribes in miraculous ways. Occasionally people hazard guesses about the antecedents of a saint. Thus some say that Nabi Saleh was a pre-Islamic Arabian prophet; others think that perhaps he was the ancestor of the Sawalha tribe. The same uncertainty seems to have prevailed over a century ago, when Robinson ([1841] 1867, 1: 215) reported that "[t]he history of this Saint is uncertain; but our Arabs held him to be the progenitor of their tribe, the Sawaliha; which is not improbable." I believe that the continuing ambiguity of the saint's identity is "built-in," and permits him to perform the various symbolic roles of tribal ancestor, saint, and emblem of Islam. This indeterminacy is also true for other saints. Thus Sheikh 'Awad is said by some Jabaliya to belong to their tribe, while others claim to know nothing about his origins. Some Muzaina consider Sheikh Abu Zaid to have been a Sawarka Bedouin from North Sinai, while others attribute Muzaina origins to him. The only saint who appears to be an acknowledged tribal ancestor is Faraj of the Muzaina (Lavie 1990: 248, 276), but his tomb is not reckoned among the *maqams*. It is named after a group, the Faranja, and not after the putative ancestor Faraj, and only in recent years was a shrine built over the tomb. Yet the fact remains that Faranja is one of the Muzaina's three pilgrimage sites, and one has to conclude that, in a sense, the saint stands for the unity of the tribe. Whether the pilgrimage is made to one or three saints, it always symbolizes the Bedouin's solidarity with three social aggregates. If the saint is to represent all of them, his identity must be indeterminate. He is and he is not a tribesman, and he is also a benevolent saint, as well as an illustrious Muslim.

The three holy tombs visited by the Muzaina until recently allow us to define more clearly the symbolic significance of the saint, for the person of each of the three saints gives special emphasis to one aspect: Faranja symbolizes the unity of the tribe, as well as its descent from the North Arabian Muzaina (Doughty

[1888] 1937, 2: 381). Nabi Saleh represents both the unity of all the Tawara, turning South Sinai into one region to which all members of the confederation have access, and as a prophet represents the inclusion of South Sinai in the Islamic world and, by extension, its neglect by the state controlling the Sinai. In addition, many Bedouin consider Saleh to be the founder of the Sawalha tribe. Nabi Harun again stands for the longstanding connection with the Santa Katarina monastery and the privileges associated with it on the one hand, and on the other the tribe's share in the community of Islam, for both Moses and Aaron are prophets in Islamic hagiography. I cannot fully explain this extended specialization of the three Muzaina saints, for in other tribes, as well as the Muzaina, all the symbolic aspects today merge in a single saint. It may be connected with the fact that the Muzaina have become the largest and most widely dispersed tribe (Lavie 1990). They control over half of South Sinai, including most of the east coast, and this encourages a tendency for the proliferation of smuggling rings, with the ensuing competition and strife. The elders of the tribe make special efforts to preserve unity, so as to keep the Muzaina predominant in the smuggling business. Therefore they stress joint descent and initiated the pilgrimage to Faranja. When smuggling activities were interrupted during the Israeli occupation, there was no longer a need to preserve peace among the tribes, and visits to Faranja were discontinued. Now, the competition between the former rival smuggling rings erupted violently at several tribal gatherings.

On a higher level of abstraction, the three Muzaina saints stand for beliefs that are deeply engrained in Bedouin thought and practices that concern core areas of their social life: the social security networks, the territorial organization of the tribe and the regionalism of South Sinai, and the universalism of Islam and reliance on God against all the external forces that affect the Bedouin and that they cannot control. This needs some further elaboration. The tribal pilgrimage to saints' tombs is the Bedouin's answer to some fundamental problems. They came up with this answer because their view of reality is filtered through a theory that the tribe is the hinge of their system of social assurance. The Bedouin participate as wage laborers in the wider economy and in a bureaucratic state. Both are distant and leave them as insecure outsiders. However, they have the tribe to fall back on. The tribe means to them several things: it is a territorial group owning resources from which they can make a living—it owns land on which they can dig wells, plant orchards, and build a house; it is the home of a descent group whose members should help and defend each other and their territorial resources; and their membership of the tribe gives them access to pastures all over South Sinai. All these together are elements in the Bedouin's alternative economy. The pilgrimage brings together the people who help to make this economy, and seeks to reunite them. At the same time it reflects the fears and uncertainties associated with the distant state, the vagaries of external wage labor, and the problems of life in general. Thus, the cult of saints refers not only to a regionalism more or less confined to the geographical boundaries of South Sinai and to the sharing of natural resources for the benefit of the Tawara tribes; it also refers to a larger entity, to the world in which the Bedouin work, and from which they obtain most of their food and other supplies and services. This world is located chiefly outside the borders of South Sinai and, even more importantly, the Bedouin do not exert influence on its activities. A distant government and other external organizations determine much of their lives, but contact with, not to mention influence over, these forces is minimal, for the bureaucratic lines of communication do not fully extend to the Bedouin, and their own appointed representatives, the chiefs, do not greatly influence officials at the center. So the Bedouin place their reliance on a "spiritual" representative, the saint, who is at least close to God and able to influence him. Two worlds are linked through the person of the saint, who is sometimes thought of as the patron of a tribe, perhaps even an ancestor, and at other times as a holy man of Islam. The saint represents both the tribe as conceptualized by the Bedouin, and the wide external world. His function is to mediate between the two worlds that together sustain the Bedouin. I suggest that tribal reunions elsewhere also develop in response to similar situations: they will appear in tribal or other economically undifferentiated regions under indirect rule, that depend on an external state and a capitalist economy over which they exert little influence. Such societies maintain a pastoral or farming economy that they fall back on in time of need, and maintain the tribe mainly in order to keep control over their territory. An organization that is self-sufficient, or that can rely on economic alternatives and on government assistance, even when it is dubbed a "tribe," does not need tribal reunions. The Syrian Rwala tribes, as described by Musil (1928) and Lancaster (1997), are so fully integrated in the state and in the market that they need neither personal nor tribal pilgrimages.

Epilogue: A Note on Robertson Smith

W. Robertson Smith argued that there is a correspondence between social organization and religious representations. In the *Lectures on the Religion of the Semites* he put it thus: "Religion did not exist for the saving of souls but for the preservation and welfare of society, and in all that was necessary to this end every man had to take his part" (Smith 1894: 29). In his work on regional cults, Richard Werbner (1977: xviii) tends to reject the "correspondence" theory, because for it "[t]he 'community of the god' is a conception of boundedness." It is true that Robertson Smith, like the Bedouin themselves, viewed the tribe as a bounded political and territorial entity, perhaps because he too considered agnation to be the backbone of the tribe. The ideology of agnation informs "bounded" activities, such as the control over rights in land, the protection of life and property, and the setting up of groups. It is to this kind of activity that Robertson Smith's (1894: 150) dictum that holiness is "a restriction on the licence of man in the free use of natural things" applies. In the Arabian context, he believed that gods were associated with permanent sanctuaries, and that their powers were confined to a certain territory (ibid.: 92). Therefore, "at most sanctuaries embracing a stretch of pasture-ground, the right of grazing was free to the community of the god, but not to outsiders" (ibid.: 144).

This prescription did not fit the customary sharing of pastures. Although "every tribe indeed has its own range of plains and valleys, and its own watering places ... from which it repels aliens by the strong hand ... the boundaries of the tribal land are merely maintained by force against enemies, and not only every tribesman but every covenanted ally has equal and unrestricted right to pitch his tent and drive his cattle where he will" (ibid.: 143). This contradiction is immediately explained away: nomads did not claim private property in pastures, and for that reason the local god did not acquire ownership over them.

The material on saints' tombs in South Sinai shows that Robertson Smith was mistaken on two counts. First, the god or saint is not simply associated with one tribe and his influence not confined to a bounded territory. On the contrary, the "local" god in ancient Arabia, like the saint in South Sinai, symbolizes the interdependence between the tribe and a wider region, particularly where pastures are concerned. Wellhausen shows that many sanctuaries in pre-Islamic Arabia had extensive spheres of influence. For instance, the sanctuary of the goddess Manat was located in Hudhail territory, but was frequented by Aus and Khazraj tribesmen, as well as others ([1887] 1961: 27–28). The sanctuary at Mecca too was not only visited by the Quraish, but also attracted pilgrims from various tribes, while the Meccans too visited other sanctuaries. In this manner, ties were forged between Bedouin stemming from different regions, links that facilitated transit and mutual access to available pastures, even in the absence of a central government.

Second, for each restriction on the use of resources there must be a corresponding opening up of resources, as exemplified in the following quote, also taken from Robertson Smith (1894: 111): "The Arabs regard rain as depending on the ... seasons, which affect all tribes alike within a wide range; and so when the showers of heaven are ascribed to a god, that god is Allah, the supreme and non-tribal deity." Evidently these tribesmen reserve certain rights in territory for themselves, but also grant rights to pasture on it to others, on a basis of mutuality. Robertson Smith cannot admit that the "tribal deity" also stands for Allah; to imply that the same people believe in two gods, one tribal and one supreme, at the same time is as far as he dare go. In South Sinai the saint is clearly associated with God. While he intercedes with God on behalf of his tribe, he also works on behalf of individuals from any tribe, and is thus never an exclusive patron of his own people. He represents both restrictions on the use of the country's resources in favor of some people and access to the remaining resources for others. There is no paradox in this, for rights are always specific, so that every prohibition has its complementary permission.

Thus in South Sinai certain rights in land, wells and roads are reserved for tribesmen, and other rights are expressly opened up to all Tawara: land everywhere is available to anyone for pasture, drinking water for men and beasts may be drawn from any well, even when surrounded by a fence, and every Bedouin can pasture animals and travel freely anywhere in the peninsula, as long as he does not infringe upon the privileges of the locals and does not establish an orchard, build a house, or seek employment in their territory.

Yet, after all is said and done, we are still left with a correspondence between social reality and its symbolic representation. If the reality is more complex than Robertson Smith's, and if it has many dimensions, that is due to the more detailed ethnography available today. If, in addition to the tribe, we now see a variety of groups and networks of relationships, that is due to relatively new theoretical insights. The brilliance of Robertson Smith's original idea, and its eminent usefulness, remain undiminished: that symbols refer to a social reality, as seen and interpreted by people; and that the symbols derive from ordinary daily life, so that anyone familiar with it can directly grasp and apprehend their multiple meanings.

Conclusion

In November 2009 I returned for a brief visit to Santa Katarina. Much had happened during my absence. The Bedouin villages in the area had become Santa Katarina City, a town of seven thousand inhabitants, of whom three thousand were Egyptians from the Nile Valley. The two largest buildings were the government center and the police prefecture. They were built on the high ground overlooking the town. There was a new shopping arcade and hotels, and numerous stores had opened all over the town. The traders from al-'Arish had been displaced by local and mainland Egyptian suppliers and store owners. Many Bedouin were constructing permanent houses, using the dark-hued local granitic stone. The local water supply had proven insufficient, and the reservoirs were replenished with water hauled up daily by tankers from Wadi Firan. We were informed that within a year or two a pipeline would ensure a regular water supply to Santa Katarina City.

The appointed mayor of the town was an old acquaintance, a Jabaliya Bedouin who had established the first local coffeehouse. He still owned the café, now one of half a dozen similar establishments, as well as a grocery store. His duties were quite circumscribed, as the urban services, which now included a telephone exchange, a small hospital, sanitation, street cleaning and policing, were provided by the pertinent government departments.

During my fieldwork most men had been labor migrants. Now most men remained at home, and were either employed locally or seemed to be waiting for work. At first sight, tourism seemed to play a major role in the local economy. The Santa Katarina monastery had become a major international tourist site, visited by a daily average of a thousand persons. The tourists derived from all over the Middle East and also from eastern Europe. There were few visitors from western Europe, and practically none from neighboring Israel. The tourists would arrive in air-conditioned buses from Sharm al-Shaikh or Cairo, spend two to three hours on a guided tour of the monastery, and continue on their way. In the hope of profiting from the brisk tourist traffic, several three-star hotels affiliated with Egyptian hotel chains had sprung up in the town. The monks too had upgraded their spartan guesthouse into a hotel, and local Bedouin had set up half a dozen guesthouses. Most of these enterprises, however, were not flourishing. They picked up the crumbs of the tourist traffic and catered to the few backpackers who wished to stay on in Santa Katarina or explore the mountains.

The drug trade had resumed in a big way; it was perhaps responsible for the obvious prosperity of some of the townspeople and the seeming lack of employment of others. Hashish still appeared to be the staple drug used by Egyptians, but hotel guests in Sinai seemed to require other drugs as well.

In such prosperous times the Bedouin's arrangements for mutual security could be expected to lose their importance. Indeed, many people told me that the Bedouin no longer kept flocks of goats and that their orchards in the mountains had dried up. Perhaps the flocks had declined; they had been very small anyway. Yet every Bedouin I asked about the state of the orchards said that although others were neglecting theirs, he was taking care of his own and would never abandon them (see also Gilbert 2010). Evidently, they expected further economic and political upheavals.

As Bedouin men now remained at home, women had lost much of their previous independence. They no longer controlled the purse strings, and spent less time working in the orchards. This change was reflected in the way they dressed: in public they still wore black dresses that enveloped their bodies, and hid the colorful dresses they wore underneath. Most women had ceased to wear the red veils ornamented with jingling coins, and instead wore dark plain shawls that completely covered their hair and most of their face. The celebrated "horned" hairdo had gone. According to some women, Islamic dignitaries had forbidden it, but perhaps it was due to the women's loss of control of the family purse.

The tribal pilgrimages had been discontinued and personal pilgrimages to saints' tombs too seemed to have become less frequent. The saints' tombs, however, were kept in a good state of repair. Perhaps the Bedouin expected that tribal pilgrimages would resume sooner or later. Apparently the Bedouin were no longer secure in the ownership of the land, for the cemeteries of each descent group were now surrounded by stone walls, and the tombs carried inscriptions with the name and date of death of the deceased man or woman.

Does this mean that my ethnography is outdated? While I readily admit that it is not an up-to-date account of the Bedouin of Mount Sinai, I would claim that my story already contains the possibilities of later developments. The changes I observed in 2009 have already been superseded by radical new developments. The Bedouin are quite clear that their lives are an endless series of adaptations to rapidly changing conditions, and that they must therefore invest great effort in maintaining a complex system of social assurance.

References

Abu-Lughod, Lila. 1986. *Veiled Sentiments: Honor and Poetry in a Bedouin Society*. Berkeley: University of California Press.

———. 1993. *Writing Women's Worlds: Bedouin Stories*. Berkeley: University of California Press.

Abu-Rabi'a, Aref. 1994. *The Negev Bedouin and Livestock Rearing: Social, Economic and Political Aspects*. Oxford: Berg.

———. 2001. *Bedouin Century: Education and Development among the Negev Tribes in the Twentieth Century*. New York: Berghahn Books.

Ahmed Mohammed 'Abdullahi. 1990. *Pastoral Production Systems in Africa: A Study of Nomadic Household Economy and Livestock Marketing in Central Somalia*. Kiel, Germany: Vauk.

Albergoni, Gianni. 1990. "Les Bédouins et les échanges: La piste introuvable." *Cahiers des Sciences Humaines* 26, no. 1–2: 195–215.

Algazi, Gadi. 2006. "Matrix bebil'in: Sippur 'al kapitalizm koloniali biysra'el shel yameinu" [Matrix in Bil'in: A Story of Colonial Capitalism in Contemporary Israel]. *Theory and Criticism* 29: 173–91.

Aljazeera TV. 2006, 5 June. "Egypt Arrests Two Bombing Suspects." www.aljazeera.net.

———. 2006, 4 October. "Egypt Busts Arms Ring." www.aljazeera.net.

Altorki, Soraya, and Donald P. Cole. 1989. *Arabian Oasis City: The Transformation of Unaizah*. Austin: University of Texas Press.

'Arif, 'Arif al-. 1934. *Ta'rikh bir al-sab' wa-qabailiha* [The History of Beersheva and its Tribes]. Jerusalem: Bait al-Maqdis.

Asad, Talal. 1970. *The Kababish Arabs: Power, Authority and Consent in a Nomadic Tribe*. London: Hurst.

———. 1979. "Equality in Nomadic Social Systems? Notes towards the Dissolution of an Anthropological Category." In *Pastoral Production and Society*, ed. L'Equipe Écologie et Anthropologie des Sociétés Pastorales, 419–28. Cambridge: Cambridge University Press; Paris: Editions de la Maison des Sciences de l'Homme.

Aswad, Barbara C. 1971. *Property Control and Social Strategies in Settlers in a Middle Eastern Plain*. Museum of Anthropology, Anthropological Paper 44. Ann Arbor: University of Michigan.

Aswany, Alaa al-. 2004. *The Yacoubian Building*. Trans. Humphrey Davies. Cairo: American University in Cairo Press.

Aziz, Heba. 1995. "Understanding Attacks on Tourists in Egypt." *Tourism Management* 16, no. 2: 91–95.

———. 2000. "Employment in a Bedouin Community: The Case of the Town of Dahab in South Sinai." *Nomadic Peoples* 4, no. 2: 28–47.

Bailey, Clinton. 1985. "Dating the Arrival of the Bedouin Tribes in Sinai and the Negev." *Journal of the Economic and Social History of the Orient* 28: 20–49.

———. 1991. *Bedouin Poetry from Sinai and the Negev*. Oxford: Clarendon Press.

———. 2009. *Bedouin Law from Sinai and the Negev: Justice Without Government*. New Haven, CT: Yale University Press.

Bandman, Yona. 1987. "Hatzi-ha'i sinai batefisa ha'istrategit shel mitzrayim 1949–1967" [Sinai: The Egyptian Strategic Viewpoint 1949–1967]. In *Sinai*, ed. Gdaliahu Gvirtzman and Avshalom Shmueli, 941–60. Tel Aviv: Ministry of Defence.

Barfield, Thomas J. 1993. *The Nomadic Alternative*. Englewood Cliffs, NJ: Prentice Hall.

Barth, Fredrik. 1961. *Nomads of South Persia: The Basseri Tribe of the Khamseh Confederacy*. Oslo: Oslo University Press.

Bartheel, Carla. 1943. *Unter Sinai-Beduinen und Mönchen: Eine Reise*. Berlin: Limpert.

Bar-Zvi, Sasson, Aref Abu-Rabi'a, and Gideon M. Kressel. 1998. *Qesem haqevarim: minhagei avelut upulhan tsadiqim beqerev beduei hanegev* [The Charm of Graves: Mourning Rituals and Tomb Worshipping among the Negev Bedouin]. Tel Aviv: Ministry of Defence and Blaustein Institute for Desert Research, Ben-Gurion University.

Bates, Daniel G. 1973. *Nomads and Farmers: A Study of the Yörük of Southeastern Turkey*. Museum of Anthropology, Anthropological Papers 52. Ann Arbor: University of Michigan.

Bauman, Zygmunt. 1995. *Life in Fragments: Essays in Postmodern Morality*. Oxford: Blackwell.

———. 2000. *Modernity and the Holocaust*. Ithaca, NY: Cornell University Press.

Bax, Mart. 1995. *Medjugorje: Religion, Politics, and Violence in Rural Bosnia*. Amsterdam: VU University Press.

Beck, Lois. 1986. *The Qashqa'i of Iran.* New Haven, CT: Yale University Press.

———. 1991. *Nomad: A Year in the Life of a Qashqa'i Tribesman in Iran.* London: Tauris.

Befu, Harumi, and Leonard Plotnicov. 1962. "Types of Corporate Unilineal Descent Groups." *American Anthropologist* 64, no. 2: 313–27.

Bell, Gertrude L. 1907. *The Desert and the Sown.* London: Heinemann.

Bencherifa, Abdellatif, and Douglas L. Johnson. 1990. "Adaptation and Intensification in the Pastoral Systems of Morocco." In *The World of Pastoralism: Herding Systems in Comparative Perspective,* ed. John G. Galaty and Douglas L. Johnson, 394–416. New York: Guildford Press.

Ben-David, Joseph. 1981. *Jebaliya: Shevet bedui betsel haminzar* [Jebaliya: A Bedouin Tribe in the Shadow of the Monastery]. Jerusalem: Kanna.

Ben-Porath, Yoram, and Emanuel Marx. 1971. *Some Sociological and Economic Aspects of Refugee Camps on the West Bank.* Santa Monica, CA: Rand.

Berland, Joseph C., and Aparna Rao, eds. 2004. *Customary Strangers: New Perspectives on Peripatetic Peoples in the Middle East, Africa, and Asia.* Westport, CT: Praeger.

Berque, Jaques. 1955. *Structures sociales du Haut-Atlas.* Paris: Presses Universitaires de France.

Birks, J. Stace, and S. E. Letts. 1977. "Diqal and Muqayda: Dying Oases in Arabia." *Tijdschrift voor Economische en Sociale Geografie* 68: 143–51.

Black-Michaud, Jacob. 1986. *Sheep and Land: The Economics of Power in a Tribal Society.* Cambridge: Cambridge University Press.

Bocco, Riccardo. 2000. "International Organisations and the Settlement of Nomads in the Arab Middle East, 1950-1990." In *The Transformation of Nomadic Society in the Arab East,* ed. Martha Mundy and Basim Musallam, 197–217. Cambridge: Cambridge University Press.

Bodemann, Y. Michal. 1998. "Von Berlin nach Chicago und weiter: Georg Simmel und die Reise seines 'Fremden.'" *Berliner Journal für Soziologie* 1: 125–42.

Boucheman, Albert de. 1935. *Matériel de la vie bédouine recueilli dans le désert de Syrie.* Damascus: Institut Français de Damas.

———. 1939. *Une petite cité caravanière: Suhné.* Damascus: Institute Français de Damas.

Bovenkerk, Frank. 2004. "The Dark Side of Dutch Drug Policy or the Failure of Half-way Legalization." In *Global Drug Policy: Building a New Framework,* 161–64. Paris: Senlis Council.

Bradburd, Daniel. 1994. "Historical Bases of the Political Economy of Kermani Pastoralists: Tribe and World Markets in the Nineteenth and

Early Twentieth Centuries." In *Pastoralists at the Periphery: Herders in a Capitalist World*, ed. Claudia Chang and Harold A. Koster, 42–61. Tucson: University of Arizona Press.

Brown, Montague. 1938. "Agriculture." In *Economic Organization of Palestine*, ed. Sa'id B. Himadeh, 109–211. Beirut: American Press.

Bruun, Ole. 2006. *Precious Steppe: Mongolian Nomadic Pastoralists in Pursuit of the Market*. Lanham, MD: Lexington Books.

Buchler, Ira R., and Henry A. Selby. 1968. *Kinship and Social Organization: An Introduction to Theory and Method*. New York: Macmillan.

Burawoy, Michael. 1975. "The Functions and Reproduction of Migrant Labor: Comparative Material from Southern Africa and the United States." *American Journal of Sociology* 81: 1050–87.

Burckhardt, Johann Ludwig. [1822] 1992. *Travels in Syria and the Holy Land*. London: Darf.

Canaan, Tewfik. 1927. *Mohammedan Saints and Sanctuaries in Palestine*. London: Luzac.

Caskel, Werner. 1954. "The Bedouinization of Arabia." In *Studies in Islamic Cultural History*, ed. Gustave E. von Grunebaum, 36–46. Memoir 76. Menasha, WI: American Anthropological Association.

Chatty, Dawn. 1980. "The Pastoral Family and the Truck." In *When Nomads Settle*, ed. Philip Carl Salzman, 80–94. New York: Bergin.

———. 1996. *Mobile Pastoralists: Development Planning and Social Change in Oman*. New York: Columbia University Press.

Christian, William A. 1972. *Person and God in a Spanish Valley*. New York: Seminar Press.

Claudot-Hawad, Hélène. 2006. "A Nomadic Fight Against Immobility: The Tuareg in the Modern State." In *Nomadic Societies in the Middle East and North Africa: Entering the 21st Century*, ed. Dawn Chatty, 654–81. Leiden, the Netherlands: Brill.

Cole, Donald P. 1975. *Nomads of the Nomads: The Āl Murrah Bedouin of the Empty Quarter*. Arlington Heights, IL: AHM Publishing.

Colonna, Fanny. 1980. "Saints furieux et saints studieux ou, dans l'Aurès, comment la religion vient aux tribus." *Annales ESC* 35, no. 3–4: 642–61.

Coon, Carleton S. 1960. "Badw." In *Encyclopaedia of Islam*. New ed. 1: 872–74. Leiden, the Netherlands: Brill.

Cunnison, Ian. 1966. *Baggara Arabs: Power and the Lineage in a Sudanese Nomad Tribe*. Oxford: Clarendon Press.

Cytryn-Silverman, Katia. 2001. "The Settlement in Northern Sinai during the Islamic Period." In *Le Sinaï de la conquête arabe á nos jours*, ed. Jean-Michel Mouton, 3–36. Cahier des Annales Islamologiques 21. Cairo: Institut Français d'Archéologie Orientale.

Dahl, Gudrun, and Anders Hjort. 1976. *Having Herds: Pastoral Herd Growth and Household Economy.* Stockholm: University of Stockholm.

Dahlberg, Andrea. 1991. "The Body as a Principle of Holism: Three Pilgrimages to Lourdes." In *Contesting the Sacred: The Anthropology of Christian Pilgrimage,* ed. John Eade and Michael J. Sallnow, 30–50. London: Routledge.

Danin, Avinoam. 1983. *Desert Vegetation of Israel and Sinai.* Jerusalem: Cana.

Davis, John. 1987. *Libyan Politics: Tribe and Revolution.* London: Tauris.

Deluz, Christiane. 2001. "Bédouins et pèlerins d'Occident au Sinaï, une difficile rencontre." In *Le Sinaï de la conquête arabe à nos jours,* ed. Jean-Michel Mouton, 183–96. Cahier des Annales Islamologiques 21. Cairo: Institut Français d'Archéologie Orientale.

Dickson, Harold R. P. 1951. *The Arab of the Desert.* London: Allen and Unwin.

Dietz, Ton, Abdirizak Arale Nunow, Adano W. Roba, and Fred Zaal. 2001. "Pastoral Commercialization: On Caloric Terms of Trade and Related Issues." In *African Pastoralism: Conflict, Institutions and Government,* ed. M. A. Mohamed Salih, Ton Dietz, and Abdel Ghaffar M. Ahmed, 194–234. London: Pluto Press.

Doughty, Charles M. [1888] 1937. *Travels in Arabia Deserta.* New York: Random House.

Dumreicher, André von. 1931. *Trackers and Smugglers in the Deserts of Egypt.* London: Methuen.

Eades, Jeremy, ed. 1987. *Migrants, Workers, and the Social Order.* ASA Monograph 26. London: Tavistock.

Eckenstein, Lina. 1921. *A History of Sinai.* London: Society for Promoting Christian Knowledge.

Eickelman, Dale F. 1976. *Moroccan Islam: Tradition and Society in a Pilgrimage Center.* Austin: University of Texas Press.

———. 1989. *The Middle East: An Anthropological Approach.* 2nd ed. Englewood Cliffs, NJ: Prentice Hall.

Eph'al, Israel. 1982. *The Ancient Arabs: Nomads on the Borders of the Fertile Crescent 9th to 5th Centuries B.C.* Jerusalem: Magnes Press; Leiden, the Netherlands: Brill.

Ernst, Hans. 1960. *Die mamlukischen Sultansurkunden des Sinai-Klosters.* Wiesbaden, Germany: Harrassowitz.

Éthérie [Egeria]. [385] 1957. *Journal de voyage.* Trans. and ed. Hélène Pétré. Sources Chrétiennes 21. Paris: Edition du Cerf.

Eutychius Alexandrinus [Sa'id ibn Batriq]. 1985. *Das Annalenwerk des Eutychios von Alexandrien.* Trans. Michael Breydy. Louvain, Belgium: Peeters. Originally written circa 935.

Evans-Pritchard, Edward E. 1940. *The Nuer: A Description of the Modes of Livelihood and Political Institutions of a Nilotic People.* Oxford: Clarendon Press.

———. 1949. *The Sanusi of Cyrenaica.* Oxford: Clarendon Press.

Fabietti, Ugo. 1984. *Il popolo del deserto: I Beduini Shammar del Gran Nefud Arabia Saudita.* Bari, Italy: Laterza.

———. 2000. "State Policies and Bedouin Adaptations in Saudi Arabia, 1900–1980." In *The Transformation of Nomadic Society in the Arab East,* ed. Martha Mundy and Basim Musallam, 82–89. Cambridge: Cambridge University Press.

Ferdinand, Klaus. 1962. "Nomad Expansion and Commerce in Central Afghanistan." *Folk* 4: 123–59.

Finkelstein, Israel, and Avi Perevolotsky. 1989. "Hitnahalut wehitnavdut bemidbariot hadarom bitekufot kedumot" [Sedentarization and Nomadization in the Southern Deserts in Early Times]. *Kathedra* 52: 3–36.

Food and Agriculture Organization (FAO). 2004. *Faostat Agricultural Data.* Faostat.fao.org/faostat.

Fortes, Meyer. 1945. *The Dynamics of Clanship among the Tallensi.* London: Oxford University Press for the International African Institute.

———. 1970. *Kinship and the Social Order: The Legacy of Lewis Henry Morgan.* London: Routledge and Kegan Paul.

Fournier, Guillaume. 2002. *Global Drug Policy: A Historical Perspective.* Paris: Senlis Council.

Fried, Morton H. 1957. "The Classification of Corporate Unilineal Descent Groups." *Journal of the Royal Anthropological Institute* 87, no. 1: 1–29.

———. 1975. "The Myth of Tribe." *Natural History* 84, no. 4: 12–20.

Galvin, Kathleen. 1985. *Diet and Nutrition of Turkana Pastoralists in a Social and Ecological Context.* PhD thesis, SUNY Binghamton.

Ganor, Eliezer, R. Markovitz, J. Kessler, and N. Roznan. 1973. *Aklim Sinai* [The Climate of Sinai]. Beth Dagon: Israel Meteorological Service.

Gardet, Louis. 1965. "Din." In *Encyclopaedia of Islam.* New ed., 2: 293–96. Leiden, the Netherlands: Brill.

Gardner, Ann L. 1994. *Women and Changing Relations in a South Sinai Bedouin Community.* PhD thesis, University of Texas.

Gardner, Ann, and Emanuel Marx. 2000. "Employment and Unemployment among Bedouin." *Nomadic Peoples* 4, no. 2: 21–27.

Geertz, Clifford. 1966. "Religion as a Cultural System." In *Anthropological Approaches to the Study of Religion,* ed. Michael Banton, 1–46. ASA Monograph 3. London: Tavistock.

———. 1968. *Islam Observed: Religious Development in Morocco and Indonesia.* Chicago: University of Chicago Press.

Gellner, Ernest. 1969. *Saints of the Atlas*. London: Weidenfeld and Nicolson.

———. 1973. "Political and Religious Organization of the Berbers of the Central High Atlas." In *Arabs and Berbers: From Tribe to Nation in North Africa*, ed. Ernest Gellner and Charles Micaud, 59–66. London: Duckworth.

Geshekter, Charles. 2001. "The Search for Peaceful Development in a Century of War: Global Restraints on 20th Century Somali Socio-Economic Development." In *What Are Somalia's Development Perspectives? Science between Resignation and Hope?* ed. Jörg Janzen, 9–34. Berlin: Das Arabische Buch.

Gilbert, Hilary C. 2010. *"Everything has its Price": Conservation, Development and Bedu in St. Katherine, South Sinai*. PhD thesis, University of Manchester.

Ginat, Joseph. 1987. *Blood Disputes among Bedouin and Rural Arabs in Israel*. Pittsburgh, PA: University of Pittsburgh Press.

Glassner, Martin I. 1974. "The Bedouin of Southern Sinai under Israeli Administration." *Geographical Review* 64: 31–60.

Gluckman, Max. 1958. "Foreword." In *Tribal Cohesion in a Money Economy*, William Watson, v–xvi. Manchester: Manchester University Press.

Goldziher, Ignaz. 1967. "On the Veneration of the Dead in Paganism and Islam." In *Muslim Studies*, 1: 209–38. London: Allen and Unwin. Article first published in 1884.

———. 1971. "Veneration of Saints in Islam." In *Muslim Studies*, 2: 255–341. London: Allen and Unwin. Article first published in 1890.

Gottwald, Norman K. 1979. *The Tribes of Yahweh*. Maryknoll, NY: Orbis.

Greenwood, Ned H. 1997. *The Sinai: A Physical Geography*. Austin: University of Texas Press.

Grunebaum, Gustave E. von. 1951. *Muhammedan Festivals*. New York: Schuman.

Hamdan, Jamal. 1993. *Sina fil-'istratijia wal-siyasa wal-jighrafiya* [Sinai in Strategy, Politics and Geography]. Cairo: Madbuli.

Hammoudi, Abdellah. 2006. *A Season in Mecca: Narrative of a Pilgrimage*. New York: Hill and Wang.

Harries-Jones, Peter. 1969. "'Home-boy' Ties and Political Organization in a Copperbelt Township." In *Social Networks in Urban Situations*, ed. J. Clyde Mitchell, 297–347. Manchester: Manchester University Press.

Hayden, Brian, and Aubrey Cannon. 1982. "The Corporate Group as an Archaeological Unit." *Journal of Anthropological Archaeology* 1, no. 2: 132–58.

Henein, Nessim Henry. 1988. *Mārī Girgis: Village de Haute-Égypte*. Cairo: Institut Français d'Archéologie Orientale.

Henninger, Joseph. 1955. "Ist der sogenannte Nilus-Bericht eine brauch-
bare religionsgeschichtliche Quelle?" *Anthropos* 50: 81–148.

Herodotus. 1947. *The History of Herodotus*. Trans. George Rawlinson. New
York: Tudor. First published in 447 BCE.

Herskovits, Melville J. 1926. "The Cattle Complex in East Africa." *American Anthropologist* 28: 230–72, 361–88, 494–528.

Hobbs, Joseph J. 1989. *Bedouin Life in the Egyptian Wilderness*. Austin: University of Texas Press.

———. 1995. *Mount Sinai*. Austin: University of Texas Press.

———. 2001. "The Sinai Bedouin at the Dawn of the Twenty-first Century." In *Le Sinaï de la conquête arabe à nos jours*, ed. Jean-Michel Mouton, 207–13. Cairo: Institut Français d'Archéologie Orientale.

Holes, Clive, and Said Salman Abu Athera. 2009. *Poetry and Politics in Contemporary Bedouin Society*. Cairo: American University in Cairo Press.

Humbsch, Robert. 1976. *Beiträge zur Geschichte des osmanischen Ägyp-
tens nach arabischen Sultans- und Statthalterurkunden des Sinai-Klosters*.
Freiburg, Germany: Schwarz.

Hussein, Nashaat Hassan. 1990. *The Sub-culture of Hashish Users in Egypt:
A Descriptive Analytic Study*. Cairo Papers in Social Science 13, no. 2.
Cairo: American University in Cairo Press.

Ibrahim, Saad Eddin. 1980. "Anatomy of Egypt's Militant Islamic Groups:
Methodological Note and Preliminary Findings." *International Journal
of Middle East Studies* 12, no. 4: 423–53.

Israel, Army. 1962. *Beduei sinai* [The Bedouin of Sinai]. Israel: Army,
Southern Command.

Jakubowska, Longina. 1992. "Resisting 'Ethnicity': The Israeli State and
Bedouin Identity." In *The Paths to Domination, Resistance, and Terror*, ed.
Carolyn Nordstrom and JoAnn Martin, 85–105. Berkeley: University
of California Press.

Janzen, Jörg. 1980. *Die Nomaden Dhofars/ Sultanat Oman: Traditionelle Le-
bensformen im Wandel*. Bamberg, Germany: Fach Geographie an der
Universität Bamberg.

Jarvis, Claude S. 1931. *Yesterday and To-day in Sinai*. Edinburgh, UK:
Blackwood.

Johnson, Douglas L. 1969. *The Nature of Nomadism: A Comparative Study of
Pastoral Migrations in Southwestern Asia and Northern Africa*. Chicago:
University of Chicago Press.

Kandiyoti, Deniz. 2002. "Post-Colonialism Compared: Potentials and
Limitations in the Middle East and Central Asia." *International Journal
of Middle East Studies* 34, no. 2: 279–97.

Kapara, Yohanan. 1975. "Ziarat Sheikh Abu Taleb" [The Pilgrimage to
Abu Taleb Shrine]. *Teva' Waarets* 17: 192–94.

Katz, Sha'ul. 1983. "Ginot meromei sinai" [Orchards in the High Mountains of Sinai]. *Nofim* 17: 5–54.

Kavoori, Purnendu S. 1999. *Pastoralism in Expansion: The Transhuming Herders of Western Rajasthan*. New Delhi: Oxford University Press.

Keller, Adolf. 1900. *Eine Sinai-Fahrt*. Frauenfeld, Switzerland: Huber.

Kershaw, Sarah. 2006. "Tribal Underworld." *New York Times*, 19–20 February.

Kerven, Carol. 1992. *Customary Commerce: A Historical Reassessment of Pastoral Livestock Marketing in Africa*. London: Overseas Development Institute.

Khazanov, Anatoly M. 1984. *Nomads and the Outside World*. Cambridge: Cambridge University Press.

Khoury, Philip S., and Joseph Kostiner, eds. 1991. *Tribes and State Formation in the Middle East*. London: Tauris.

Kilani, Mondher. 1992. *La construction de la mémoire: Le lignage et la sainteté dans l'oasis d'El Ksar*. Geneva: Labor et Fides.

Kister, Meir J. 1991. "Makam Ibrahim." In *Encyclopaedia of Islam*. New ed., 6: 104–7. Leiden, the Netherlands: Brill.

Kliot, Nurit, and Shemuel Albeck. 1996. *Sinai—anatomia shel preida* [Sinai—Anatomy of an Evacuation]. Tel Aviv: Ministry of Defence.

Kressel, Gideon M. 1982. *Rivei-dam beqerev beduim 'ironiim* [Blood Feuds among Urban Bedouin]. Jerusalem: Magnes Press.

Labib, Mahfouz. 1961. *Pèlerins et voyageurs au Mont Sinaï*. Cairo: Institut Français d'Archèologie Orientale du Caire.

Lancaster, William. 1981. *The Rwala Bedouin Today*. Cambridge: Cambridge University Press.

———. 1997. *The Rwala Bedouin Today*. 2nd ed. Long Grove, IL: Waveland Press.

Lancaster, William, and Fidelity Lancaster. 1987. "The Function of Peripatetics in Rwala Bedouin Society." In *The Other Nomads: Peripatetic Minorities in Cross-Cultural Perspective*, ed. Aparna Rao, 311–22. Cologne: Böhlau.

Landau-Tasseron, Ella. 1997. "Unearthing a Pre-Islamic Arabian Prophet." *Jerusalem Studies in Arabic and Islam* 21: 42–61.

Lane, Edward William. 1895. *An Account of the Manners and Customs of the Modern Egyptians*. London: Gardner. First published in 1836.

Lange, Katharina. 2003. "Zwischen den Kategorien—Nomaden, Halbsesshafte, Sesshafte? Das Beispiel der Welde." *Orientwissenschaftliche Hefte* 9: 253–87.

Lavie, Smadar. 1990. *The Poetics of Military Occupation: Mzeina Allegories of Bedouin Identity under Israeli and Egyptian Rule*. Berkeley: University of California Press.

Lazarus-Jaffé, Hava. 1976. "The Religious Problem of the Islamic Pilgrimage: The Islamization of Ancient Rituals." *Proceedings of the Israel Academy of Sciences and Humanities* 5, no. 11: 1–22.

Leder, Stefan, and Bernhard Streck, eds. 2005. *Shifts and Drifts in Nomadic-Sedentary Relations.* Wiesbaden, Germany: Ludwig Reichert.

Levey, Martin. 1971. "Hashish." In *Encyclopaedia of Islam.* New ed., 3: 266–67. Leiden, the Netherlands: Brill.

Levi, Shabetai. 1980. *Emuna vepulhan shel habeduim biderom sinai* [Belief and Cult of the Bedouin in South Sinai]. Tel Aviv: Society for Nature Protection, David Cliffs Field School.

———. 1987. *Habeduim bemidbar sinai* [The Bedouin in the Sinai Desert]. Tel Aviv: Schocken.

Levy, Reuben. 1962. *The Social Structure of Islam.* Cambridge: Cambridge University Press.

Lewis, Norman N. 1987. *Nomads and Settlers in Syria and Jordan, 1800–1980.* Cambridge: Cambridge University Press.

———. 2000. "The Syrian Steppe during the Last Century of Ottoman Rule: Hawran and the Palmyrena." In *The Transformation of Nomadic Society in the Arab East,* ed. Martha Mundy and Basim Musallam, 33–43. Cambridge: Cambridge University Press.

Lida, Ofra. 1979. *Degem shimushei hakarka' shel habeduim betarfat al-qadren* [Patterns of Land Use by Bedouin in Tarfat Qadren]. Seminar paper, Ben-Gurion University.

Linant de Bellefonds, Yvon. 1978. "Kabr." In *Encyclopaedia of Islam.* New ed., 4: 354–55. Leiden, the Netherlands: Brill.

Lindner, Rudi Paul. 1982. "What Was a Nomadic Tribe?" *Comparative Studies in Society and History* 24, no. 4: 689–711.

Lipman, Jonathan N. 1997. *Familiar Strangers: A History of Muslims in Northwest China.* Seattle: University of Washington Press.

Little, Peter D. 2003. *Somalia: Economy without State.* Bloomington: Indiana University Press.

Lofland, Lyn. 1973. *A World of Strangers: Order and Action in Urban Public Space.* New York: Basic Books.

Macleod, Arlene Elowe. 1992. *Accomodating Protest: Working Women, the New Veiling, and Change in Cairo.* Cairo: American University in Cairo Press.

Mafeje, Archie. 1975. "Religion, Class, and Ideology in South Africa." In *Religion and Social Change in Southern Africa: Anthropological Essays in Honour of Monica Wilson,* ed. Michael G. Whisson and Martin West, 164–84. Cape Town: David Philip.

Maine, Henry. [1861] 1917. *Ancient Law.* London: Dent.

Marx, Emanuel. 1967. *Bedouin of the Negev.* Manchester: Manchester University Press.

―――. 1977a. "Communal and Individual Pilgrimage: The Region of Saints' Tombs in South Sinai." In *Regional Cults,* ed. Richard P. Werbner, 29–51. ASA Monograph 16. London: Academic Press.

―――. 1977b. "The Tribe as a Unit of Subsistence." *American Anthropologist* 79, no. 2: 343–63.

―――. 1980. "Wage Labor and Tribal Economy of the Bedouin in South Sinai." In *When Nomads Settle,* ed. Philip C. Salzman, 111–23. New York: Bergin.

―――. 1984. "Changing Employment Patterns of Bedouin in South Sinai." In *The Changing Bedouin,* ed. Emanuel Marx and Avshalom Shmueli, 173–86. New Brunswick, NJ: Transaction.

―――. 1985. "Tribal Pilgrimages to Saints' Tombs in South Sinai." In *Islamic Dilemmas: Reformers, Nationalists and Industrialization,* ed. Ernest Gellner, 104–31. Berlin: Mouton.

―――. 1987. "Labour Migrants with a Secure Base: Bedouin of South Sinai." In *Migrants, Workers, and the Social Order,* ed. Jeremy Eades, 148–64. ASA Monograph 26. London: Tavistock.

―――. 1990. "The Social World of Refugees: A Conceptual Framework." *Journal of Refugee Studies* 3, no. 3: 189–203.

―――. 1992. "Are There Pastoral Nomads in the Middle East?" In *Pastoralism in the Levant: Archaeological Materials in Anthropological Perspectives,* ed. Ofer Bar-Yosef and Anatoly M. Khazanov, 255–60. Madison, WI: Prehistory Press.

―――. 1996. "Are There Pastoral Nomads in the Arab Middle East?" In *The Anthropology of Tribal and Peasant Pastoral Societies: The Dialectics of Social Cohesion and Fragmentation,* ed. Ugo Fabietti and Philip C. Salzman, 101–15. Pavia, Italy: Collegio Ghislieri; Como, Italy: Ibis.

―――. 1999. "Oases in South Sinai." *Human Ecology* 27, no. 2: 341–57.

―――. 2004a. "Bands and Other Corporate Hominid Groups in Acheulian Culture." In *Human Paleoecology in the Levantine Corridor,* ed. Naama Goren-Inbar and John D. Speth, 89–104. Oxford: Oxbow.

―――. 2004b. "Roving Traders among the Bedouin of South Sinai." In *Customary Strangers: New Perspectives on Peripatetic Peoples in the Middle East, Africa, and Asia,* ed. Joseph C. Berland and Aparna Rao, 57–69. Westport, CT: Praeger.

―――. 2004c. *The Social Context of Violent Behaviour: A Social Anthropological Study in an Israeli Immigrant Town.* London: Routledge. First published in 1976.

―――. 2005a. "The Bedouin's Lifeline: Roving Traders in South Sinai." In *Social Critique and Commitment: Essays in Honor of Henry Rosenfeld,* ed. Majid Al-Haj, Michael Saltman and Zvi Sobel, 193–206. Lanham, MD: University Press of America.

——. 2005b. "Nomads and Cities: The Development of a Conception." In *Shifts and Drifts in Nomadic-Sedentary Relations*, ed. Stefan Leder and Bernhard Streck, 3–15. Wiesbaden, Germany: Ludwig Reichert.

——. 2006a. "The Political Economy of Middle Eastern and North African Pastoral Nomads." In *Nomadic Societies in the Middle East and North Africa: Entering the 21st Century*, ed. Dawn Chatty, 78–97. Leiden, the Netherlands: Brill.

——. 2006b. "Tribal Pilgrimages to Saints' Tombs in South Sinai." In *Archaeology, Anthropology and Cult: The Sanctuary at Gilat, Israel*, ed. Thomas E. Levy, 54–74. London: Equinox.

——. 2008. "Hashish Smuggling by Bedouin in South Sinai." In *Organized Crime: Culture, Markets and Policies*, ed. Dina Siegel and Hans Nelen, 29–40. New York: Springer.

Matthews, Victor H. 1978. *Pastoral Nomadism in the Mari Kingdom, ca. 1830–1760 B.C.* Dissertation Series 3. Cambridge, MA: American Schools of Oriental Research.

Mayer, Philip. 1963. *Townsmen or Tribesmen.* Cape Town: Oxford University Press.

McCabe, J. Terrence. 1994. "The Failure to Encapsulate: Resistance to the Penetration of Capitalism by the Turkana of Kenya." In *Pastoralists at the Periphery: Herders in a Capitalist World*, ed. Claudia Chang and Harold A. Koster, 197–211. Tucson: University of Arizona Press.

——. 2004. *Cattle Bring Us to Our Enemies: Turkana Ecology, Politics, and Raiding in a Disequilibrium System.* Ann Arbor: University of Michigan Press.

Meillassoux, Claude. 1972. "From Reproduction to Production." *Economy and Society* 1, no. 1: 93–105.

——. 1981. *Maidens, Meal and Money: Capitalism and the Domestic Community.* Cambridge: Cambridge University Press.

Meri, Josef W. 1999. "The Etiquette of Devotion in the Islamic Cult of Saints." In *The Cult of Saints in Late Antiquity and the Middle Ages: Essays on the Contribution of Peter Brown*, ed. James Howard-Johnston and Paul A. Hayward, 263–86. Oxford: Oxford University Press.

Meshel, Zeev. 1971. *Derom sinai* [South Sinai]. Jerusalem: SH.H.L.Y.

Mitchell, J. Clyde. 1956. *The Kalela Dance.* Manchester: Manchester University Press.

Montagne, Robert. 1947. *La civilisation du désert: Nomades d'Orient et d'Afrique.* Paris: Hachette.

Moore, Sally F. 1978. *Law as Process: An Anthropological Approach.* London: Routledge and Kegan Paul.

Mouton, Jean-Michel. 2000. *Le Sinaï médiéval: Un espace stratégique de l'Islam.* Paris: Presses Universitaires de France.

Mouton, Jean-Michel, ed. 2001. *Le Sinaï de la conquête arabe à nos jours.* Cahier des Annales Islamologiques 21. Cairo: Institut Français d'Archéologie Orientale.

Murray, George W. 1935. *Sons of Ishmael: A Study of the Egyptian Bedouin.* London: Routledge.

Musil, Alois. 1927. *Arabia Deserta.* New York: American Geographical Society.

———. 1928. *The Manners and Customs of the Rwala Bedouins.* New York: American Geographical Society.

Nandris, John G. 1990. "The Jebaliyeh of Mount Sinai, and the Land of Vlah." *Quaderni di Studi Arabi* 8: 45–90.

Nassar, Heba. 2008. *Temporary and Circular Migration: The Egyptian Case.* CARIM Analytic and Synthetic Notes 2008/09. San Domenico di Fiesole, Italy: European University Institute.

Niebuhr, Carsten. [1774–78] 1968. *Reisebeschreibung nach Arabien und andern umliegenden Ländern.* 3 vols. Graz, Austria: Akademische Druck- und Verlagsanstalt.

———. 1799. *Travels Through Arabia and Other Countries in the East.* 2 vols. Perth, Scotland: Morison.

Nir, Yaacov. 1987. "Shivtei habeduim biderom sinai—mivnam hahevrati-mishpahti" [The Social and Family Structure of the Bedouin Tribes in South Sinai]. In *Sinai,* ed. Gdaliahu Gvirtzman and Avshalom Shmueli, 2: 807–17. Tel Aviv: Ministry of Defence.

Nordstrom, Carolyn. 2007. *Global Outlaws: Crime, Money, and Power in the Contemporary World.* Berkeley: University of California Press.

Palmer, Edward H. 1871. *The Desert of the Exodus.* 2 vols. Cambridge: Deighton, Bell.

Palmer, Henry S. 1906. *Sinai: From the Fourth Egyptian Dynasty to the Present Day.* London: Society for Promoting Christian Knowledge.

Patai, Raphael. 1971. *Society, Culture, and Change in the Middle East.* Philadelphia: University of Pennsylvania Press.

Peletz, Michael G. 1995. "Kinship Studies in Late Twentieth-Century Anthropology." *Annual Review of Anthropology* 24: 343–72.

Perevolotsky, Avi. 1981. "Orchard Agriculture in the High Mountain Regions of Southern Sinai." *Human Ecology* 9, no. 3: 331–57.

———. 1987. "Territoriality and Resource Sharing Among the Bedouin of Southern Sinai: A Socio-Ecological Interpretation." *Journal of Arid Environment* 13: 153–61.

Peters, Emrys L. 1976. "From Particularism to Universalism in the Religion of the Cyrenaica Bedouin." *Bulletin of the British Society for Middle Eastern Studies* 3, no. 1: 5–14.

————. 1990. *The Bedouin of Cyrenaica: Studies in Personal and Corporate Power*, ed. Jack Goody and Emanuel Marx. Cambridge: Cambridge University Press.

Prescott, Hilda F. M. 1957. *Once to Sinai: the Further Pilgrimage of Friar Felix Fabri*. London: Eyre and Spottiswoode.

Procopius Caesariensis. 1954. *Procopius, vol. 7: Buildings*. Trans. H. B. Dewing. London: Heinemann. Originally written circa 555.

Quran. 1955. *The Koran Interpreted*. Trans. Arthur J. Arberry. 2 vols. London: Allen and Unwin.

Ramphele, Mamphela. 1993. *A Bed Called Home: Life in the Migrant Labour Hostels of Cape Town*. Cape Town: David Philip.

Raswan, Carl R. 1936. *The Black Tents of Arabia*. London: Paternoster Library.

Read, Margaret. 1942. "Migrant Labour in Africa and its Effects on Tribal Life." *International Labour Review* 45: 605–31.

Reifenberg, Adolf. 1955. *The Struggle between the Desert and the Sown: Rise and Fall of Agriculture in the Levant*. Jerusalem: Publishing Department of the Jewish Agency.

Richards, Alan, and John Waterbury. 1990. *A Political Economy of the Middle East: State, Class, and Economic Development*. Boulder, CO: Westview.

Robinson, Edward. 1867. *Biblical Researches in Palestine and the Adjacent Regions*. 3 vols. London: Murray.

Rosen, Steven A. 1988. "Finding Evidence of Ancient Nomads." *Biblical Archaeology Review* 14, no. 5: 46–53.

Rosenfeld, Henry. 1965. "The Social Composition of the Military in the Process of State Formation in the Arabian Desert." *Journal of the Royal Anthropological Institute* 95: 75–86, 174–94.

Rosenthal, Franz. 1971. *The Herb: Hashish versus Medieval Muslim Society*. Leiden, the Netherlands: Brill.

Rusch, Walter, and Lothar Stein. 1988. *Siwa und die Aulad Ali*. Berlin: Akademie-Verlag.

Russell Pasha, Thomas. 1949. *Egyptian Service, 1902–1946*. London: Murray.

Salzman, Philip Carl. 1972. "Multi-Resource Nomadism in Iranian Baluchistan." In *Perspectives on Nomadism*, ed. William Irons and Neville Dyson-Hudson, 60–68. Leiden, the Netherlands: Brill.

————. 1980. "Introduction: Processes of Sedentarization as Adaptation and Response." In *When Nomads Settle: Processes of Sedentarization as Adaptation and Response*, ed. Philip Carl Salzman, 1–19. New York: Bergin.

————. 2004. *Pastoralists: Equality, Hierarchy, and the State*. Boulder, CO: Westview.

Sapir, Edward. 1934. "Symbolism." In *Encyclopaedia of the Social Sciences,* 14: 492–95. New York: Macmillan.

Sassen, Saskia. 2003. "Global Cities and Survival Circuits." In *Global Woman: Nannies, Maids, and Sex Workers in the New Economy,* ed. Barbara Ehrenreich and Arlie Russell Hochschild, 254–74. New York: Holt.

Schapera, Isaac. 1947. *Migrant Labour and Tribal Life.* London: Oxford University Press.

Schneider, David M. 1968. *American Kinship: A Cultural Account.* Englewood Cliffs, NJ: Prentice Hall

Schneider, Jane C., and Peter T. Schneider. 2003. *Reversible Destiny: Mafia, Antimafia, and the Struggle for Palermo.* Berkeley: University of California Press.

Scholz, Fred. 1995. *Nomadismus: Theorie und Wandel einer sozio-ökologischen Kulturweise.* Stuttgart, Germany: Steiner.

Schwartz, Sabine. 1986. *Ökonomie des Hungers.* Berlin: Reimer.

Schwarz, Klaus. 1970. *Osmanische Sultansurkunden des Sinai-Klosters in türkischer Sprache.* Freiburg, Germany: Schwarz.

Segev, Tom. 2005. *1967 weha'aretz shinta et paneiha* [Israel in 1967]. Jerusalem: Keter.

Shack, William A., and Elliott P. Skinner, eds. 1979. *Strangers in African Societies.* Berkeley: University of California Press.

Sharp, John. 1987. "Relocation, Labour Migration, and the Domestic Predicament: Qwaqwa in the 1980s." In *Migrants, Workers, and the Social Order,* ed. Jeremy Eades, 130–47. ASA Monograph 26. London: Tavistock.

Shmueli, Avshalom. 1984. "The Desert Frontier in Judea." In *The Changing Bedouin,* ed. Emanuel Marx and Avshalom Shmueli, 17–38. New Brunswick, NJ: Transaction.

Shoup, John. 1990. "Middle Eastern Sheep Pastoralism and the Hima System." In *The World of Pastoralism: Herding Systems in Comparative Perspective,* ed. John G. Galaty and Douglas L. Johnson, 195–215. New York: Guildford Press.

Shuqair, Na'um. 1916. *Ta'rikh sina' al-qadim wal-hadith wa-jighrafiatiha* [The History and Geography of Ancient and Modern Sinai]. Cairo: Al-Ma'arif Press.

Siegel, Dina, Henk van de Bunt, and Damián Zaitch, eds. 2003. *Global Organized Crime: Trends and Developments.* Dordrecht, the Netherlands: Kluwer.

Simmel, Georg. 1950a. "The Metropolis and Mental Life." In *The Sociology of Georg Simmel,* trans. and ed. Kurt H. Wolff, 409–24. New York: Free Press.

———. 1950b. "The Stranger." In *The Sociology of Georg Simmel,* trans. and ed. Kurt H. Wolff, 402–8. New York: Free Press.

Smith, Michael G. 1974. *Corporations and Society.* London: Duckworth.

Smith, W. Robertson. 1894. *Lectures on the Religion of the Semites.* London: Black.

Southall, Aidan. 1961. "Introductory Summary." In *Social Change in Modern Africa,* ed. Aidan Southall. London: Oxford University Press.

Spencer, Paul. 1988. *The Maasai of Matapato: A Study of Rituals of Rebellion.* Manchester: Manchester University Press for the International African Institute.

Sperling, Louise, and John G. Galaty. 1990. "Cattle, Culture, and Economy: Dynamics in East African Pastoralism." In *The World of Pastoralism: Herding Systems in Comparative Perspective,* ed. John G. Galaty and Douglas L. Johnson, 69–98. New York: Guildford Press.

Spiegel, Andrew D. 1980. "Rural Differentiation and the Diffusion of Migrant Labour Remittances in Lesotho." In *Black Villagers in an Industrial Society: Anthropological Perspectives on Labour Migration in South Africa,* ed. Philip Mayer, 109–68. Cape Town: Oxford University Press.

Spooner, Brian. 1973. *The Cultural Ecology of Pastoral Nomadism.* Module in Anthropology 45. Reading, MA: Addison-Wesley.

Stein, Lothar. 1967. *Die Šammar-Ǧerba: Beduinen im Übergang vom Nomadismus zur Sesshaftigkeit.* Berlin: Akademie-Verlag.

Stephens, Angela. 1992. "Modern Men, Medieval Trade." *Cairo Today* 13, no. 3: 70–82.

Stewart, Frank H. 1988–90. *Texts in Sinai Bedouin Law.* 2 vols. Wiesbaden, Germany: Harrassowitz.

———. 1991. "Notes on the Arrival of the Bedouin Tribes in Sinai." *Journal of the Economic and Social History of the Orient* 34: 97–110.

———. 2003. "The Contract with Surety in Bedouin Customary Law." *UCLA Journal of Islamic and Near Eastern Law* 2, no. 2: 163–280.

Stichter, Sharon. 1985. *Migrant Laborers.* Cambridge: Cambridge University Press.

Sweet, Louise E. 1965. "Camel Raiding of North Arabian Bedouin: A Mechanism of Ecological Adaptation." *American Anthropologist* 67: 1132–50.

Tapper, Richard. 1991. "Anthropologists, Historians, and Tribespeople on Tribe and State Formation in the Middle East." In *Tribes and State Formation in the Middle East,* ed. Philip S. Khoury and Joseph Kostiner, 48–73. London: Tauris.

Tapper, Richard, ed. 1983. *The Conflict of Tribe and State in Iran and Afghanistan.* London: Croom, Helm.

Tayib, Muhammad Suliman al-. 1993. *Mausu'at al-qaba'il al-'arabyya* [Encyclopedia of Bedouin Tribes]. Cairo: Dar al-Fikr al-'Arabi.

Turner, Victor W. 1973. "The Center Out There: Pilgrim's Goal." *History of Religions* 12, no. 3: 191–230.

United Nations Office on Drugs and Crime. 2005. *World Drug Report 2005.* www.unodc.org/unodc/en/world_drug_report.html.

United States Energy Information Administration. 2007. *Sudan.* www. eia.doe.gov/cabs/Sudan/Oil.html.

Van Velsen, Jaap. 1961. "Labour Migration as a Positive Factor in the Continuity of Tonga Tribal Society." In *Social Change in Modern Africa,* ed. Aidan Southall, 230–41. London: Oxford University Press.

Waardenburg, Jaques D. J. 1979. "Official and Popular Religion as a Problem in Islamic Studies." In *Official and Popular Religion as a Theme in Religious Studies,* ed. P. H. Vrijhof and J. D. J. Waardenburg, 340–86. The Hague: Mouton.

Watson, William. 1958. *Tribal Cohesion in a Money Economy.* Manchester: Manchester University Press.

Weber, Max. 1947. *The Theory of Social and Economic Organization,* ed. Talcott Parsons. London: Hodge.

Weir, Shelagh. 1976. *The Bedouin: Aspects of the Material Culture of the Bedouin of Jordan.* London: World of Islam Festival Publishing.

———. 1985. *Qat in Yemen: Consumption and Social Change.* London: British Museum Publications.

Weissbrod, Tuvia. 1987. "Hamahtsavim besinai" [The Mineral Resources in Sinai]. In *Sinai,* ed. Gdaliahu Gvirtzman and Avshalom Shmueli, 287–96. Tel Aviv: Ministry of Defence.

Wellhausen, Julius. [1887] 1961. *Reste arabischen Heidentums.* Berlin: de Gruyter.

Werbner, Pnina. 2002. *Imagined Diasporas among Manchester Muslims.* Oxford: Currey.

Werbner, Richard P. 2004. "Marx, Emanuel." In *Biographical Dictionary of Cultural and Social Anthropology,* ed. Vered Amit, 340. London: Routledge.

Werbner, Richard P., ed. 1977. *Regional Cults.* ASA Monograph 16. London: Academic Press.

Westermarck, Edward. 1926. *Ritual and Belief in Morocco.* 2 vols. London: Macmillan.

Wilson, Charles W., and Henry S. Palmer. 1869–71. *Ordnance Survey of the Peninsula of Sinai.* 5 vols. Southampton, UK: Ordnance Survey.

Wilson, Godfrey. 1941–42. *Economics of Detribalization in Northern Rhodesia.* 2 vols. Livingstone, Zambia: Rhodes-Livingstone Institute.

Wolpe, Harold. 1972. "Capitalism and Cheap Labour-Power in South Africa: From Segregation to Apartheid." *Economy and Society* 1, no. 4: 425–56.

Yamba, C. Bawa. 1995. *Permanent Pilgrims: The Role of Pilgrimage in the Lives of West African Muslims in Sudan.* Edinburgh, UK: Edinburgh University Press for the International African Institute.

Zaitch, Damián. 2003. "Recent Trends in Cocaine Trafficking in the Netherlands and Spain." In *Global Organized Crime: Trends and Developments,* ed. Dina Siegel, Henk van de Bunt, and Damián Zaitch, 7–17. Dordrecht, the Netherlands: Kluwer.

Zalat, Samy, and Francis Gilbert. 2008. *Gardens of a Sacred Landscape: Bedouin Heritage and Natural History in the High Mountains of Sinai.* Cairo: American University in Cairo Press.

Zambelis, Chris. 2006. "Egypt Attacks may Indicate Emerging Sinai Bedouin Insurgency." *Terrorism Focus* 3, no. 19. http://jamestown.org/terrorism/news.

Index

www.ingramcontent.com/pod-product-compliance
Lightning Source LLC
Chambersburg PA
CBHW060039030426
42334CB00019B/2399